History's Daughter

Lines written by Terence MacSwiney to his daughter on her birth in 1918

Baby, Baby, sweet and wise
Deeper than the morning skies
Is the wonder of your eyes.

Lines written as he embarked on his hunger strike in 1920

I feel the shadow of a danger hovering
Over my wife and child …

History's Daughter

A MEMOIR FROM THE ONLY CHILD OF TERENCE MacSWINEY

Máire MacSwiney Brugha

THE O'BRIEN PRESS
DUBLIN

This paperback edition first published 2006 by
The O'Brien Press Ltd,
12 Terenure Road East, Rathgar, Dublin 6, Ireland.
Tel: +353 1 4923333; Fax: +353 1 4922777
E-mail: books@obrien.ie
Website: www.obrien.ie
Reprinted 2007.
Originally published in hardback 2005.

ISBN: 978-0-86278-986-2

British Library Cataloguing-in-Publication Data
Brugha, Maire MacSwiney, 1918-
History's daughter : a memoir from the only child of Terence MacSwiney
1.Brugha, Maire MacSwiney, 1918- 2.MacSwiney, Terence J. (Terence Joseph), 1879-1920 - Family
3.MacSwiney (Family) 4.Ireland - Biography
I.Title
941.7'082'092

3 4 5 6 7 8 9 10
07 08 09

Letters in preliminary pages:
Page 1 Terence MacSwiney's poem to his daughter in his own hand; *page 3* letter from Terence MacSwiney
to his daughter on her first birthday 1919; *page 4* letter from Terence's wife, Muriel Murphy MacSwiney,
to Terence's sister immediately after his death; *page 6* letter from Muriel to Terence when he was in prison.
Photographs on preliminary pages:
Page 1 Máire as a young child; *page 2* Máire with her aunts Mary and Annie MacSwiney
Photos taken by Emma Byrne: pages 22, 29, 49, 55, 87, 142, 150-1, 172,
185, 246-7, 248, 252-3, 277, 281, 284

Editing, typesetting, layout and design: The O'Brien Press Ltd
Printing: MPG Books Ltd

Acknowledgements

Firstly, I would like to thank journalist Des Fisher who originally suggested I should write my story. I was not prepared to undertake the task. However, I did not reckon with the persistence of Des. So I finally gave in, though by then I had lost my sight, which posed a real difficulty. To overcome this problem, my daughter-in-law Catherine Jennings Brugha was pressed into action. I dictated the whole story and she typed it into the computer. She was indefatigable. Without her help the book could not have been written. Catherine shaped the story into chapters and used her artistic skills to incorporate the photographs and memorabilia. I would like to thank my son Cathal, who worked along with Catherine and who did the difficult job of editing the first draft.

I wish also to express my appreciation to O'Brien Press for the beautiful production of this book, especially Michael O'Brien, Íde ní Laoghaire, Emma Byrne, Rachel Pierce and Colm Ó Riagáin. There were many more wonderful people who helped it come to fruition, including Andrea Mc Tigue, Kate Hayes, Eleanor Murphy, Andrew O'Rorke, Paula Jennings, Geraldine Jennings, Máire and Cathal MacSuibhne. I got great help from my Cork friends, especially Aoife Sloane-Minihane, Aingeal and Breandán Ó Buachalla, Tony Duggan, and the Lord Mayor's Office, Cork. *Gabhaim buíochas le Diarmaid Ó Mathúna agus Antoin Daltún chomh maith.*

We used many photographs and letters I had in our home. For others I would like to thank Hugh O'Donnell, Seamus Helferty of the Archives Department at University College Dublin, and, for permission to use images: Stella Cherry in the Cork Public Museum; Padraig Barry of the Crawford Municipal Art Gallery, Cork; Jacquie Moore of the Office of Public Works; Aoife McBride of the National Museum; and Tony O'Connell, Cork. I would like to thank my other children, Deirdre, Terry and Ruairí, for their help on the book, and their spouses, Bernard Stuart, Máire Nic Eoghain Brugha and Nicola Brennan, and my ten grandchildren for their ongoing support.

As I write this acknowledgement before the reprinting of my book in paperback I would particularly like to thank my husband Ruairí who died on 20 January 2006 for his immense patience during its writing, and for the sixty wonderful years of marriage that we had together.

Máire MacSwiney Brugha, 11 February 2006

the loss of Terry is wors

than for any of it th

CONTENTS

TELEGRAMS:—
"GRIFFINOTA, LONDON

FOREWORD

This is Máire MacSwiney Brugha's story in her own words. The decision to write it was made in January 2004 following encouragement from my brother Ruairí and myself. Over the years many others had asked her to write her story. These included the journalist Des Fisher; past pupils of Scoil Íte (Máire's aunts' school in Cork); people who had links with the Irish War of Independence and its aftermath; and others who got to know her during her husband Ruairí's political career which became, to an extent, her public life. A particular motivation came from her need to put the record straight about why she decided, at the age of fourteen, to return from Germany against the wishes of her mother, Muriel Murphy MacSwiney, and make her life in Ireland. Even though Muriel lived to her ninetieth year, she refused to communicate with her daughter. Muriel's record of these events is at variance with Máire's and was beginning to find its way into the public arena. So this book began as a necessary factual account.

There were some difficulties with regard to writing the book. The first was my mother's age. We started when she was eighty-five years old. Now eighty-six, her main role is to care for eighty-seven-year-old husband, Ruairí Brugha, as he does for her. She is almost totally blind. For six months she dictated her story to my wife, Catherine, who both typed it and clarified it with her as they went along. Without Catherine's help this book would not have been written. In between sessions on the computer my mother would lie awake at night, forming sentences and paragraphs, sometimes writing them on paper despite the difficulties with her eyesight.

The story was buried for most of her life, for many reasons. As she herself explains, she lived a double life: one in Ireland as the daughter of Terence MacSwiney, the internationally famous hero from the War of Independence; the other growing up in Germany, almost as an orphan. As a student in University College Cork, she never shared with her friends the story of her estrangement from her mother. When she did so on the radio some half-century later, it came as a great shock to her friends that they had known so little about her hidden life.

She spent the first years of her life learning, forgetting and re-learning three languages like a native: Irish, English and German, with French always in the background. Máire saw language merely as a necessary tool for survival. In her career she excelled at teaching Latin. She studied Old and Middle Irish, as well as German literature. When RTÉ did a programme in Irish about her and her husband, with contributions from her children and grandchildren, native speakers in the Gaeltacht judged Máire's Irish to be the best of all. However, she never regarded the speaking of Irish as a patriotic gesture, unlike her father, who had a great love of and commitment to the Irish language, and Irish culture and music.

The turbulence of her early life — being moved from country to country, from home to home, from carer to carer — taught her the habit of adjusting. She didn't have a mother on whom she could unburden her emotions, so she buried them. She herself says that she was happy. However, repeatedly having to fit into new circumstances caused her to suffer anxieties that remained with her throughout the years. She says that she dealt with the facts and moved on. Her habit of focusing on dealing with the next problem, and not dwelling on her feelings about the past, made it difficult, at the start, to uncover her thoughts about the incidents that shaped her life.

The two people she reveals as being most significant to her in these personal recollections are her aunt, Mary MacSwiney, and her husband, Ruairí Brugha.

Máire's half-sister, who is eight years younger than she and who lived with her for less than three years, has asked that her privacy be respected; she is therefore not mentioned in the story.

Máire has included short biographies of both Terence MacSwiney and Cathal Brugha, along with some extracts from MacSwiney's writings, to give a background to the historical influences she came from and married into, and to help the reader who would like to know more about them.

Cathal M. Brugha, April 2005

EARLIEST
MEMORIES

LEFT: **My mother, Muriel, with me at two months.** ABOVE: **My father; the first time he saw me he was in prison in Belfast.**

My earliest memory is of standing on a beach surrounded by big, black rocks and looking at the waves breaking on the sand. I was told later it must have been Oysterhaven, a seaside resort near Cork. I was with the Fleischmanns, friends of my aunt, Mary (Máire) MacSwiney, who were on a holiday there. At the time, the autumn of 1920, my father, Terence MacSwiney, the Lord Mayor of Cork, was on hunger strike in Brixton prison, so all the family were in London while I must have been staying with my mother's mother, Grandmother Murphy. I was two years old.

The Murphys owned the Cork distillery. They lived in a large house, called *Carrigmore*, in Montenotte and must have been one of the wealthiest families in Cork. They were surrounded by luxury, with a full staff from butler to housemaid, including a nursemaid for me. I have no distinct recollection of my stay there at that time but I remember well when my mother and I visited later.

I was born on 23 June 1918, in Cork. When my mother was expecting me it was taken for granted that the baby would be a boy, so I was referred to as Traolach Óg. As my Aunt Máire was leaving after visiting my mother in the nursing home, she met one of their acquaintances on her way in to visit. My aunt informed her, 'It is only a Máire'! I was known as Máire Óg to distinguish me from my aunt,

Mary MacSwiney, known within the family as Min or Máire. I called her Aunt Máire.

The first time my father saw me was when my mother, accompanied by Aunt Annie MacSwiney, visited him in prison in Crumlin Road jail in Belfast in 1918; I must have been about three months old. My mother asked the prison attendants to please go and heat the baby's bottle, which was quickly attended to as my mother had an

imperious manner and a pronounced Oxford accent. The first vision of his baby daughter must have been a moving event for my father. After the visit he wrote the poem, 'Máire':

Máire

Baby, baby, sweet and wise
Deeper than the morning skies
Is the wonder of your eyes.
While we pause before this wonder,
All life's cares must drop asunder
In the spell you hold us under.
Ah, we had been sad, reviewing
Barren years and fruitless rueing.
Lo! you give our lives renewing.
Night had flashed to us a warning;
Ah, we prayed, and God, not scorning
In your eyes restored the morning.

LEFT, TOP: The hearse carrying my father's body is tended by a member of Cumann na mBan. LEFT, BOTTOM: My father holding me in his arms in the doorway of Scoil Íte, the school run by his sisters. ABOVE: He is wearing his *fáinne* on his tie in this photo of a rare occasion when we were together as a family.

When I was born my parents decided they would speak only Irish to me. When my father returned home to Cork from prison in Belfast, in 1918, he had a little *fáinne* made for me (a gold brooch in the shape of a ring indicating that the wearer could speak Irish), which he pinned to my baby frock before I could speak at all.

I don't recall my father. He died when I was two years old. Apparently he often spoke to me on the telephone from his office at Cork City Hall. My mother later wrote that, when she was speaking to anybody on the telephone, '... the baby would snatch the receiver out of my hand and think it was her father, and she would whisper, just whisper to him.' On my first birthday he wrote me another poem. It is called 'Máire Plays' and is more lighthearted and playful. Another one, 'Athair's Prayer', written in August 1919, is more solemn and full of foreboding:

Máire Plays

(one year old)

Quick, *a mháthair*, take that knife
How on earth did Máire get it, –
Heavens! oh, I'll lose my life!
The paper – Lord, she can't have eat it!

No – or she'd be surely sick –
See a trifle will elate her –
There! She's jumping – stop her quick
She'll upset the perambulator.

God preserve us! take that string –
She herself will surely throttle. –
Stop! What's that she's going to fling –
There I knew! – Smash goes her bottle!

Hush – she's keeping quiet now.
Let her be or else you'll fret her.
Heavens, keeping quiet! How?
See she's tearing up my letter!

Oh her mischief, sunny sprite,
And our hurry scurry after.
And she understands it quite –
Hear the glory of her laughter!

But see the tiny hands now drooping
Drowse along her eyelids creep –
And we a spell of calm recouping
In the beauty of her sleep.

Athair's Prayer

Here, far away from those I love, to Thee
I cry, oh Lord, Thy saving hand to raise,
To guard them from all peril and to be
Their hope and refuge in uncertain days.

I feel the shadow of a danger hovering
Over my wife and child – yet have no fear
If but Thy mercy like a garment covering,
Close round their path – if Thou be ever near.

With Thy great sacrifice I offer mine.
I offer all that Thou may'st give them all:
Thy truth, Thy constancy, Thy love divine,
Thy saving strength whatever may befall.

Oh, but my sacrifice is poor – yet still
Thou hast said 'all for all'; and all I yield,
Strong in the faith that by Thy sacred will
My loved ones from all peril Thou wilt shield.

The press of labour through each trying day
I offer all its burden, and I strive
For patience, zeal and constancy, and pray
Only for them to be preserved alive.

But if Thy will is death – Thy will be done;
And be the time, the place, the manner Thine,
with all the sorrow of the things undone –
for them I offer all before Thy shrine.

But if Thou wilt that rather I should live
But see my projects perish – still I trust
Thy dispensation – all my dreams I give –
Be each brave project shattered in the dust.

Or let it be thy will, I should achieve
Some noble work – fruitful in many ways –
Let mine be all the labour, and I leave
Glory aside – to others give the praise.

I can give all for them, for Thou hast deigned
One breath to give me of Thy love divine,

And in my sacrifice I am sustained
For Thou hast strengthened me, oh Lord, with Thine.

Both life and death, all joy, all praise, all pain,
I lay them all, O God, before Thy feet
That those I love Thy promise full may gain –
The purpose of my life is then complete.

LEFT: The poem my father wrote about me in his own hand, written 9 November 1919. 'Athair's Prayer', above (see page 1 for hand-written version), was written on 25 August 1919.
LEFT, BOTTOM: My father playing with me in the play-pen!

17

My father, Terence MacSwiney, died on 25 October 1920 in Brixton prison, London, after seventy-four days on hunger strike. I did not know until many years later that his death was worldwide news. Shortly after his death President Éamon de Valera asked my mother and my aunt, Mary MacSwiney, to go to the United States to look for support and recognition for the Irish Republic. The grieving widow, who was very beautiful, and Aunt Máire, who had never given a public speech in her life, went to get support for the Republic, and obviously to raise funds. Money had been collected originally for the Irish Republic by issuing £100 bonds; my father had bought

IRISH PILGRIMS PLAYING THE MELODIES OF OLD IRELAND
at the Door of Brixton Prison to Cheer the Lord Mayor of Cork in the Final Days of
His Hunger Strike.
(*Times Wide World Photos.*)

CERTIFIED COPY OF AN ENTRY OF DEATH

GIVEN AT THE **GENERAL REGISTER OFFICE**

Application Number Y534464

	REGISTRATION DISTRICT				Lambeth			
1920 DEATH in the Sub-district of Norwood					in the County of London			

Columns:-	1	2	3	4	5	6	7	8	9
No.	When and where died	Name and surname	Sex	Age	Occupation	Cause of death	Signature, description and residence of informant	When registered	Signature of registrar
80	Twenty Fifth October 1920 Hm. Prison Brixton	Terence James Mac Swiney	Male	40 Years	Volunteer Officer of 4 Belgrave Place Cork Ireland	Heart Failure from dilated Heart & acute delirium following Scurvy due to exhaustion from prolonged refusal to take food	Certificate received from Geo. Perceval Wyatt Coroner for Counties of Surrey & London Inquest held 27th October 1920	Thirtieth October 1920	J. Tee. Registrar.

CERTIFIED to be a true copy of an entry in the certified copy of a Register of Deaths in the District above mentioned.

Given at the GENERAL REGISTER OFFICE, under the Seal of the said Office, the .... 19th .... day of .... June 2003

DYA 149177

See note overleaf

LEFT, TOP: Irish musicians play at the door of Brixton prison in the final days of my father's hunger strike.
LEFT: Peter, Annie, Seán and Mary standing on either side of their brother's body lying in state in Southwark Cathedral.
TOP: My father's death certificate.
ABOVE: Headlines on the *Boston Evening Globe.*

one of these bonds in my name.

It was not long before Mary MacSwiney discovered that she was a natural orator. *The Boston Globe* reported on her great power as a speaker, her remarkable diction and her comprehensive knowledge of American history in relation to Ireland. The following story shows she could also think on her feet. At one of her meetings she spoke to the Daughters of the American Revolution, an organisation of upper-class Republican women. One woman stood up at the end of the speech when questions were being asked and said, 'Miss MacSwiney, could you explain to me about ambushes. I don't think it very fair to hide behind a bush and shoot at people. I hear the Irish are hiding and shooting

at the Black and Tans, it doesn't sound very fair.'

My aunt replied, 'In order to explain it to you, I will describe an ambush.' She went into great detail describing an ambush, and at the end asked the lady what she thought of that. The lady said, 'Well, yes, I can understand it, but I still don't like it, it doesn't seem right to me.' My aunt asked again did she understand and the lady said that she did. Mary MacSwiney replied, 'Well, I'm glad you do as I have just described the main ambush of the American War of Independence.' She had described in detail the stand at Concord Bridge in 1775!

ABOVE: **Muriel and Aunt Máire arriving in New York in 1920 to look for support and recognition for the Irish Republic. My mother did not wish to go to America and was glad to have Máire to accompany her.**
RIGHT: **Muriel contacting the Irish Consulate on 29 December 1922, in New York.**

As the end of 1920 approached the lecture tour was still in progress, and Mary MacSwiney sent word to President de Valera that she would have to return to Cork in the New Year to reopen her school; she was headmistress of St Ita's school in Cork (later called Scoil Íte), which she ran with her sister, my Aunt Annie. My mother stayed on in America for quite a considerable time longer. She was given the Freedom of the City of New York on 21 December 1920, and was the first woman to receive this honour, although it was given to her as the wife of Terence MacSwiney, as she herself appreciated.

ANNE DONAHUE
379 FIFTH AVE.
NEW YORK

After my mother returned from the United States, early in 1921, we lived in Cork for a short while. I distinctly remember us living with a family in a farmhouse in Ballingeary (in Irish, Béal Áth' an Ghaorthaigh), where only Irish was spoken. I remember my mother, after a visit to the city, bringing back hair ribbons for the little girl of the family and for me.

Sometime after my third birthday, in June 1921, my mother moved to Dublin. We were living in a house or a flat in Dublin — my mother

LEFT, BOTTOM: (*Left*) The doll given to me by the people of Catalonia after my father's death. (*Right*) The scroll giving the Freedom of New York to my mother. LEFT, TOP: Photo of me taken for the American media. RIGHT: My mother in a Celtic costume with me in Dublin in 1922. BELOW: O'Connell Street, Dublin, that same year. Kingston's, where my husband's family later had their shop, was part of the building that replaced the turreted building in the photo, on the corner of Cathedral Street.

and I and a live-in home help. Máire Ní Cheallaigh, secretary to President de Valera, told me that we had lived on Mespil Road next door to her aunt, Kathleen O'Connell, who had been previous secretary to de Valera.

I have one very distinct recollection from that time. It has to do with my refusal to eat my supper. My mother said that if I didn't eat my egg, she would be gone next morning. I thought this was unlikely to happen, so I refused to obey her. But, sure enough, she *was* gone next day. It was two weeks after my fourth birthday when she left, and I didn't see her again for about eighteen months. This, however, had nothing to do with my disobedience.

I found out in later life whereto my mother had vanished. Civil war had broken out in Dublin. Oscar Traynor had set up a Republican

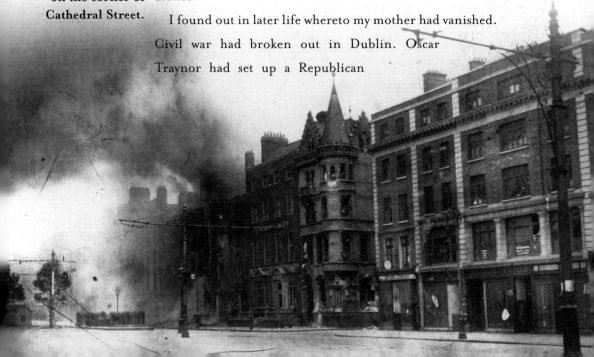

defence in the Hammam Hotel in O'Connell Street and was joined by Éamon de Valera and subsequently by Cathal Brugha. They took up positions to defend the Republic. My mother joined them, as did some other women volunteers. My mother had, in fact, gone to Dublin, with other Cumann na mBan women, to be stationed at the Hammam Hotel. She, Linda Kearns and Kathleen Barry refused to leave when word came that it was going to be shelled, but they eventually crawled out through a hole in the wall and into the Gresham Hotel. By all accounts my mother then went on a lecture tour in the United States. This was my experience of the outbreak of civil war in Ireland: the complete disappearance of my mother!

Máire Ní Cheallaigh and Madame O'Rahilly (always known as 'Madame', she was the widow of Michael O'Rahilly, known as 'The O'Rahilly', who was killed near the GPO in Dublin in 1916) related to me the events that took place subsequently. I was told that the girl

LEFT: **My mother (centre) and Aunt Máire (far right) at the funeral of Cathal Brugha, 1922.** BELOW: **A letter to Aunt Máire from Muriel while she was still in London after my father's death. In it she worries that I will suffer most, in the long run, from the loss of Terence.**

in whose charge my mother had left me was from the country and hardly knew Dublin. As well as that, she spoke very little English as she was from the Gaeltacht. After a few weeks with no sign of my mother returning, she began to worry about what was to happen to me. Apparently, she had a friend or a sister who was working in the house of Madame O'Rahilly. The girl confided in her friend. Her friend said she would ask Madame what she was to do.

Madame O'Rahilly lived with her five sons in a lovely house at the corner of Herbert Park. She said to the girl, 'Bring her to me.' She had always wanted a daughter, so I was very welcome in her home. I spent the following eighteen months in the loving care of Madame O'Rahilly and her family. It was one of the happiest, if not the happiest, years of my childhood and the longest period that I spent in a family situation.

Many years later I learned from reading my mother's account of these events that she had asked some people in America, who were travelling to Ireland, to bring me back to her on their return to the States. I must commend my Aunt Máire that she refused to let me travel with them to America to join my mother, who was apparently living in hotels and moving about constantly. I was soon to learn not to be upset by her frequent disappearances.

The youngest O'Rahilly son was Rory, who was about two-and-a-half years older than me

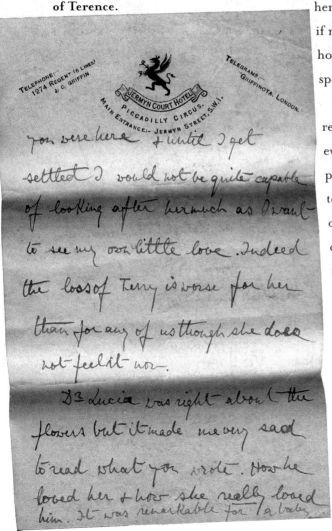

LEFT: I spent eighteen months in the loving care of Madame O'Rahilly, and here I am with her youngest son, Rory.

and so we were always together. I have many happy memories of this period. The two of us would invade the kitchen looking for 'cookies', as Madame O'Rahilly, who was an American lady, called them. The cook, Sarah, would chase us out. She was a small, rotund woman with a pointy nose and a pointy chin. In later years, when reading *Grimm's Fairy Tales*, I always pictured the witch as looking like Sarah in the O'Rahilly household.

At this time Mac O'Rahilly, the eldest, was a teenager. He had a motorbike with a sidecar attached. He used to take Rory and me for a ride, probably in Herbert Park. One of us would be put down in the hold and the other sitting up. The noise and the speed terrified me, but the other two thought it was great fun. The best memory of all is of my fifth birthday. There was a room next to the hall door that seemed to be full of toys and presents. Grandmother Murphy had sent from Cork a bright scarlet coat with big white buttons and a little white hat to match. I was so happy with it, and a photo was taken of Rory and myself with me wearing this outfit.

When my mother returned from America after another lecture tour, in August 1923, she took me from Madame O'Rahilly to live with her. The first thing I remember was that she took the red coat and had it dyed navy. I asked her why she did this, because I was very upset. Her answer was, 'Poor children can't have pretty clothes.' This was my first experience of what one might call the socialist philosophy. I also asked her why we couldn't ride in a motor car. I got the same answer: 'Poor children can't ride in motor cars.'

My mother was always very concerned about the poor and the underprivileged. I think she was reacting against her upbringing in a wealthy family. She also disapproved strongly of the Catholic Church because of its attitude to girls who became pregnant outside marriage. She held these beliefs throughout her life, moving further and further to the left and forbidding me to have any contact whatsoever with the Church.

During that summer she rented a house, of which I have vivid memories. It was a newly built, small, semi-detached house in a row of houses facing the sea. Beyond the road in front of it was a low wall overlooking the strand. I later identified it as probably Sutton.

My strongest memory of this period is of another confrontation with my mother, again involving my refusal to eat my supper. This

time she threatened me with *'an fear dubh'* ('the black or 'boogie' man');
that's how I know we spoke Irish. Again, I didn't believe her. However,
as I was coming down stairs I could see in the open doorway that she
had fetched *'an fear dubh'* and brought him to see me: she must have
gone a few houses up the road to find a chimney sweep and brought
him down to confront me with him. I can only remember being
astonished rather than frightened. What the chimney sweep thought
about it I don't know, except that he was probably being offered a job
to clean our chimney. These erratic threats indicate that my mother
did not understand how to bring up a child.

That was the last time I lived with my mother, except for occasional
summer holidays when I was in boarding school in Germany. These we
spent in hotels – in Paris, in Normandy, on a walking tour of the
Black Forest – all very enjoyable, but not living with her in a normal
home situation.

BELOW: Plaits were very popular in Germany and it took me two years to grow my hair long enough for them.

GERMANY

In the autumn of 1923, when I was five years old, my mother decided to leave Ireland and move to Germany. Why did my mother choose Germany as her destination? She had been attending a doctor there for her depressions. My mother always suffered from her nerves and from depression, even before her marriage and my father's death. After they were married, when depressed she would retire to bed and shut out the world. My father would then bring me to my grandmother's house, where I was well looked after by my nursery maid.

In January 1920 my father had made a will in which he made his sister, Mary, legally co-guardian with my mother. I used to think that he made this arrangement while on hunger strike in England in late 1920, but I later discovered that he actually did it before he became Lord Mayor of Cork. Obviously he was anxious for my future and, I think, worried that my mother would not be able to look after me if anything should happen to him.

My recollection of the journey to Germany is of sitting in a train, possibly the boat-train. While we sat on the train in the station, my mother suddenly got up to fetch something from outside, leaving me sitting alone in the compartment. This was the first time I really panicked, believing the train would leave without her; I never felt that I could rely on her. Of course, she returned on time.

Another incident comes to mind, which must have occurred in the early stages of our stay in Germany, when I knew no German. I remember being brought to what must have been a police station, and sitting on a wooden table while strange men, probably policemen, interrogated me as to my name and where I came from. I couldn't understand them, but I gave my name in Irish, Máire Ní Shuibhne, which was a great puzzle to them. In the end my mother must have found me because I don't remember any more.

When we arrived in Germany, in December, my mother brought me to Wiesbaden, where we stayed in a hotel. She must have taken a suite because I distinctly remember the sitting-room and bedroom in the hotel. My mother brought a German lady to live with us in the hotel, somebody she had befriended, a Fräulein Plumpe. My first distinct memory is of Christmas. There was a Christmas tree with toys beneath it; I got a little stove. Next came New Year. The festivities included fireworks on the street outside our windows after I had been put to bed. I was terrified by the red, green, blue and yellow lights from the fireworks moving along the ceiling of the bedroom. I hid under the bedclothes, as I didn't know what was happening. No one came to rescue me.

Next morning, I remember coming downstairs to the main hall in the hotel, where I learned my first two words of German. Everybody was calling to one another, 'Prosit Neujahr'. I was quite preoccupied with adjusting to my new surroundings: I was anxious to please and never caused any trouble.

In January 1924 my mother brought me to the school she had chosen for me. This was a very modern, avant-garde boarding school for girls, called Odenwaldschule. It had been founded by an educationalist by the name of Paul Geheeb and put more emphasis on a 'liberal' approach to education rather than just teaching.

I have a vivid memory of the first day my mother brought me to the school. I felt somewhat uneasy. I was five years of age and could not speak German. I felt I couldn't trust my mother. I asked her not to go away and leave me there. She said she wouldn't, which was very wrong of her because she *was* going to leave me there. In any case she went off, and I can still hear myself screaming when I discovered myself alone in this strange environment, not understanding a word. My mother could not cope with life or its problems. Her only way of dealing with difficult situations was to walk away from them, which is what she did when she left me in Odenwaldschule. I settled in, however, as I was accustomed by now to unpredictable circumstances.

We learned a great deal about nature study and cultural subjects, for example, ancient Greek history as well as its mythology and even its architecture. By the time I was eight I could tell the difference between a Doric, a Corinthian and an Ionic column. I could tell the differences between trees by their leaves and bark. There was also a practical side to our education, concentrating on crochet, knitting and cross-stitch embroidery at a very early age. (These were the only skills I brought to my homemaking efforts as a young married woman.) I still knit in the continental rather than the Irish way. On the other hand, very little emphasis was placed on spellings and arithmetic tables. This was to present me with a great problem five years later when my mother moved me – suddenly and without warning – away from the Odenwaldschule to another situation.

Odenwaldschule was a very big boarding school, laid out in ten or twelve separate houses suitable for the different age groups. Our house was for the youngest, the *Kindergarten*. We had a *Hausmutter* (house mother) and were treated like a little family. I was very happy in the

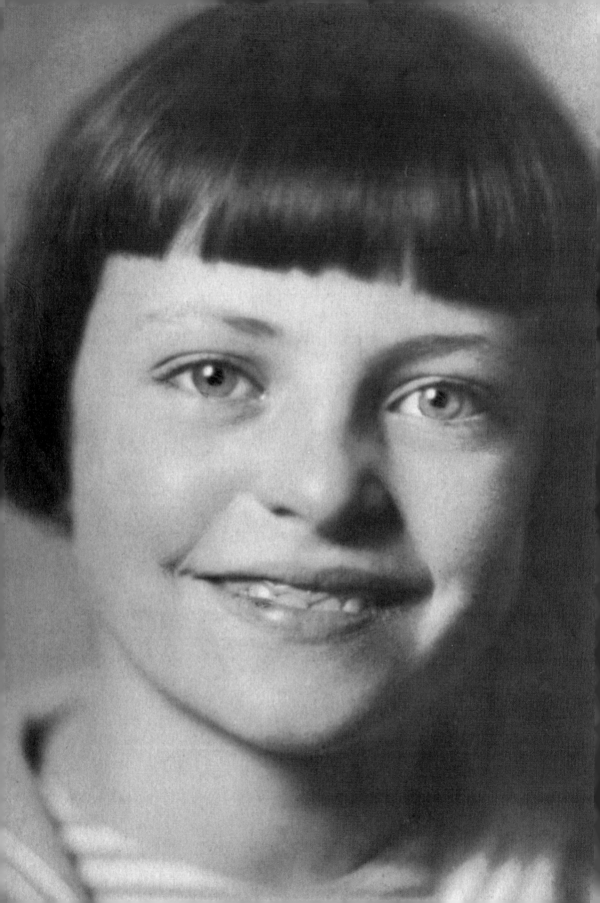

LEFT:
In summer 1927 my mother took me to Darmstadt, where this photo was taken. At school in the Odenwaldschule my foreign-sounding name proved no problem: they christened me *Spatz*, and that is how I signed the back of this photograph.

school and have many fond memories of my five years there. I rapidly learned German and forgot my English. My foreign-sounding name proved no problem: one look at me, a thin little child, and the others christened me *Spatz*. '*Spatz*' is the German for 'sparrow', and I answered to that name for the remainder of my stay in the school. I even wrote it on my copybooks. I became indistinguishable from other little German children.

One of my earliest recollections is of having small skis strapped to my boots and being put standing at the top of what would have been a very gentle slope, but which looked to me like the side of a mountain, and being given an encouraging nudge in the back. Off I went, yelling the whole way, until I came to the bottom and sat on my bum! This was my first introduction to *skilaufen* – skiing. Normally our winter amusement was tobogganing on fairly steep slopes, two to each toboggan. I remember one occasion when we apparently hit a stone and I flew off into the snow onto my back and was winded, and I thought I was going to die.

As regards the teaching of religion, there was no specific doctrine taught. However, at night, before we went to bed, our *Hausmutter* would gather the little ones around and we would sing hymns. I still remember this one:

Weisst du, wieviel Sternlein stehen
an dem blauen Himmelszelt?
Weisst du, wieviel Wolken gehen
weithin über alle Welt?
Gott der Herr hat sie gezählet,
dass ihm auch nicht eines fehlet
an der ganzen grossen Zahl
an der ganzen grossen Zahl.

Do you know how many stars are in the heavens?

Do you know how many clouds go

all across the wide world?

The Lord God has counted them,

so that not one is missing

of the whole large number,

of the whole large number.

I remained in the school for the Christmas holidays and sometimes Easter holidays. Some other children were also there and the staff made every effort to give us a happy Christmas.

Christmas in Germany started at the beginning of December. First came Advent. The custom was to make a wreath of pine branches with four broad red ribbons attaching it to the ceiling light. On the wreath were four thick red candles that were lit in succession each Advent Sunday, while we stood around singing Christmas carols. Finally came the high point: *Heiliger Abend*, Christmas Eve.

As he did for all other German children, St Nicholas came to bring me sweets and fruit on 6 December, after I left my shoes outside the bedroom door. If you had been bold, he would leave a little *rute* (bunch of twigs), but he always generously tied a few sweets to it. In general, children were never allowed to see the Christmas tree in the house until Christmas Eve, when it was fully decorated with the pres-ents underneath and the candles lighting. But at the Odenwaldschule instead of a Christmas tree decorated in the house, we were led into the forest through deep snow to look for the tree with lighted candles. It was magical. But I don't remember any Christmas presents while I was in there, nor did I miss them.

Apart from singing '*Stille Nacht, Heilige Nacht*', one of our favourite Christmas hymns was:

O Tannenbaum, O Tannenbaum,

wie treu sind deine Blätter!

Du grünst nicht nur zur Sommerszeit,

nein auch im Winter, wenn es schneit.

O Tannenbaum, O Tannenbaum,

Wie treu sind deine Blätter.

Sung in English as:

Oh Christmas Tree, Oh Christmas Tree,

how steadfast are your branches!

Your boughs are green in summer's clime

and through the snows of wintertime.

Oh Christmas Tree, Oh Christmas Tree,

how steadfast are your branches!

**BELOW:
Summer 1928,
my tenth birthday,
with garlands
around my head.**

The Communist party later adopted the tune of this very old German hymn for its anthem, 'The Red Flag'.

Birthdays were celebrated in a very special way for us young ones. A garland of flowers was placed around our setting at the table in the refectory. For us, the small children, a wreath of flowers would also be placed on our heads. One year the wreath for me was made of dark cherries — I still remember trying to catch them in my mouth. I can't remember any birthday presents.

An epidemic must have struck the Odenwaldschule when I was very young. I don't know what it was except that a symptom was a very high fever. I remember we were all lying on mattresses in the big hall like sardines in a tin and, in turn, we were wrapped in sheets steeped in ice-cold water to break the fever. I recovered completely from whatever it was, but we understood that one or two of the older girls died. I was so young that I was not really frightened.

One of my less pleasant memories is of having to take cold showers every morning, after which we would stand on a bench wrapped in towels. There was one girl there who was a little older than me and very plump. I thought it was unfair that she should have to be naked in front of the rest of us. I recalled this memory years later when I heard Prince Charles say in an interview that he had not been very happy in school, and that he especially did not like the cold showers. Apparently Kurt Hahn, the founder of the school Prince Charles went to, Gordonstoun in Scotland, was a disciple of Paul Geheeb, who founded the Odenwaldschule.

A memorable occasion while I was in that school was a full eclipse of the sun. It was summertime and we were brought up to a clearing in the woods and given pieces of smoked glass through which to look at it.

One summer we were brought to pick blueberries, which were growing wild. I once made the mistake of sitting down on them and getting my white dress all stained blue.

My five years in Odenwaldschule were happy. I had learned to adjust to whatever situation I found myself in. I had always been moved around and had never lived in a normal family situation. An exception was my year with the O'Rahillys, but even there I knew I was not a member of the family. I didn't really know what normality was, therefore I could not miss it.

BELOW: Summer 1929, my eleventh birthday, again with garlands. Obviously the camera was taken out for birthdays!

SUMMER HOLIDAYS WITH MY MOTHER

The school closed down completely during the summer holidays, so I had to stay with my mother. I remember her as a very beautiful and charming woman with a lovely smile. I never saw much of her except for the four summer holidays when I was at boarding school from the age of five. When she was not around I did not miss her, but when we were on holidays together we had a loving relationship.

The first time my mother had to take charge of me was in the summer of 1924. I was just six years old. I do not remember having any expectations about the holiday. I understood that I was going back to Ireland to visit my Grandmother Murphy. My mother never spoke about her family or my father's family, as far as I recall. I think she disapproved of her family, and this was the last visit she made to them.

My mother and I travelled by boat to Cork, probably the *Innisfallen*. When we were together she spoke only Irish to me. (At that time I had not forgotten my Irish, as I was less than a year out of Ireland.) We had a cabin; I was on the top bunk and my mother on the lower one. I got seasick because I had eaten chocolate before we embarked.

I remember the boat docking at the quayside in Cork where my grandmother was waiting for us in her big, black, chauffeur-driven car. My mother put me sitting in the car with my grandmother while she went back to collect the luggage. My grandmother began to speak to me. She was very upset when she discovered that I could not understand her. It was then we found out that I had forgotten all my English, even though I was only nine months out of Ireland.

BELOW:
My six-year-old signature is boldly written above those of Éamon de Valera, my mother Muriel, Erskine Childers, Aunt Máire and Dorothy Macardle! This invitation to Sinéad Ní Bhriain was to welcome de Valera as President of the Irish Republic to a Sinn Féin meeting held at Scoil Íte in 1924.

Sinn Féin.

Cómairle Ceanntair Concaiġe.

Fáiltiú

roim

Éamonn De BaleRa,
uactarán poblacta na h-éireann

as

Scoil Íte, 14-9-24, an a 8 p.m.

ainm........Sinéid Ní Ḃriain........

MÁIRE

Éamon de Valera

Erskine Childers

Máire Nic Suibhne

Dorothy Macardle

Some days later I was brought down to my aunts' school, St Ita's (later Scoil Íte), where they had brought a little girl from an Irish-speaking family to play with me. This girl was Máire de Róiste, and she was later to become my best friend when I finally returned to Ireland and went to school in St Ita's.

When we were in *Carrigmore*, my grandmother's house, my mother and I slept in the same big bedroom, facing east. In the morning the beautiful bright sunshine streamed in through the windows. All my memories of *Carrigmore* relate to this period. I remember standing in the front garden playing with a flower, which I found out later was a snapdragon.

I recall sitting alone at a huge, mahogany dining-room table with a plate of food in front of me, which I would not eat. I always had a very poor appetite. (Many years later Dr Bryan Alton tried to find out why I suffered from indigestion; x-rays showed scars which indicated that I must have had TB in the stomach when a child.) Everybody else had left the dining-room. There was a hot-water container under my plate to keep the food warm. On the other side of the hall was the big sitting-room, which was forbidden territory for me. One day I was discovered in this room, examining some very valuable chess pieces. A quick stop was made to that activity. Upstairs was my nursery, which appeared to me to be crammed with toys. Toys never figured large in my life, so I did not take much note of them.

After that summer we returned to Germany and school and never again went back together to Ireland. I did not see Ireland again for eight years. I forgot everything about it, even where it was; children in Germany always mixed up Iceland and Ireland – and so did I! Soon I forgot whatever Irish I had had and could speak only German. My mother now communicated with me in German. I do not remember any letters or presents from my aunts in Cork at this time. They could not write to me because they did not know where I was for quite some years. I grew up just like any other little German girl.

My mother was living in Paris from the time she left me in the Odenwaldschule. She mixed with journalists and writers who were of extreme communist persuasion, which view she also adopted. On one of the holidays that I spent with my mother, at about the age of seven, she tried to introduce me to the communist ideals. She bought me a little child's picture book. The story was about six children who were all given the same amount of sweets and when they were examined later it was discovered that one of the children had amassed all the sweets and the others were left with none. My mother asked me, 'Wasn't that very unfair that one should have everything and the others nothing?' I thought it over and decided that the other five children must have been very stupid. It was then that I decided that communism was illogical!

LEFT: **Barefoot at** *Carrigmore.* **I remember the snapdragons in the garden. This was probably the last time I visited my Grandmother Murphy. Although she lived for many more years, I never got an opportunity to see her again.**

When it came to the week-long autumn and spring mid-term breaks most of the other children would go home. During one break, two of the teachers took a small group of us in the *Kindergarten* hiking through central medieval Germany for the week. I remember one evening, at the end of a day's hiking, falling asleep while walking and being supported by the two teachers who minded us on our trip. Each of us had a little rucksack with a grey sleeping bag and hood. We slept in the haylofts of barns. The hay was very scratchy. At the end of the week we were brought back to school by train. This way I got to see various medieval German towns.

We sang all the German wandering songs as we marched along the road – that's how I know so many of them. One of our favourites was:

Muss i denn, muss i denn
zum Städtele 'naus, Städtele 'naus,
und du, mein Schatz, bleibst hier?
Kann i gleich nit allweil bei dir sein,
han i doch mein' Freud' an dir;

wenn i komm, wenn i komm,

wenn i wiedrum komm, wiedrum komm,

kehr i ein, mein Schatz, bei dir.

Must I go, must I go

From the little town, from the little town,

And you, my darling, stay here?

Though I can't be with you all the time

You are still my joy.

When I come back, when I come back,

I'll come to your house, my darling.

Elvis Presley later used this tune for 'Wooden Heart'; he apparent-ly picked it up while serving in the US Army in post-war Germany.

When school finished for the summer of 1925, my mother brought me on a hiking holiday in the Black Forest. I was seven. She collected me from school. We were both wearing rucksacks. I can remember walking down a slope through a meadow of long grass and flowers in bloom, in the brilliant summer sunshine. My mother had brought sheets of paper on which she had written short sentences in German in order to teach me how to read. I learned to read within a week. Along the way we walked, the tree trunks had coloured symbols — triangles, squares and circles — to mark the route. I remember one place where we stayed because I got a bee sting under my foot; the bee had crept into my sandal. It was a farmhouse with a big open farmyard.

The following two summer holidays I spent with my mother in France. We were very much alone together. These were very happy times for me. I loved being with my mother because she was a very lov-ing, charming person. From these visits Paris became very familiar to me, and I have always felt at home there.

I recollect meeting Seán and Geraldine Neeson from Cork, who were on their honeymoon in Paris in 1926. Geraldine had been my mother's bridesmaid, and they must have kept in touch. We visited the Louvre with them. I was very struck by the statue of the 'Winged Victory', standing at the top of a staircase, which was headless and armless. I called her 'my angel without a head'. When I returned as an adult and saw her again, she seemed very small in comparison to my memory of her.

My memory of my holiday at the seaside in Normandy, in 1927, is also very vivid. In the hotel dining-room a large plate of mussels was put in front of me, which turned me off them for life. Once, on a Normandy beach, I wandered off and found myself with a lady who was feeding a small child behind a beach cabin. She was speaking French, which I understood very well but couldn't speak, so communications between us were limited. She dropped a scissors in the sand, which I helped her to find. Finally my mother found me. These frequent visits to France enabled me to learn to speak the language quite easily later in life.

That same year we stayed in a small hotel on the outskirts of Paris and my mother had a lady friend with her. I developed the measles, which I obviously brought from school. My mother or her companion had to stay with me while the other went to see the city; I felt that I was spoiling their holiday.

These four holidays, in Ireland, Germany and France, were the only times that I lived with my mother. My mother probably spoke to me of my father, but I do not remember. I know I did not ask her any questions. She must have been grieving but I, being a young child, would not have noticed it. She was suffering from extreme depression at times and this probably caused her erratic behaviour. After I left the Odenwaldschule, at the age of ten, I never lived with her again.

HEIDELBERG

During those years while I was abroad, my aunt and legal co-guardian, Mary MacSwiney, became very concerned as to my whereabouts and what was happening to me. She finally traced me to the Odenwaldschule and wrote to the school authorities inquiring about me. When my mother found out that my aunt had discovered where I was, she informed the school that she was going to remove me immediately. This animosity towards my Aunt Máire stemmed, I think, from my mother's resentment of the fact that my father had made her my legal co-guardian.

It was Easter 1928 and the end of the school year. I should have been moving on to the *Hochschule* (secondary school), as I was approaching my tenth birthday in June. The Odenwaldschule was a very unusual school and I appreciate what I learned there. As a private school, it was free to focus on providing a liberal education. However, the lack of a proper knowledge of the 'three Rs' proved a great disadvantage when I had to fit into a 'normal' school. Before I left, the teachers tried to prepare me for the entrance exam that I would have to pass to get into the State *Hochschule*. I remember sitting alone in my school bedroom trying to learn all this stuff off by heart.

My mother had been in a psychiatric hospital in Heidelberg, where she was being treated for depression. In the bed next to her was a very nice lady, Tilde Illig, whom she befriended. They must have stayed in

RIGHT: Frau Illig was a kind lady who was very good to me. ABOVE: My letter to her daughter Tilde, signed Goldspatz, her pet name for me.

A happy moment in
Heidelberg at twelve
years of age.

touch because when my mother took me away from the Odenwaldschule, she brought me to stay with Tilde's mother in Heidelberg. Frau Illig was a kind old lady who was very good to me. She was already looking after her granddaughter, Ursula, a girl two years younger than I and the daughter of Tilde's brother, Otto, who lived in Berlin. My appearance in her home may have put Ursula out a bit.

I loved Frau Illig's daughter Tilde, but rarely saw her because she lived in Strasbourg. Frau Illig had two other daughters, Else and Erika, both secondary school teachers: one taught French, and the other English. They tested me to see if I could do the entrance exam to the secondary school. They quickly discovered that my spelling and arithmetic were inadequate. I would have to go to the *Volksschule* (primary school) for another year.

I found that year very difficult, a real culture shock after the Odenwaldschule. Now I had to face the real world. The first problem was my name. Up to now I had used the name *Spatz*. I knew I was Máire Ní Shuibhne, but I couldn't spell my surname. So I tried to write it phonetically, in German, on my copybook: H-I-N-G-E. Some years later, when I went to live in Garmisch, our school teacher made some reference to Ramsey MacDonald, who was then Prime Minister of Britain. Then the teacher, to my amusement, drew attention to the similarity of my name, MacSwiney, to MacDonald. This confirmed for me that my surname was MacSwiney. Another new experience was the fact that if one made a mistake in spelling or anything one got a slap. I still remember the shock when first I got a slap across my hand for making a mistake in spelling! I was absolutely determined to learn enough as quickly as possible to get out of there and into the secondary school.

My mother never realised the difficulties I faced having to fend for myself. One time she came to visit me in Heidelberg for a short while,

staying in a small hotel nearby. She was living in Paris at that time. After this she paid occasional short visits but she would only ever meet me at the railway station, and only for an hour or two. I would have no forewarning of these train station *rendezvous*, but whenever she sent for me I was always delighted to see her. I remember at that time asking her to get a flat and take me to live with her. She said it was out of the question. It is likely she was not well and therefore did not feel up to it.

The following Easter I sat and, luckily, passed the entrance exam to the secondary school. I can still remember the extreme anxiety I felt lest I should fail to pass. The *Hochschule* was situated within the old Heidelberg University City, to which I travelled by tram from the Illigs' flat in Heidelberg. We first had to learn to write Latin script, as we had used only German script until then; this was to enable us to learn French.

I remember my first lesson in French. The teacher wrote these words on the blackboard: *'Le Lit'* and *'La Pie'* ('the bed' and 'the magpie'). This was to teach us that there were two different genders in French. The fact that we were already accustomed to using three genders in German — masculine, feminine and neuter — didn't occur to us. I made new friends in the class and was very happy there. In the

LEFT:
My mother visiting me in Heidelberg at a small hotel near where I lived.
ABOVE AND BELOW:
The photograph album Else Illig compiled for me.

summer holidays we picked redcurrants and blackcurrants for jam. Frau Illig was a wonderful cook and it was a very happy home. We lived in a block of flats with a garden and a children's playground in the centre. Our flat had a veranda off the kitchen, facing south. In the summer we went to the swimming baths on the Neckar River. One day one of my companions gave me a push into the deep end of the pool. We had already been shown the breaststroke. I sank down deep under the water. It was a case of sink or swim. I rapidly learned how to swim.

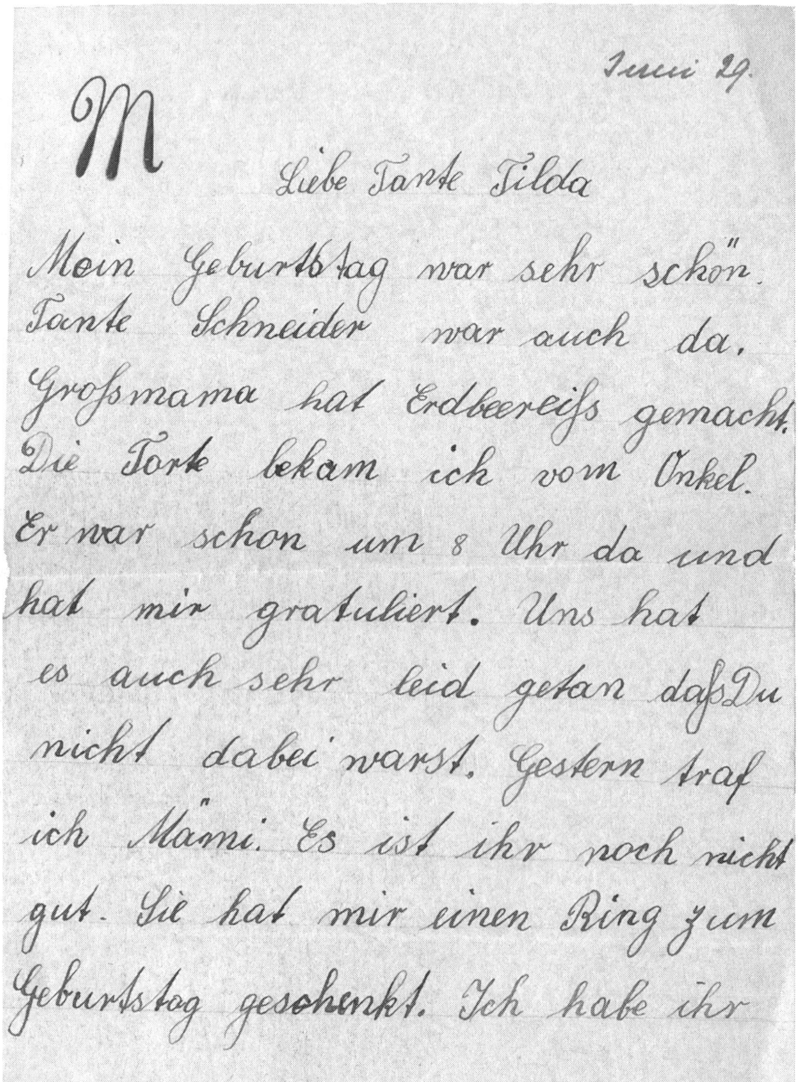

Juni 29.

M

Liebe Tante Tilda

Mein Geburtstag war sehr schön. Tante Schneider war auch da. Großmama hat Erdbeereis gemacht. Die Torte bekam ich vom Onkel. Er war schon um 8 Uhr da und hat mir gratuliert. Uns hat es auch sehr leid getan daß Du nicht dabei warst. Gestern traf ich Mami. Es ist ihr noch nicht gut. Sie hat mir einen Ring zum Geburtstag geschenkt. Ich habe ihr

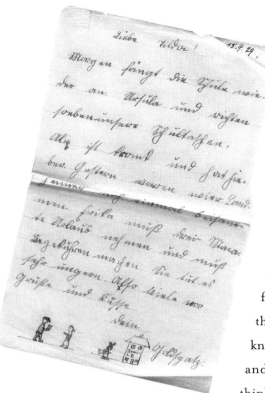

A strict instruction my mother gave to anybody who was to take charge of me was that I was to be completely kept away from any knowledge of the Catholic Church and its teachings. The Odenwaldschule had no problem with this as it was non-denominational. When I got to Heidelberg and attended ordinary school, however, we had to deal with the regulatory filling-out of forms. Apart from the usual data required there was also a question on religion. I didn't know what to put down. I asked my mother and she said, 'Put down *Freidenker*' (free thinker!). So that is what I wrote down. It didn't mean anything to me. Then there was the form

LEFT AND ABOVE: A letter I wrote to Tilde Illig after my eleventh birthday. RIGHT: Studying in Frau Illig's house. It was a happy home.

dealing with smallpox vaccination. Every child had a certificate to prove that they had been vaccinated by the age of two. It was discovered that I had no certificate and had not been vaccinated. They couldn't believe that this was possible: what kind of a barbaric country did I come from? Many years later, when I was back in Ireland, I asked why I had not been vaccinated. It was explained to me that it was a matter of principle — vaccination in those days was mainly carried out for

people going into the British
Army, therefore some Irish children were not vaccinated.

At the age of twelve every child in Germany had to get
a booster shot, which was carried out in school.
Whatever about not having the original vaccination,
I got the booster shot and it almost killed me. I had
a very strong reaction to it.

Erika Illig asked my mother to arrange for her to
visit Cork to improve her English. She stayed with my
mother's friend, Geraldine Neeson. Meanwhile, my aunt,
Mary MacSwiney, was always concerned as to my welfare and
my whereabouts; possibly it was through the Neesons that
she found out where I was staying. She would ask people

going to Germany to look me up, so I had several visitors from Cork. First came Violet (Vi) Stockley, the daughter of Professor Stockley, Professor of English in University College Cork (UCC). As Vi's mother, Madame Stockley, was half-French and half-German, Vi spoke both French and German fluently. I had no difficulty communicating with her. Another visitor was Seán Neeson, whom I had met when I was on holidays in Paris. I could not communicate with Seán as he knew no German and I no English. He had a beautiful singing voice and used to sing Irish ballads for us. One of his favourites was 'Úna Bhán'. It was a very sad song and sounded like a dirge to me.

Both these people were friends of my mother as well as the MacSwineys, so I do not think my mother would have had any objections to these visits. However, I think she worried about the many contacts my aunt had made with me. My mother did not want Aunt Máire, or anybody in Ireland, to know where I was. She may have been worried that my aunt might have some rights regarding responsibility for my welfare and upbringing.

My stay in Heidelberg was about to come to an abrupt end. I had spent a year in the girls' secondary school and had gone to the second class, having completed a year of French. The Illigs were a Catholic family. Frau Illig's granddaughter was being prepared for her First Communion, which was made at the age of ten in Germany. I learned the 'Our Father' from listening to her. My mother was afraid that I was being contaminated by the Catholic religion. At Easter 1930 she decided to move me at a moment's notice. I was fond of Frau Illig and her three daughters, Tilde, Else and Erika, particularly Tilde, but I never saw them again.

LEFT: **I looked like any other German schoolgirl.**

BAVARIA

In 1930 my mother brought me to the beautiful village of Grainau in southern Bavaria, in the heart of the German Alps, five kilometres from Garmisch-Partenkirchen. The local physician, Dr Kaltenbach, and his wife took in as boarders children who were sent to the Alps for health reasons. There were only three or four children there with me at that time.

This was a very happy household. I was particularly fond of Frau Kaltenbach, and I think she also was fond of me. Later, she showed concern for me and was a great help when I needed it. However, the upheaval was once more traumatic, mainly as far as school was concerned.

The Kaltenbachs were probably Protestant, but there was no religion visible in the house. However, all the people around them were very staunch Catholics. The maid working in the house brought me to midnight Mass one Christmas. We walked the three kilometres through the snow to the next village. The church was typical Bavarian Baroque, full of statues and gilt. It was the first time that I had been in a church as far back as I could remember. I sat down as a spectator and did not feel any particular interest, but I knew my mother would have disapproved strongly of this adventure.

I attended school in Garmisch, which was a short train journey away from Grainau. The only school for girls was a convent school, so as far as my mother was concerned, that was out. Therefore, I had to attend the boys' school, a *Gymnasium*, which meant that it taught the classics. It was non-religious. There were three or four other girls in the class with me, who may have been

Protestant. I had to catch the train at 7.05 in the morning, therefore I left the house at 6.30am for the half-hour walk to the station. I had no complaints as I regarded that as normal. In the winter, when the snow was deep, I used to do the trip to the station on skis. This was the obvious method of travel. As I was one of the first people out at that hour of the morning onto the freshly fallen snow, to try and walk would have been impossible as one would sink down into snow up to half-a-metre deep. School started at 8.00am and finished sometime after lunch. We used to leave the skis in the station and collect them on our return. I was the only one getting on the train at Grainau. I never once missed that train, whatever the weather. This was to be my school for the next two years, from the time when I was just twelve until I was fourteen.

I looked like any normal German schoolgirl; I had plaits down my back. In the winter we all wore skiing outfits. In the summer we dressed in local costume. Women and girls wore cotton dresses with frills around the waist, with a little coloured apron. In cooler weather there was a black woollen jacket, close-fitting around the waist, with brass buttons and green-and-red edging across the top: this was called a *Berchtesgartner*. Later this outfit was adopted as the costume of the Hitler girl guides, called Bund Deutscher Mädel, or BDM. I suppose, after that, people didn't wear it as it was identified too much with that organisation. Men and boys wore *Lederhosen* with ornamental braces decorated with an ivory-coloured stag's head. On Sundays they wore snow-white shirts.

The two districts of the village, Obergrainau and Untergrainau, were two to three kilometres apart. It was a rural area, with the farm-ers mainly engaged in dairy farming. One could hear the cowbells

LEFT:
Grainau, Bavaria,
where one could
hear cowbells
ringing in
the fields.
RIGHT:
The rear of the
house of Dr and
Frau Kaltenbach
where I lived.

ringing all day in the fields. In the spring and early summer, some of these fields were blue, covered in *Enzian* gentian and later *Alpenrosen*. We seldom saw *Edelweiss* in the wild as it grew higher up in the cracks of the Alpine rocks. In the summer we played in the woods and in winter we went tobogganing. Skiing didn't seem to be for recreation, but rather for practical purposes when the snow was deep.

The summers were hot, most evenings ending in a summer storm, with a lot of lightning and the thunder reverberating from the mountaintops. We knew the distance of the thunder by counting the seconds between the lightning and the thunder. The lightning did not bother us, as we knew it would strike the mountaintops first. Although I did hear that a fireball once went through an open window of a house and out the other side. In any case, every house had a lightning conductor. When I came back to Ireland, I found it quite strange that the houses had no lightning conductors – and quite worrying until I learned that thunderstorms were rare in Ireland.

While we were waiting at the station for our train home, the boys often bought the Nazi newspaper, the *Völkischer Beobachter* (the 'People's Observer'). We girls didn't take much notice, but we could see what was in it: big, black headlines underlined in garish red. It did have an effect on the boys. They used to get all fired up. The main news was of the struggle on the streets of German cities between the communists and the Nazis. It was practically a civil war, with many people killed every night.

In later years I heard people speak of this conflict as being between the Nazis and a democratic system. I used to look back to what I had experienced as a young girl. The conflict was not between democracy and Fascism. Germany had never recovered after the Treaty of Versailles. The country was in complete collapse, with high unemployment, a wrecked economy and no hope for the future. Because democracy under the Weimar Republic had failed them, the young looked to either communism or Fascism for strong leadership. War broke out before the decade was over. We had been told it was to defeat Fascism and allow democracy to prevail, but that was not the choice before the German people. They only had the choice to follow the lead either of the Nazis or of the communists. If communism had prevailed, all Germany would have become a communist state under Russian influence and the frontiers of the USSR would have reached almost to the French borders. This was the situation that was arrived at when Roosevelt, Churchill and Stalin met at Yalta, on the Black Sea, towards the last year of the war. Roosevelt and Stalin saw eye to eye and were cooperating with one another. Apparently, Churchill tried to prevent this wholesale hand over of Middle Europe to Stalin, but as he was one against the other two, he failed.

At school I had my own problems. There are slight variations in the curriculum across the various German *Länder* (regions). In Heidelberg the first foreign language taught was French, whereas in Bavaria it was English. Accordingly, I had to abandon my year's French from my former school and try to catch up with the English class. The fact that I must have spoken the language until the age of five did not seem to be of any help; I always lagged behind. My main occupation was reading. I was an avid reader and started with *Kinder – und Hausmärchen* by Jacob and Wilhelm Grimm, later moving on to adventure stories. I remember reading *Alice im Wunderland*. I don't remember my mother writing me any letters at this time.

We lived our quiet daily routine. For us children life was divided between school and homework. In these circumstances you don't see much of your surroundings, but three incidents stood out for us during this period. One summer's evening we saw, high up in the sky, what looked like a small silver ball glinting in the sun and drifting over the Alps, to disappear beyond the mountains. We were later told that this was the first manned balloon flight into the stratosphere. The Frenchman Auguste Piccard was at its helm.

Another time we were brought on a hike to a deep ravine in the mountains. The path was narrow, slippery and wet. We only had a rope guideline on one side, with a waterfall pouring down from overhead. It was quite scary.

The third incident was the most interesting. We were brought on an excursion from the school to Austria, to view a deep fissure that had opened up in the ground following an earthquake some distance away. This was quite unusual as earthquakes were rare in this area. It was because of this trip that I knew where and how near the Austrian border was. This was important when later I needed to get myself out of Germany quickly and back to Ireland.

In winter Grainau lay almost asleep under deep snow. One year we

Unter grainau 1931

LEFT:
Frau Tilly
Fleischmann and
her son, Aloys,
outside the Hotel
Waxenstein,
with me in the
traditional outfit,
including the
Berchtesgartner.

were completely snowed in and a path had to be dug for us from the main road to the house. All that spring we walked up this path to our house, with high walls of snow and ice on either side. We had a huge St Bernard dog whose bark was enormous and frightening; his wagging tail could knock down a child. When Dr Kaltenbach arrived home the dog would put its paws on his shoulders and it stood a head above him. The dog's name was Barry. None of us was afraid of him as we understood he was only welcoming us home.

All the houses were built of wood with shallow, sloping roofs. The farm animals were kept on one side, under the same roof. Stoves heated these houses. On my return to Ireland, I was horrified by the open fires in the rooms; I was sure they would burn down the house. Our house was heated by a huge stove, which went from floor to ceiling and was covered in green tiles. This was built into the wall between the sitting-room and the hall, one side heating the room and the hall side heating the rest of the house. Wooden logs fuelled the stove. These logs were stacked around the outside of the house in the summer, protected by the overhanging eaves of the roof. As the air was dry, even when it snowed, these logs never became wet. It was often my job to go out and collect wood for the stove. I got great practice testing the blocks for weight: the lighter they were, the drier. This ability to check the difference in weight came in handy later in life – in a supermarket I could check the egg-boxes for weight to see which was the best value!

The village was surrounded by the Alps, with the Zugspitze, the highest mountain in Germany, in the distance. Right across the valley, looking down on our house, was the Waxenstein towering over us. Peeping from behind was the sharp-pointed Alpspitze. Snow never melted completely up there in the summer and always remained on the Zugspitze.

Once more my Aunt Máire discovered where I was staying. When she heard that her friend, Frau Tilly Fleischmann and her son, Aloys Fleischmann, were visiting Munich, she asked them to call to see me. My aunt was always glad to get news of me from these various visitors. After the Fleischmanns' visit, my aunt started to write to me.

ESCAPE

Ayear later, at Easter 1931, my mother turned up again and asked to meet me at the station in Garmisch. She always met me in the waiting-room at train stations, either the station in Heidelberg or the station in Garmisch, never at the place where I was living. She told me she wanted me to move back to Heidelberg to live with her and another friend. I had happily settled down again and liked where I was. I said emphatically that I was not moving. I think that is when I grew up. I decided to take charge of my own life. I was just approaching my thirteenth birthday.

I wouldn't budge. It was the first time I remember being angry with my mother. I had spent only one year with the Kaltenbachs and was very happy there. She retorted by saying she wouldn't pay for me any more, which apparently included school fees. My mother was living on her inherited dowry, which was substantial, but having to pay for my care in an expensive school, and afterwards with two different families, must have been a drain on her resources. I didn't fully understand all the complications of the situation. As a foreigner, my mother had to pay school fees and the Kaltenbachs also had to be paid. I stood my ground and decided to stay. My mother had to leave without me. I didn't look to see her get on the train. That was the last time I met my mother. I took the train back to Grainau.

I went home and told Dr and Frau Kaltenbach what my mother had said. I think Frau Kaltenbach was very concerned about my future.

She said they would keep me anyway, but could not pay for my clothes and school fees. Some time after school reopened, I was called in to the headmaster's office, Herr Hollahra, to be told my school fees hadn't been paid.

Frau Kaltenbach felt that I should get in touch with my Aunt Máire. As it was coming into winter, she suggested that I write asking her to send me the material to make a winter coat. My aunt used to write back in English, which Dr Kaltenbach was able to translate for me. By this time I knew where Ireland was, but it still appeared a strange place. This idea was strengthened by the appearance of the notepaper on which my aunt wrote; it was Ancient Irish Vellum. Her principles would allow her to buy only Irish goods. This notepaper was very thick; on the Continent, the thinner the notepaper the more elegant it was. Again, the material for the coat had to be Irish-made. She sent heavy, rough Donegal homespun tweed. It was a dark red and black scratchy material. This was of an early variety, not like the elegant fine tweed of later years. This added to my peculiar impression of what was Irish. In Germany, fine material was considered elegant!

In February 1932 I was brought to the cinema for the first time. It was in Garmisch, and the film was *Snow White and the Seven Dwarfs*. For me, the highlight of my visit to the cinema was the newsreel. It mainly depicted the events in Dublin when Éamon de Valera and his party were first elected as the government in Ireland. There were crowds milling about, cheering and waving, in an area I was later to learn was College Green, opposite Trinity College. I was thrilled to see that this mythical country called Ireland actually existed.

Later, in the spring, Frau Kaltenbach suggested that I write asking could I visit Cork during the summer holidays. In order for me to be able to do so, my aunt had to write to my mother for permission. My aunt gave her word of honour that she would return me to Grainau in the autumn in time for school. I am positive that if the visit had been allowed, my aunt would have complied with this condition. I too wrote to my mother for permission for this visit to Ireland. The answer she gave was an emphatic 'No'. At that point, Frau Kaltenbach suggested that I write to my aunt asking her to come and visit me.

About this time, my aunt had received a small legacy from an American lady who had admired her for her public speaking during her American tour in the autumn of 1920, after my father's death. She immediately thought, Now I can visit Máire. She had no money and couldn't normally have afforded to travel. Now she made arrangements for the journey. As she did not recognise the Free State, she would not go through the normal channels to acquire a passport. She went straight to de Valera to provide her with one. From then on Mr de Valera was extremely helpful, assisting my aunt with her plans in every way.

My aunt informed Frau Kaltenbach that she was coming to Germany to visit me. My aunt brought Madame Stockley to accompany her because she spoke fluent German and French; she acted as interpreter since my aunt spoke no German, though she did speak French. The two ladies arrived in our village of Grainau, where they stayed at the only hotel. They also brought with them Madame Stockley's sister, Fräulein Mädi Kolb. Before coming to Grainau, my aunt had spent a few days in Munich where she consulted a lawyer as to her legal position *vis-à-vis* me. (The previous summer, 1931, when Frau Fleischmann and her son, Aloys, had visited me, I remember her bringing me to see Cardinal Faulhaber, the Archbishop of Munich and Freising, who was known for having given sermons that were critical of anti-Semitic Nazi propaganda. Of this meeting I have a very vague impression. My aunt may have asked him for advice.) The lawyer's advice was that my mother's guardianship took precedence over my aunt's. He suggested that it would be no harm if my aunt got my name on her passport; at the time, a minor could be written into the passport of an adult relative.

RIGHT: Grainau, surrounded by the Alps with the Zugspitze, the highest mountain in Germany, towering over it in the distance.

When the three ladies had booked into the little hotel in the village, they came to the house of the Kaltenbachs to see me. We all had tea together, but my aunt and I could not communicate with one another as neither of us spoke the other's language. Madame Stockley interpreted.

Some days later, Aunt Máire made her sad farewell, giving me some German money in case I could at any time try to make the journey to Ireland. I realised this was an unrealistic suggestion and we parted company, they to return to Ireland the following day.

In the meantime, my mother got wind of this visit. She informed the Kaltenbachs that she was sending a male acquaintance to collect me immediately and bring me back to Heidelberg. It was the summer of 1932, fifteen months after my mother and I had parted company at the Garmisch railway station. As promised, she immediately sent somebody to fetch me back to her. This gentleman had been introduced as Herr Borcher, but I knew him later as Herr Pullmann. He had arrived at the same time as my aunts, but checked into a hotel in Garmisch. As the three ladies were leaving that evening, he came to the house. My aunt and he exchanged unfriendly glances in the hall as they passed one another. He announced that I was to be packed and ready the following morning to travel back with him to Heidelberg.

Next morning my aunt fully intended to return with her two companions via Munich to Ireland. I was getting ready to be collected for the journey by my mother's messenger, Herr Pullmann. I went into Frau Kaltenbach's bedroom to say goodbye to her. I was wearing a little summer frock and was holding my hairbrush as I had been brushing my long hair, which I wore in plaits. I was fond of her and was very upset that I had to leave her and yet another home where I had been happy. I was very emotional and tearful. Frau Kaltenbach looked at me and said, 'If I were you, I would run to the aunt in the hotel and ask her to take you back with her to Ireland.' But she asked me never to tell anyone that she had suggested it. I followed her suggestion out of desperation: the only way I could see myself having a future was to take the chance of persuading my aunt to take me with her as she was leaving that morning to go back to Ireland.

The Kaltenbach house backed onto a wood, through which was a short-cut to the hotel. I was very familiar with these woods. Without hesitation I ran out the back door, still only dressed as I was in my light summer frock. I was holding my hairbrush. I did not even go upstairs to get my coat. I ran through the woods by the short-cut to the back of the hotel, hoping that they had not yet left. I must say, I would never have thought of taking this initiative. Frau Kaltenbach was a calm and dignified woman and I owe everything to her, all my future life, and I will never forget what she did for me. As the rest of the household was still in bed I had no chance to say goodbye, not even to Dr Kaltenbach.

When I arrived at the hotel, the three ladies were sitting on the veranda in the sunshine having their breakfast. They had ordered the only hackney cab in the village to bring them to the station in Garmisch for the return journey via Munich to Ireland. At this point I had to take full charge; there was no time to lose as my mother's friend was going to arrive at any moment to collect me. As my aunt could not understand what I was trying to say, I tried to explain to Madame Stockley, in German, what we needed to do. She seemed completely incapable of taking it in, or translating it, or explaining it to my aunt. I was worried that my mother's messenger would arrive. I was desperate. So I kept saying, 'Schnell! Schnell!' My aunt later said to me that she never forgot that word of German.

I had decided what we should do. There was a back road from Grainau to the Austrian border, just half-an-hour's drive away. I finally got through to my aunt when the hackney cab arrived to take them to the station.

We all got into the cab and my aunt put me lying down on the floor at the back seat and covered me with a rug. It was an open Landau model so if I had been sitting up, I would have been seen driving through the village. At least I had got through to my aunt. Right enough, as we were driving out of the village my mother's messenger passed us by in his taxi on his way to pick me up.

I took charge of the proceedings. The way to Garmisch was to turn right on the main road for a short journey of about five kilometres to the station. I told our driver to turn sharp left instead, in the direction of the Austrian frontier. When we neared the frontier my aunt made me sit up in the cab. At the frontier post I got out and spoke to the men on duty. I explained that the two Irish ladies and I would continue to Austria, but that the cab driver and the other lady would return immediately as soon as he left us at the nearest railway station. Madame Stockley's sister, Mädi, and the cab driver had no passports. My aunt and Madame Stockley had their Irish passports, and I was able to accompany them because my name was now on my aunt's passport. My mother later claimed that Aunt Máire had this done in Dublin, *before* she came to Germany. This could be true, if she had it done in anticipation of bringing me back to Ireland for a holiday. My mother maintained that this was illegal. But since my aunt was also my legal guardian, it probably was in order.

All this could not have been done had my father not organised to have my aunt as co-guardian. Going over these events now, it strikes me that at every point at which things could have gone wrong, miraculously, they did not. I have a strong feeling that my father was watching over me, not only at that crucial time, but all the years I was more or less on my own in Germany.

The frontier-post guard made no fuss. I think they were accustomed to waving local people through, as there is no difference in either race or dialect between Southern Bavarians and Austrians.

Once we crossed the frontier I left my aunt in charge of everything;

she knew what to do. She told the driver to take us to the nearest railway station where the express train from Vienna to Geneva would stop, which he did. The cab driver must have been rather bewildered as he had only been engaged to take these three elderly ladies the short, twenty-minute drive from their hotel in Grainau to the railway station in Garmisch. Madame Stockley's sister, Mädi, was very agitated as she was a rather timid elderly lady and was afraid of any complications resulting from my unorthodox departure. When we got to the correct station my aunt gave the cab driver most of the German money she had and sent him back with Mädi to catch her train from Garmisch home to Munich.

I felt very lonely leaving the Alps and familiar surroundings while driving to Austria, going to a foreign country of which I knew nothing. It was a case of between the devil and the deep blue sea: I really had no alternative, as staying in Germany held no future for me. It was an instinctive decision. I completely trusted my aunt, even though I did not know her very well. I did not think of the consequences.

I don't know how far we drove. It was a dull, drizzly day and I felt very depressed. Once again I was going from familiar surroundings to a strange country and completely unknown circumstances. But whatever happened, I knew I had no alternative. I was now fourteen years of age and I could not continue to roam around at my mother's whim; I had to settle down if I was to have a future. We caught the express train and arrived in Geneva early the next morning.

My aunt brought me to the house of Seán Lester, who was the Irish representative at the League of Nations in Geneva. One of the main reasons she had to do this was to borrow some money, since she had given most of her money to the cab driver and Mädi. As we crossed his threshold she said to me, 'Máire, we are safe now, we are on Irish soil.' I think by then I could understand some English but could not speak it, so communication between us was fairly limited. She also

told me that Mr Lester had three little daughters who spoke Irish. This meant nothing to me as, alas, my own Irish was long since gone! I met one of his daughters, Dorothy, many years later when I was living in Dublin and attended a book launch in the Mansion House. She had married Douglas Gageby, editor of *The Irish Times*. She told me she was a daughter of Seán Lester and one of the three little girls who had met me that day in Geneva. I was delighted to meet Dorothy after all those years.

While we were in Geneva, my aunt brought me to meet Mademoiselle Etienne Beuque. She was an invalid and staying with her family in Lausanne on holidays. She had been gathering material to write a biography of my father and was delighted to see me. Another thing my aunt did was to buy me a silver-grey raincoat with a hat to match. I was still dressed only in my summer frock. Whatever happened to the hairbrush, I wonder.

Apparently, when Herr Pullmann discovered that I had left, he alerted the police. They started to look for us all over Germany, thinking my aunt and I were *en route* back to Ireland in the normal way. The only people they could interview were the cab driver, who didn't understand what had gone on, and poor timid Mädi, who was terrified of the police and everything to do with them. Madame Stockley accompanied my aunt and me as far as Geneva. Then she felt it her duty to return to Munich to look after Mädi, whom she found had been subjected to the full interrogation of the police inquiry, for which she was not a good subject.

LEFT:
My aunt bought
me this silver-grey
raincoat with hat to
match in Geneva.

That night, my aunt and I took the overnight express train from Geneva to Paris. We had a *couchette* in a *wagon lit* and she got some pillows at the station. I was looking forward to seeing my beloved Paris again. However, we arrived early in the morning at the Gare de Lyon in drizzly rain and took a taxi immediately across Paris to the Gare du Nord, seeing nothing of the city. I was very disappointed. From there we caught the boat-train to Calais and then the ferry to Dover. On the train from Dover to Fishguard my aunt ordered breakfast. It was my first experience of an English breakfast. I was confronted with a strange-looking fruit. Was it an orange, or a lemon? Then I put my spoon in and tasted it. It tasted horrible! I later discovered it was a grapefruit. Truly I was going to have some strange experiences!

At Fishguard we continued our journey on the *Inisfallen*, the mail-boat to Cork. As we sailed into Cork harbour, passing Spike Island on one side, my aunt began to tell me a story about my Uncle Seán. My schoolgirl English was just sufficient to follow the story. My aunt explained to me that Uncle Seán had escaped from prison on the island and had swum across the harbour. Things were getting stranger by the minute. I could not believe what I was hearing. What kind of a country was I coming to? Normal people did not go to prison in Germany, nor escape from prison. But I did not care, as I knew that I was home and that I was safe. I wrote to Frau Kaltenbach to tell her of my safe arrival in Ireland and she wrote back and kindly sent me my belongings.

Now, once more, I had to start a whole new life in what was, to me, a foreign country. Of course, the unorthodox way in which I returned home to Ireland had its consequences. My mother took my aunt to court to try to win custody over me. She was convinced that my aunt had kidnapped me and that the Catholic Church was involved. The Catholic Church had nothing whatsoever to do with my return to Ireland. It was my own decision. When later I seemed hard in my resolution not to comply with my mother's wishes, it was then I recognised the inevitable; it had become, as it were, a case of *sauve qui peut*. I *had* to rescue myself.

COURT CASE

After a few days in Cork we had to go to Dublin in order for my aunt to attend the court for the decision on my custody. The case dragged on all that summer and must have been very stressful for my mother, especially as she felt she was being blocked at every turn. In a way, there seemed to be some truth in that. De Valera, and with him any authorities involved, was anxious to keep this matter out of the public domain. This was to protect my father's name and memory. It was legally possible to hold the case *in camera* because I, 'the minor', had property. The 'property' I held was my father's £100 Republican Bond, which he had taken out in my name in the early days of the Republican government, set up in 1919. The First Dáil floated these Bonds in 1919 to finance that government. Because of this, my mother may have had reason to believe that the State had intervened on my aunt's behalf.

The Catholic Church had absolutely nothing to do with it, however. My mother had an obsession about the part she supposed the Church had played. The Church's position may have had some indirect bearing on the case, insofar as it was perfectly obvious that, had he been alive, my father would have brought me up a Catholic, but that was the extent of the influence. From later correspondence I discovered that my mother had called on her friends and acquaintances in the Labour party to give her some moral support. I understood

that she had been in touch with Jim Larkin and others. Though they were very sympathetic, nobody was prepared to get directly involved.

My erratic upbringing, moving frequently from place to place, did not help my mother's case. In the end, the presiding judge, Judge Meredith (later a Supreme Court judge), made the sensible decision to ask me directly what my wishes were. He took me into his private chambers. By now I had passed my fourteenth birthday and was well able to

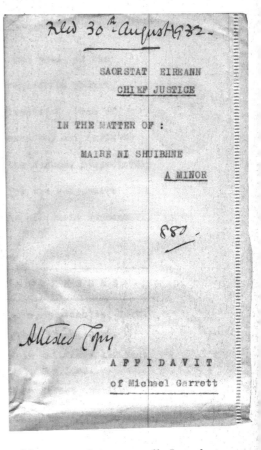

LEFT: My new family, the MacSwineys — Seán, me, Máire, Annie. This photo was taken to send to the other MacSwineys — Kit in Tokyo, Peg in Ashville, North Carolina, and Peter in New York — as proof that I had finally come home!
RIGHT: An affidavit sworn for the case to establish my legal guardianship.

understand English, though I could not speak it very well. I made it very clear to him, in my limited English, that I wanted to stay in Ireland with my Aunt Máire. That was the only time that I was brought to the court.

In making my aunt my co-guardian, my father had understood that my mother was not well and would probably be unable to look after me, which must have been of great concern to him. In the end the case went against my mother and my aunt was granted custody over me. However, there were conditions attached to this. First, I was made a ward of court and placed under police protection, which seemed to me rather unnecessary at the time. I learned later that my mother had plans to 're-kidnap' me, so perhaps it was necessary after all.

Secondly, an order was made that I was not to be involved in any way in Republican activities. For this I was eternally grateful because returning to Cork as the daughter of Terence MacSwiney, it might have been expected, in Republican circles, that I would be drawn into the Cumann na gCailíní, the Republican girl guides, and other such movements. (This was a common difficulty faced by the children left behind after the armed struggle — to live up to the expectations of

A íoſa, a Ḋia ḃílıſ, ταḃαıſ ḋó ſíοτċáın ſíοſſαıḋe.

It is not to those who can inflict most,
but to those who can endure most that
the victory is certain.

ní'l a ſáſú ſo ve gſáḋ ag vuıne aſ bıτ,
a beaτa a ταḃαıſτ ſuaſ aſ ſon a ċαſαv

ı nÐıl-Cuıṁne aſ
ΤΟΙRÐΕΑLḂΑĊ mαc SUIḂNε,

Ταοıſeaċ aſ ċéαv vſıong Coſcaıge
ın aſm na Saoſ-ſτáıτe,
áſv-ṁaoſ Caτſαċ Coſcaıge
a v'ſulang báſ aſ ſon a Τí e ḃúττaıſ
ı gCaſcaſ Bſıcſτon. ı Saſanaıḃ
an 25aḋ lá ve ṁí Ðeıſe ſoġṁαıſ. 1920.
.ı. 4aḋ blıaḋaın na Saoſ-ſτáıτe.

Τſόcαıſe Ðé aſ a anam-ſan aguſ aſ
anmannaıḃ na bſıſéan a ſuaıſ báſ
aſ ſon na h-Éıſeann.

others.) The reason for this order of the court was my mother's contention, as part of her case, that if I were put in the care of my aunt, I would be involved in all such activities. Thus it was explicitly laid down that all such things would have to be excluded if my aunt were to be granted custody.

Being now a ward of court meant a garda escort frequently

accompanied us. We noticed this when one day the O'Rahilly family brought me for an outing to Portmarnock. Two gardaí escorted us on motorbikes, a little distance behind. My aunt may have found this difficult to accept considering her attitude to the Free State and its officials. It shows how she once again put my welfare before her political principles. When I returned to Cork at the end of that summer, the garda presence seemed to fade away.

LEFT: **My father's mortuary card with the old Irish spelling of Terence.** THIS PAGE: **his prison badge, cutlery set and hat.**

The few summer weeks that we had to be in Dublin for the court case we stayed with my aunt's friends, the O'Donels, in Eccles Street. This was home from home for my aunts. There were three O'Donel sisters, Gerry, Jo and Lil, originally from Swinford, County Mayo. It was always pointed out to me that the name was spelt with one 'n' and one 'l'.

The eldest, Gerry, a trained nurse, kept a nurse's home and co-op at 27 Eccles Street, and a registry for private nurses. Nurses went from her establishment to doctors and nursing homes. Most importantly, Gerry O'Donel's home, one of the Georgian houses on Eccles Street, was a centre where many well-known Republicans met. I thought of this as a 'salon' for Republicans. There, one was likely to meet many of the well-known people of the time.

The second sister, Jo O'Donel, was also a nurse. She ran a private hospital at 62 Eccles Street. She had the top floor converted into an operating theatre in order to nurse wounded IRA volunteers during the Civil War. Some years later she bought number 63 next door and set up a private maternity home. Many years later my children were born in number 63. (Coincidentally, my son, Cathal, was to work there in the 1970s, in the building in which he was born, when he was a lecturer with the Dublin Institute of Technology.) My gynaecologist told me this was the only private nursing home with an operating facility.

Gerry and Jo were quite different characters: Gerry being more loving and kind-hearted; Jo more practical and focused. They often spent their spare time playing Bridge, Jo with skill and understanding, Gerry with a more vague and haphazard approach. The result was often confusion and an explosive experience – a pantomime to watch. Jo would exclaim in exasperation, 'Good God, Gerry, did you not see me leading with the two of hearts?'

Lil was the youngest and married to Peadar O'Donnell, the famous writer and socialist Republican activist. He described Lil as a vivacious redhead who visited him in Mountjoy jail where he and other Republicans were imprisoned. Peadar had always maintained, jokingly, that he had taken on the three women. It was through Peadar that I met quite a few of the socialists of the time. I can remember quite distinctly George Gilmore, who later fought in the Spanish Civil War on the Republican side. I also remember a Frau Grabisch, an elderly lady interested in the Irish cause; I heard her name mentioned on RTÉ recently.

Gerry was a devout Catholic and the first to introduce me to the practice of that religion by presenting me with a Rosary of little red glass beads. She went to daily Mass and Communion accompanied by Aunt Máire and myself, so I was plunged straight into Catholicism from the very beginning. We would walk up Nelson Street, through an archway to the back of Berkeley Road and to the church. I was later to learn that this was the church to which Cathal Brugha was brought after he died in the Mater hospital in 1922. Later, this was where all our children were christened, as they were born in Jo's nursing home nearby.

Peadar O'Donnell was always in and out of O'Donels'. When I got to know him better I admired him greatly and he became a lifelong friend of my husband, Ruairí, and myself. Peadar was a person of great humility and he had a wonderful sense of humour. Years later, when I was living in Dublin, he used to tell us of the time when he was holding a meeting in College Green in connection with the Republican Congress, a movement then considered by the Catholic Church to be communist and very dangerous! At that time a Catholic political organisation was formed called Maria Duce, and its members went to the College Green meeting in protest and to attack Peadar and his friends. Peadar told how he climbed up a lamppost while they prayed below, waving their Rosary beads at him. I learned later that Frank Duff, the founder of a Catholic religious organisation, the Legion of Mary, was a great friend of Peadar's. Peadar was certainly a very broadminded person whose humanity and tolerance made him acceptable to all sorts of people.

This was the Ireland I was first introduced to, during the month the case of my custody between my mother and my aunt was conducted. Another memory of that time in Dublin was a visit, with my aunt, to the de Valera home on Cross Avenue in Blackrock. As always, I was very shy and diffident. The whole family sat around the table. Young Terry de Valera, playing with a dog under the table, relieved the situation for me; this distraction freed me from having to participate in the general proceedings.

At the end of August my aunt and I returned home to Cork.

MY RELATIONS

There were a few short weeks still available before the opening of school. This time was filled mainly with visiting friends, or with visitors calling to the house to see the new arrival from foreign parts – perhaps to give me the 'once over'. Cork people are notoriously curious! Of the visits I especially remember, one was to the home of the Fleischmanns. Frau Tilly Fleischmann had been born in Cork, with her two sisters, of German parents, called Schwarz. They had been given a bad time during the 1914–1918 war and were ostracised. Apparently, only the MacSwineys, the Stockleys and a few others had befriended them.

Frau Fleischmann was a gifted pianist and performer, as well as an eminent teacher of pianoforte. We heard she had been either a pupil of Liszt or had studied under one of his pupils. Only daughters of families with means could afford to be taught by her. Her pupils included my mother, Muriel Murphy, Jenny O'Brien (later known as Sinéad Ní Bhriain), daughter of the O'Brien Woollen Mills family in Douglas, and Geraldine O'Sullivan (later Neeson), daughter of a well-to-do merchant in Cork. Thus Frau Fleischmann was influential in bringing together these three women who, by their friendship, brought about the link between my mother and the MacSwiney family.

Frau Fleischmann's husband was Aloys Fleischmann (Senior) from Bavaria, who, when I met him, still spoke in broad Bavarian German (to which I was well accustomed) and not very good English. Aloys Senior was the choir master and organist in the North Cathedral in Cork. I believe his pupils often had difficulty understanding his English! Their only son was also Aloys, later to become Professor of Music in UCC and promoter of ballet and the Cork Choral Festival.

My recollection of that visit is mainly of Aloys's kindness in entertaining me — a difficult youngster who could not speak the language — while our elders chatted and drank tea. After all, Aloys was a grown young man at the time.

I had, of course, met Aloys and his mother the previous year in Grainau, when they were on a visit to Munich. He was then twenty years old and had just got his degree, Bachelor of Music, of which his mother was very proud. I still have a lovely photograph taken with them, with my German Alps in the background (shown on page 60).

The other memorable visit we paid was to a big, imposing house in the outskirts of Cork City, on the banks of the River Lee. On our arrival, there was some concern when it was discovered we would be thirteen sitting down to table at supper. This was completely out of the question as it was believed it would bring bad luck. I was banished (I felt) to eat with the younger children in another room. I felt completely baffled and somewhat upset; I had never heard of this strange superstition of the Irish!

Apart from these visits, if anybody called to see me in St Ita's I would sit them down and play cards because of my inability to hold a conversation in English. I had recently been taught how to play Rummy and 110. Everybody was always very obliging.

The one great disappointment was that my Grandmother Murphy, who was then coming near the end of her life, had not been told of my return; the family decided she was not well enough to be informed. I think it would have been a great disappointment to her not to have seen me if she had understood that I had returned home. Throughout the nine years I was away, my whereabouts in Germany was a cause of concern to my grandmother as well as to Aunt Máire. My mother did not keep in contact with any of her relations in Cork, so they were all in the dark regarding my life abroad. In fact, my grandmother used regularly drive down to my aunts Máire and Annie in St Ita's to enquire if they had any news as to my whereabouts. In this way these elderly ladies became quite close because of their mutual concern for me.

When my mother got involved with the MacSwineys and there emerged the possibility of her marrying my father, Terence, it caused consternation in the Murphy family. I found amongst the MacSwiney papers a reply from the bishop of Cork to Grandmother Murphy, who had requested him to intervene in the proposed marriage. The bishop's reply was to the effect that he was unable to intervene in this matter,

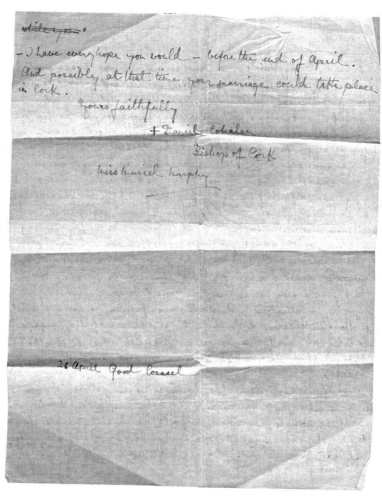

state you.

— I have every hope you would — before the end of April.
And possibly at that time your marriage could take place
in Cork.

Yours faithfully

+ Daniel Cohalan

Bishop of Cork

Miss Muriel Murphy

26 April Good Counsel

LEFT AND RIGHT:
The letter from
Bishop Daniel
Cohalan to my
mother asking
her to postpone
her wedding.

although he did write to my mother asking her to postpone the wedding so as to give her mother time to adjust to the idea.

My father got to know my mother during some musical evenings that Frau Fleischmann held, during which time they became very close. She visited him when he was in Wakefield Detention Barracks in England after the 1916 Rising. They got engaged, but my mother could not get married until after her twenty-fifth birthday on 5 June 1917, when she would receive her settlement. In those days women didn't inherit the family business, but instead were given a handsome settlement on reaching maturity at twenty-five. So they fixed the wedding day for 9 June.

LEFT:
My father admired my mother's fearlessness and commitment to the cause.
BELOW:
The little church near Bromyard where my parents were married in 1917. My father paid the fee to have this church registered for weddings so that they could get married there.

My father, at the time, was in an open prison in Frongoch, in North Wales. He had freedom of movement, but was not allowed to leave the area. There was some confusion in Frongoch regarding his identity. He was known to be an officer, and therefore presumed to be a British officer on leave from the First World War. As a consequence, apparently, he got invited to garden parties in the area.

My parents were married in a small Catholic chapel in Bromyard, Herefordshire; theirs was the first marriage to be held in that church. They were married by Fr Augustine OFM, a Capuchin priest from Cork. My father had a volunteer uniform made and sent over to him, which he wore under his overcoat until the beginning of the ceremony, in case there would be any objection. (There was some wonder among the locals who turned up as to why he was wearing such a heavy coat on a very hot day.) His best man was Richard (Dick) (later General) Mulcahy. They had become good friends during their joint activities promoting the Irish language. My mother's bridesmaid was Geraldine O'Sullivan, who later married Seán Neeson. It was a small gathering, but my aunts, Máire and Annie, were in attendance. After they were married I think my grandmother became reconciled to the

fact and was very helpful to her daughter in looking after me whenever my mother fell ill. Of course, within three years of marriage, in
1919, my father became Lord Mayor of Cork, which would then have
made a very respectable son-in-law!

During my first years in Cork, Aunt Mabel, my mother's older
sister, used to invite me regularly to lunch at her beautiful residence,
Ringmahon, which was south of Cork City, overlooking the Lee. She
would send for me in her chauffeur-driven car, driven by White. (In
those days, people in service were always known by their surnames.) I
would sit in the back of the car like royalty, feeling very conspicuous.
Aunt Mabel was married to her second cousin, James Murphy, who
belonged to the Murphy brewery branch of the family; our branch was
the Cork distillery. My aunt and I would lunch in her huge dining-
room at a large mahogany table, all alone. Portraits of the Murphy
ancestors surrounded us. She would point out to me, 'That is your
great-uncle James' and so on, all the way around the walls. To me,
who grew up with no knowledge of my family, I found it a little

overwhelming. After lunch she would show me her beautiful garden, which White and his staff looked after. Aunt Mabel was also a very competent amateur photographer, with a dark room to develop her own film. Her husband, James, died before her, and after her death, in the 1950s, this beautiful house was sold as part of her estate. Ben Dunne, of Dunnes Stores, got it for very little and lived there with his family for quite a few years. Sadly, it was later knocked down and a modern estate built on the land.

All the Murphy family were educated in England, as were most of the well-to-do Irish Catholics in Cork. My mother and her sisters were sent to the Holy Child Sisters in London, and the boys to Stonyhurst or Ampleforth. Aunt Nora entered the Holy Child convent, which is why I never met her. I got to know Aunt Edith, who had entered the Irish Sisters of Charity and was Reverend Mother in the nearby Tramore convent for a time. On her visits to the Cork convent in Peacock Lane, Aunt Edith would ask me to come and visit her. It was through her that I heard about my mother's earlier years. Muriel had always been a worry to her elderly parents and as a teenager rebelled against her wealthy and privileged position. At one time they sent her to Oxford for a short period, hoping this might benefit her. By the time she met the MacSwineys, my mother was already of a very independent and liberal way of

LEFT:
My parents on their wedding day, with Máire, Annie, Fr Augustine, Geraldine Neeson and Richard Mulcahy.
RIGHT:
Grandmother Murphy's mother-of-pearl rosary beads, my only memento of her.

thinking. On one of my visits to Aunt Edith in the convent, the Angelus bell began to ring. She immediately sank to her knees and started praying, 'In the name of the Father ...', expecting me to join in. I had to stop her and shamefacedly tell her that I could only say the prayer in Irish. She graciously suggested that we would each say our own in silence.

My mother's eldest brother and head of the family was Nicholas, known to me as Uncle Nico. He should have taken over the management of the Cork distillery business, but didn't feel inclined to take on this task. Instead, he went to live in England with his young wife and had two children, Beryl and Stephen. They were born and grew up in England. Beryl and I must have got married at roughly the same time because Aunt Mabel took a beautiful photograph of me with my daughter, Deirdre, aged three months, wrapped in a white christening shawl. This shawl was commissioned by Aunt Edith to be made by the nuns in the convent. Aunt Mabel took another photo around the same time of Beryl with her daughter in a similar christening shawl.

Since Nicholas would not take over the business his younger brother, Norbert, took it on. He had two sons, Tony and Ronnie, the eldest of whom died young. When Norbert wished to retire, my cousin, Stephen Murphy, was asked to come over from England and run the distillery. Stephen bought a beautiful house in Montenotte, on a height, overlooking the Lee. It was situated very near the Murphy ancestral home of *Carrigmore*. I first got to know Stephen when, on the death of Uncle Norbert, he rang to give me the particulars of the funeral in Glanmire. Ruairí and I drove to Cork and I met Stephen for the first time. Norbert was buried in the impressive Murphy family grave in St Finbarr's cemetery in Cork. It was all very imposing. By the end of the same week Aunt Edith had died in the convent of the Irish Sisters of Charity on Wellington Road. Stephen rang again and we returned for the second funeral that week. She was buried in the cemetery on the convent grounds.

Stephen and I, from the very beginning, were *en rapport*. Throughout the years we became very friendly. Any time I went to Cork I was invited to his house to lunch, or I visited him in his offices where he was doing a lot of research into Murphy family history. Some years after he took over the business, the Cork distillery was amalgamated with Jameson's and Powers in Dublin to become the Irish Distillers Group so as to compete internationally, especially on the American market. The old Cork distillery in Midleton was abandoned (now rejuvenated as a visitor centre), and next to it a big new distillery was built to manufacture all the products of the Irish Distillers Group. Stephen remained one of the main directors and managers of this. I decided, in later years, to buy a few shares in the company simply to enable me to attend the AGMs in Dublin so that I could meet Stephen there. We always had great chats. The table would be covered with all the products of the company and Stephen would ask me what I would like to drink. I had always to reply, 'Sorry, Stephen, I do not drink any of the products you people produce. I drink wine.' He would then chase around looking for something suitable and come back with a 'spritzer'.

When our second son, Terry, was getting married to Máire Owens, who was from Cork, her parents, Denis and Maura Owens, asked me was there nobody in Cork of my family that they could invite to the wedding. I told them, 'Well, none of my MacSwiney family is left.' Then it occurred to me: 'I have a cousin called Stephen Murphy.' So they invited him and his fiancée. Stephen came to the wedding and he told me that when he saw Terry and his bride as they walked down the aisle in the Honan Chapel, he saw immediately that Terry was the image of the Murphys. Stephen enjoyed the wedding festivities and remained friendly with some of my Cork friends. Sadly, he died fairly young of cancer. He was buried from St Patrick's Church in Cork. That funeral was the first and only time I met my cousin Beryl, his sister, and that was the end of my contact with the Murphys.

"NA PLANÉIDÍ" ("Stars without Stripes")

Review of the Planetary System held by its Sovereign, the Sun

AUNT MÁIRE

Mercurí (Mercury) ... Eiblín De Nógla

Bénus (Venus) ... Fionnghula Ní Conchubair

An Domhan (the Earth) ... Póilín Ní Churtáin

An Ge... (the Moon) ... Eiblín Ní Scanláin

Má... ... Úna Ní Churtáin

Iúpi... ... Máire Ní Fhícheallaigh

Comédie Française—

Scenes du "Voyage de Monsieur Pe

Personages:

M. Perrichon ... Nollai

M. Armand Desroches ... Eit

Daniel Savary ... Máire

Jean (un domestique) ... Caitlí

Mme. Perrichon ... Eiblín

Henriette (sa fille) ... Áine

Act III.—Un Salon.   Act IV.—Ja

(Synopsis of the Play will be read in English)

Céilidhe an Feithideacháin
(Little Butterfly's Ball)

An Feithideachán (the Butterfly) ... Eibl

An Dubán Alla (the Spider) ... Mái

I spent from 1932 to 1945, thirteen years, in Cork. My Aunt Máire lived for only ten of them. She and my Aunt Annie used to talk to me about my father. I really thought it was just private family history. The first time I understood that he was a public figure was when my Uncle Seán was a member of the Cork Corporation in the 1930s. He came home one Monday night from a meeting and told my aunts that the Corporation had voted unanimously that Wellington Road, where the MacSwineys lived and where St Ita's school was situated, was to be renamed MacSwiney Road. My aunts said, 'Is that so?' A few weeks later they asked what had happened the resolution, only to be told that the City Manager, Mr Monahan, had vetoed it. A few years later Seán again told them that Cork Corporation had once more unanimously passed a resolution to name a street after Terence MacSwiney. At that time there was no legal obstruction to changing the name of a road, but again Mr Monahan would not allow it. My aunts told me about my father's love of the Irish language and his hunger strike and death. This was the first time I had heard about it. It was only in later life, after I had got married and settled in Dublin, that I began to realise fully that my father was a historical figure, known all over the world.

My aunts' school reopened in the September after my homecoming, in 1932. My aunt, Mary MacSwiney, was a remarkable woman of great intellect and strength of character. Her father, John MacSwiney, was a descendant of the MacSwiney clan who had lived in Doe Castle

RIGHT:

My Aunt Máire was a remarkable woman of great intellect and strength of character.

90

(Caisleán na dTuath) in Donegal. The MacSwineys were chieftains to the O'Donnells. They fought battles for the O'Donnells, but also, to cement their relationship, fostered their sons to one another's families. This could be described as the first record of the MacSwiney involvement in education.

Eoghan Óg MacSwiney, who held the castle between 1570 and 1592, provided refuge for survivors of the Spanish Armada in 1588, and was foster father to Red Hugh O'Donnell, who was entrusted to his care in 1587. When the McCarthys of Muskerry, in County Cork, asked The O'Donnell for assistance to repel the first English invasion of Munster, these MacSwineys moved south where they settled and built three castles, not to be evicted until the arrival of Oliver Cromwell in 1649.

As a young man, John MacSwiney went to Italy to serve in the Papal Guard in the war against Garibaldi. He arrived too late for the war, and returned not to Ireland but to London, where he took a job as a teacher in 1870. There he met another teacher, Mary Wilkinson, an

LEFT:(L–R): The four MacSwiney sisters in their youth, Peg, Annie, Mary (Máire) and Kit. RIGHT: The young family of John and Mary MacSwiney. *Standing* (L–R): Peter, Kit and Mary, with Terence in front. Peg on her mother's lap and Annie and Seán with their father. Note that each is wearing a Papal Cross.

Englishwoman brought up in the Victorian era. Their three eldest children, Mary, Peter and Kit, were born in London and spent their early childhood there. The family then transferred to Cork. The first child born in Cork was my father, Terence. John had been persuaded to join his brother-in-law in Cork to set up a small snuff and tobacco factory on Wellington Road. This was unfortunate as he suffered from asthma and such an environment was injurious to his health.

I think my aunt, Mary (Máire) MacSwiney, got her independence and self-confidence from her English background. She once said to me, 'I cannot understand the slave-mindedness of the Irish.' I later thought this lack of confidence of the Irish came from centuries of British domination. One didn't usually come across English people who lacked self-confidence.

Mary attended St Angela's school on Patrick's Hill, run by the

ABOVE:
My parents, Terence and Muriel, with his two sisters, Máire and Annie, and me a few months old.

Ursuline order. After leaving school and getting her degree, she went to Cambridge University to obtain her Diploma in Higher Education. This was the time of the Suffrage Movement, in which she took part. On leaving Cambridge she took up a teaching post in England, at Hillside Convent in Farnborough, a boarding school run by Benedictine nuns, and might even have entered the order, but duty dictated otherwise. Her mother, who had been left a widow at an early age, died suddenly of pneumonia, leaving the other five children, some of them still young, and a household to be cared for. My aunt gave up her chosen life and returned to Cork to take up duty. 'Duty' always loomed large in the MacSwiney family.

Mary MacSwiney took up a teaching position in St Angela's, her *alma mater*, where she mainly taught Latin and History. The nun in charge of the school at this time had been a classmate of hers. One day, this nun called my aunt to her office to tell her that there had been some complaints from parents regarding her teaching of Irish history. 'What's wrong with it?' Aunt Máire asked. She was told, 'The parents consider it too Irish!'

After the 1916 Rising — in which my father was to have taken part except that it was called off in Cork by countermand from Dublin headquarters — the Royal Irish Constabulary (RIC) rounded up any people who might have been involved. One of these was Mary MacSwiney. They arrested her at the school.

Máire O'Connor, later Mrs Tyrell, who was one of the first pupils to attend St Ita's, was a pupil of St Angela's at that time. She told me she saw Miss Mary, as my aunt was known in the school, being arrested and marched down the corridor, flanked by RIC men, to the great excitement of the class. All the pupils could see this unbelievable event through the glass of the partitions to the corridor. My aunt was released after a few weeks. But this was too much for the school and, on her release, she was once again sent for by the headmistress. Being an old friend of my aunt's the nun tried to break the news gently to her by saying, 'You know, Min, [she was known by that name as a girl] we have to cut down on staff owing to reduced numbers.' 'Well, since I am a senior member of the staff that would not apply to me,' Aunt Máire replied. She always believed in the direct approach. The question of the dismissal was then explained to her more explicitly.

Following this episode, friends of similar outlook suggested that she should open her own school. This she set about doing. A committee of prominent men, mainly from the Cork business world, was established to look after the school's financial affairs. One of the committee members was TJ Murphy, who owned a grocer's shop opposite the Cork GPO. He lived with his family in a large residence, called *Springfield*, in Tivoli, overlooking the Lee, which is now the Silver Springs Moran Hotel. I remember visiting there after my return to Ireland. My aunt acquired premises from Mr Murphy at the low rent of £40 a year, which he never increased while my aunts were alive. His daughter, Natalie, was one of the first pupils. Aunt Máire asked her sister, Annie, to return from England to join her in the venture. St Ita's opened its doors on 4 September 1916, at 4 Belgrave Place, Wellington Road.

In the beginning the school was well attended, as most people

LEFT AND RIGHT: A programme for a Christmas show at Scoil Íte in 1919, three years after the school opened.

clár

English Drama—

"The Wisdom of Foolishness"

Dramatis Personæ :

Sir Thomas More	...	noūlaiġ ní ṁuṗċaḋa
Erasmus "	...	eiḃlín De Dappa
William Roper ...	...	máire ní Ḋonnaḃáin
Lady More	...	eiḃlín ní Leatleaḃaiṗ
Pattison (Jester to Sir Thomas More)	máire ní ṁuṗċaḋa
King's Officer ...	...	síle ní Ċonċuḃaiṗ
Executioner ...	...	Caitlín ní Ċataṗaiġ

Daughters to Sir Thomas More :
Meg—máire ní Ċonċuḃaiṗ, Bess—ḟronnúla ní Ċonċuḃaiṗ,
Daisy—úna ní Cuṗcáin, Cecy—uṗṗala ḃuiṗeṗ

Mercy Giggs (adopted child of Sir T. More)—síle ní ṁuṗċaḋa

Peggy (a serving maid) ... Caitlín ní Ċataṗaiġ

REPORT.

DISTRIBUTION OF PRIZES.

Finale—Dán Diaḋa íce naoṁċa

áṙd scoil naoṁ íte

★

bṙonnaḋ na nDuaiṙeanna,

nodlaiġ, 1919

were nationalistically minded. After 1921, however, many who sided with the Treaty stayed away. But MacSwiney friends and Republicans remained on, including TJ Murphy's three daughters and the children of some of the academic staff in UCC, such as the Fleischmanns and the Stockleys. Many years later Aunt Máire described to me how she sat in the school, waiting to see who would turn up on the first day after the summer holidays in 1921. By degrees others returned because it was considered the best school in Cork and, since no political influence was apparent, the numbers built up again. It was quite a big school when I arrived there in 1932.

Mary MacSwiney's friend, the Hon. Albinia Brodrick, who renamed herself Gobnait Ní Bhruadair, once came up to St Ita's during the 'Tan war, when the IRA was at its height. She reported she had heard that the 'boys' were going to burn out her brother, Lord Midleton, adding 'and Min, he was always so good to his people.' My aunt is said to have replied, with her devastating logic, 'Gobnait, you must remember they were never "his people".' This is not to say that my aunt, I'm quite sure, approved of anybody being burnt out.

After the passing of the Treaty and the setting-up of the Free State in 1921 the bishop of Cork, and possibly the Catholic Church in general, I don't know, excommunicated all those who had sided with the Republic. Among these were my two MacSwiney aunts, who attended daily Mass and were the most devout Catholics I was ever to know. Of course, no priest would pass over them when they came to the altar for Holy Communion. The disapproval of Bishop Daniel Cohalan of my Aunt Máire's stance once went too far, however. He accused her of having embezzled some money, which had been collected for the Republican prisoners' dependants' fund. She immediately decided to take action. She attempted to bring a case against him in Ireland, but was informed she would have to get his 'canonical immunity' lifted in Rome; she fought the case in Rome for years, neither winning nor losing. However, she heard from various sources over the next few years that when the bishop was administering confirmation throughout the Cork diocese, in his address to the children and the congregation he would include high praise and admiration for Miss Mary MacSwiney. My aunt's reaction to this was, 'That's not good enough. The bishop should have withdrawn the remarks he made, which were a defamation of my character.' According to the doctrines of the Church, to be absolved from any wrongdoing there are three conditions: sorrow, confession of sins and atonement, and my aunt held strictly to those principles.

During the ten years that I spent under the guidance of my Aunt Máire, she had a profound influence on my life. Throughout my whole lifetime I never again met anyone to surpass her in integrity and intellectual ability.

Scoil Íᴛᴇ

Scoil Íte, as St Ita's became known before I came home to Cork, was a school of renown and the only lay school in the city, all the others being conducted by Christian Brothers or nuns. The school took in small boys, as was the custom in those days, up to the age of seven when they made their First Communion. This included many of the boys from the small Jewish community in Cork, as the school was acceptable to them. As well as that, other prominent Cork citizens of a very different political outlook from my aunt sent their children to the school, appreciating the quality of the education. They understood that no politics or republicanism permeated the school's curriculum. Perhaps they also felt it provided a certain 'pol-ish' as my aunts, being partly English, spoke with an English accent.

The lower (primary) classes were well attended, and the *Kindergarten* class was full. The *Kindergarten* was presided over by Miss Nora Cassily, known to us as Iníon Ní Chaisligh, a qualified Froebel *Kindergarten* teacher. She was otherwise known as "Bhean

RIGHT:
My Aunt Máire was concerned about my welfare while I was in Germany, so she found out where I was staying and sent me this photo of Annie and herself.
BELOW:
Children playing in a percussion band outside Scoil Íte.

Uasail'; all the teachers were addressed as 'A Bhean Uasail'. This later became the title by which she was known all over Cork, where many a prominent businessman and academic would look back with fond memories of their beginnings in school under her tutelage.

Wonderful stories came out of that *Kindergarten*. One was when the priest came up from the nearby St Patrick's Church to examine the children being prepared for First Communion. 'Now, children,' he said, 'copy everything I am doing.' And so he started off, 'In the name of the Father ...' Just then, a fly settled on his bald head and twenty-six little hands followed his direction. 'Bhean Uasail was in the background, collapsing with laughter.

Another time she asked the children to draw a picture of the 'Flight into Egypt'. The children proceeded with the task. They presented their accomplishments, which were always highly praised, but one in particular puzzled her. It had a big black blob down in the corner. She asked the child to explain and he said, 'Don't you know, the angel said to St Joseph, "take Mary and the child and flea into Egypt".'

Another achievement of Iníon Ní Chaisligh was to translate the children's names into Irish when they started school. It was the policy of the school to revert the anglicised names (such as McCarthy, Murphy, Barry) to their original Irish. As she was the first person the

LEFT:
The pupils of
Scoil Íte
playing outside the
school premises.
ABOVE:
A class *c.* 1930.

children encountered, the task was left to her. One day Aunt Annie discovered that this was being carried out to the point where Iníon Ní Chaisligh was attempting to translate every single name. Aunt Annie protested that the idea was to translate Irish names back to their original, not to change foreign names. It seems that Professors Fleischmann and Stockley escaped this fate, however David Jackson, son of a well-known Jewish family in Cork, became Daithí Jackson.

When, in later years, we had large past-pupils' reunions in Cork, Iníon Ní Chaisligh was the guest of honour and presided over the proceedings like a matriarch. We once presented her with a painting to commemorate her years of service to the school; she had been an integral part of it.

Others who acted as 'associate' teachers were such eminent people as Madame Stockley, wife of Professor Stockley of UCC, Geraldine Neeson, and Clare Kelleher, who became Mrs Hutson, wife of the Director of the School of Art. Madame Stockley was half-French and

taught us French drama, and whatever about the drama, she insisted on impeccable French pronunciation! This was no problem for me as I grew up familiar with the language, but imagine what it meant to the children born and bred in Cork. Geraldine Neeson taught us choir and plainchant. Mrs Hudson taught art.

All these well-known people added to the ambience of Scoil Íte and helped to give it a high reputation for culture as well as education. Years later I was told that the Professor of Education in UCC, a Mrs O'Sullivan, declared that after a month or so of teaching H. Dip. students, she could pick out those in her class who were past pupils of Scoil Íte. Of course, the mainstay of the staff were the two Misses MacSwiney.

Annie was younger than Máire and taught English and Maths. She was an excellent teacher, with a degree in Science from Newman College, later University College Dublin (UCD). It was there she became friends with Hannah Sheehy, who later became Mrs Sheehy

ABOVE:
Our school outing to the seaside at Garryvoe in 1933 was great fun. The teacher, Áine Ní Mhuirithe, made all the preparations.

Skeffington. Her husband, Francis Sheehy Skeffington, was murdered by the British in 1916.

Aunt Annie (Eithne Ní Shuibhne) insisted that English was spoken properly in the school. Miss Annie, as she was always known, was a very good English teacher, specialising in grammar and parsing. I also took to this subject as, once more, its logical structure appealed to me. Her teaching of Shakespeare was excellent. The play on the curriculum that year was *Julius Caesar*, my first introduction to the author. We started with Anthony's oration over Caesar's dead body, 'Friends, Romans, countrymen, lend me your ears ...', which we had to learn off by heart. At first, I was reluctant to learn it because I was too shy to recite it in front of the class, but she insisted – no exceptions would be tolerated. So I gave in on the condition that I would not have to recite it in class, to which she agreed. Next day, all the other pupils recited their work in turn, and then she called on me. Imagine my consternation! But I stumbled through it in my terrible German accent. I was furious with her after school. She had given me a promise. But, she said, exceptions could not be made, especially for her niece. I did not always see eye to eye with Aunt Annie!

Miss Annie also taught elocution and always maintained, 'If you speak a language, you may as well speak it correctly.' I heard it was often said jokingly in Cork: 'There go the two Republican ladies with their Oxford accents.' Of course, they were not the only such Republicans at the time.

In fourth year we studied for the Matriculation, or Matric, the university entrance exam. The mock exam papers came from Caffrey's in Dublin. One year, a question on the History paper was: 'Name the six counties of Northern Ireland bordering on the Free State.' My Aunt Annie sat down and wrote a letter to Caffrey's: 'In this school the children are not taught Irish history according to the dictat of a British Act of Parliament. Therefore, I am rewriting the question as follows: "Name the counties bordering on Ulster."'

The most important person in Scoil Íte was the founder and principal, Mary (Máire) MacSwiney, who was known in the school as 'Miss Mary'. Her aim was to give Irish girls an education that included being proud of their country and their language.

Aunt Máire had very definite theories of education. The most important aim was to give her pupils a foundation in character development. For instance, she had very clear ideas about truth and insisted on always adhering to the truth. Sometimes children came from other schools, at the age of twelve, for secondary education and were accustomed to telling little fibs. My aunt was firmly convinced that any child could be taught, within months, if not weeks, always to tell the truth. The method she applied was simple. If a child were questioned on the disappearance of a small item in the class and the child's immediate reaction was, 'I didn't do it', my aunt would then say, 'I accept that you are telling me the truth because you wouldn't lie.' Within weeks any child, no matter whether she was accustomed to telling small lies or not, would always tell the truth. Many years later I was sitting in Bewley's café on Grafton Street with a friend of mine, Elda Golden, who was married to Eddie Golden, the Abbey Theatre actor, and who was a former pupil of Miss Mary. She said to me, 'You know, Máire, I find it quite difficult that I am unable to lie, living as I do in normal society.'

I had the same problem, but it was the obverse of that coin: I believe that whatever people are telling me *is* the truth. Years later, when I was attending confession in Clarendon Street Church, in Dublin, the priest, perhaps feeling there was not sufficient substance in my tale, suggested that, maybe, I had told lies occasionally. I nearly shot out of the confessional like a rocket. I said, 'I beg your pardon, Father, I don't lie. I was brought up not to lie.'

Another strong principle that my aunt taught us was under no circumstances to do injury to anybody by taking away their character.

She very carefully taught us the difference between calumny and detraction. Calumny meant that you told somebody a lie about somebody else, in which case you could go back subsequently and tell the person, 'What I told you about that person was not true'. In this way, you could undo the damage and fulfil the need for restitution. Detraction, however, was a more serious matter. If what you had said to the detriment of the character of a person were true, you were faced with a greater difficulty: how could you go back and say, 'What I told you about that person was not true'? How, then, to undo the damage? My aunt always insisted we must never, ever injure anybody by taking away his or her good name.

As for any other questions of how Scoil Íte girls conducted themselves, the answer always was: 'Scoil Íte girls know how to behave.' The question of sex education didn't arise in those days. Those were different times and, of course, that attitude would not be acceptable today. If such an education had been required however, my aunt would have found a competent person to carry out this function.

RELIGIOUS EDUCATION

The most important aim of Mary MacSwiney's educational theory was to give young Catholic girls a sound basis to their religious education. Her instructions were of great significance in introducing me to the Catholic faith. She took the whole school for religious instruction. She knew her theology and doctrine better than many priests or bishops, and the centre of her faith was the Eucharist and the Mass.

Every child had to have a missal, which they brought to school every Friday morning. Then, between 12.30 and 1.00pm, Miss Mary would read the Gospel and Epistle of the following Sunday's Mass to all the girls beyond *Kindergarten*, explaining everything carefully, interpreting it

in every detail. We were taught the liturgy of the seasons, especially Easter. Instruction focused on the Blessed Sacrament. Everything was explained: the three nights of Tenebrae, the readings of the Gospels, all the ceremonies of the Church, and all the Easter ceremonies. Every year, the students had to take a diocesan exam on these subjects. A priest would come to each school to examine the children orally. They had to be word-perfect in Bible stories, parables and catechism. While I was at school, Scoil Íte always came first in the diocese in these examinations.

My aunt was also years ahead of her time in her interpretation of the Catholic doctrine. She very definitely taught us that everybody — be they Protestant, or living in the darkest jungle of Africa and therefore having no knowledge of Christ — would go to Heaven, provided they lived according to their conscience, knowing right from wrong. I never realised at the time that in other schools children were being taught that only Catholics could go to Heaven. During the 1960s, at the time of the Vatican Council when news was coming back to Dublin about the new ecumenism, my friend Elda and I were again drinking coffee in Bewley's café, this time on Westmoreland Street. Elda looked up at me and said, 'Máire, didn't Miss Mary teach us that in the thirties?'

My aunt never spoke of Hell as fire and brimstone. She explained Hell as being the loss of the sight of God. To her, Purgatory was the temporary loss of the sight of God: having seen Him for a moment after death, one was then deprived of His presence until the end of Purgatory. In many other ways her teaching was so well grounded that Scoil Íte girls, even if they emigrated to England or abroad, were always able to defend their faith.

When I first arrived, I was given to understand that one gives up something for Lent. Most children gave up sweets, but I didn't like them. I asked my aunt what I should give up. She asked me what did I like. I said, 'Sausages'. She replied, 'Then you can give up sausages.' Part of the Easter Saturday ceremony was the lighting of the Pascal fire and the light being brought into the church while the 'Lumen Christi' was sung, until the procession reached the high altar and the Pascal candle was lit. Next day, Easter Sunday morning, at High Mass the priest intoned the 'Gloria', the organ was played and all the bells were rung. That was the sign that Lent was over. We then went home and ate sausages!

I think we in Scoil Íte received a very different religious training from what was available in other schools, where there seemed to be more blind faith and unquestioning obedience. My aunt preferred an intellectually strong Catholicism, and based her teaching on Teresa of Avila rather than on Thérèse of Lisieux or any traditional 'piety'. She was probably also influenced by the years she spent teaching in the Benedictine school in England.

SCHOOL FINANCES

At Scoil Íte politics never entered into the atmosphere, but because Mary MacSwiney would not recognise the Irish Free State we were not under the Department of Education. We did not do the Intermediate or Leaving Certificate exams. Nobody from the Department was allowed to set foot inside the door, with the result that quite a few parents took their children out in order to have them sit the Intermediate or Leaving Certificate. The school did do Matriculation for the purpose of getting into university. It was *de rigueur* that the pupils do that. Some families were actually split on the issue. For instance, the father of my good friend, Bríd Cronin, kept her in Scoil Íte up to and including her Matric, whereas her sister, Máire, was sent to her aunt, a teaching sister with St Mary of the Isles, Sisters of Charity, in order to do her Intermediate.

As she did not recognise the Free State, Aunt Máire would not take a halfpenny from the Department of Education, which was the mainstay of the financial support of any school. The teachers' pay had to come out of the children's school fees. The school was run on a shoestring. First of all, the building still belonged to Aunt Máire's good friend, TJ Murphy, and only rent was paid on it and that was fixed. But the problem was the rates, which went up and up. Other expenses were the coal for the fires and the electricity. The problem with the school fees was that you had to keep them relatively in line with school fees elsewhere, as nobody would pay more unless they were very dedicated altogether. You also had to pay your teachers a reasonable amount, although Scoil Íte teachers always, I feel, were paid less than any other school. I surmise they did it for less than they would have got elsewhere for the simple reason that they felt it was an honour to teach in Scoil Íte. I am sure the staff worked at a disadvantage.

Another way they lost out, and I know they lost out, was that they worked in a non-registered school, so they were non-registered teachers. A teacher became registered after working in a designated school for a year, and was then entitled to a higher salary and a pension. My aunt never put an obstacle to any teacher's wish to leave. I don't suppose such a thing as a contract existed. The staff was excellent. Many were past pupils and others were friends of the MacSwineys and understood the principles and the ethos of the school. Anybody who was in Scoil Íte was there because they wanted to be there. I have never known a teacher to leave Scoil Íte to teach anywhere else.

My aunts took no salary and had no money. Maids in those days were paid very little. We had a maid in the kitchen, which was on the ground floor at the back of the building, and she produced food at given intervals. She was paid whatever was paid to maids, but no more. Definitely not higher paid. She was a wonderful woman.

Aunt Máire would go down town on a Friday evening to purchase the week's supplies. She was used to housekeeping as she had taken charge of her family when her mother had died suddenly. I don't think Aunt Annie ever learned to cook. In those days Aunt Máire did not cook, although she was capable of doing so. The maid did the cooking. My aunt made trifles for the annual school reunions and she always baked a Christmas cake for her friends in Dublin, the O'Donels. As a result, the only skill I had in the kitchen was to bake a Christmas cake and make a trifle.

There was no extra money, ever. I still remember all the money laid out on the table in the drawing-room. The money was divided out for the expenses of the school and whatever was left they used for their own basic needs. Aunt Máire went down to Patrick Street once a week to Mr Flynn, the butcher. He was strongly Fine Gael. The butcher's shop was open at the front, it had no glass at all – to me horrifying, having never seen such a thing in Germany. But it was clean, with sawdust on the floor. Mr Flynn would stand outside the shop and talk with my aunt for the best part of half an hour, discussing politics. He had the greatest respect for her, even though they were at opposite extremes politically. At the end of it, all she would buy was three chops.

MY NEW LIFE

I entered Scoil Íte in September 1932, aged fourteen. I had to contend with the seemingly impossible task of going from the absolute beginning to Matric standard in only three years. The task was enormous, as almost every subject was completely new to me.

Aunt Annie introduced me to Euclid. I was very good at geometry. First of all, I had an even playing field as the class was just starting the subject that year. Secondly, it was logical. MacSwineys were very logical and I had inherited this trait, plus my brains, I hope, from them. The other maths subject I could handle was algebra as I had learned it for two years in Germany. Not much of arithmetic was of any use to me. The imperial rather than the metric system was used. I took one look at roods, perches and chains and said this was not for me. I had mastered inches, feet and yards as part of daily life, but anything beyond that I ignored. I did take the precaution to learn two basic figures: 1,760, which I understood was yards in a mile, and 4,840, that was square yards in an acre. Any question that appeared on an examination paper which didn't involve these, I ignored.

The class was small and we got individual attention. I had learned only European history and geography, whereas here it was all Irish-based. The class also started Latin that year. That presented no problem. My English, however, was not up to standard. The children in my class would sometimes laugh at my accent, but I learned to speak English very quickly. I found it a very easy language to learn. I did not mind them teasing, or having fun at my expense. After all, I was a curiosity! They would hold up an object and ask me, 'What is this?' To which I would reply in my newly acquired English, with an appalling German accent, 'A ruler', whereupon great laughter ensued. I could never pronounce the letter 'r', so a word with two 'r's they used with glee. To this day I have difficulty pronouncing an 'r' between two vowels.

A major problem was Irish. I had completely forgotten it and I didn't even try to relearn it at first because it seemed to be impossibly difficult. I could not master it. But as I had been born in Ireland, I could not matriculate without it. The school lessons were not taught through Irish. My aunts knew very little Irish as they had started their teaching careers in England. Many of the staff had a very limited knowledge of the language, with some notable exceptions. The children were encouraged to speak Irish if they could possibly do so. In every classroom there was a sheet of paper on the wall with the children's names and on this was written, 'Níor labhras aon fhocal Béarla inniu' (I spoke no English today), in which case you could put a cross after your name. At the end of term there was a prize for the best performer. Somebody challenged me to get a cross. I took up the challenge and just kept my mouth shut all day so that I could put up my cross.

This was the beginning of my new life. I felt safe, secure and happy, surrounded by friends and those who loved me, and at last I was somebody with an identity, called Máire Óg. But it wasn't the end of my problems. Owing to my mother's insistence that under no circumstances was I to be contaminated by any contact with the Catholic Church, I had never received the Sacraments, except Baptism. Now I had to be prepared for my First Communion. My aunt arranged that Fr Augustine, the Capuchin priest who had married my father and mother, privately instruct me. He did it very carefully and with great understanding. He was a very holy and religious man with a deep devotion to the Blessed Sacraments, which he set out to pass on to me. I remember saying to somebody years later that there were things the Catholic Church taught that I did not quite believe, such as Limbo, but the one belief I clung to was the most unbelievable and impossible, and that was transubstantiation. This is the thing that distinguishes us from all the other Christian Churches. Fr Augustine taught me one prayer: 'Lord increase my desire to receive you, Lord increase my faith.' I still say it after Communion. I made my First Communion that autumn, in the private chapel of the Irish Sisters of Charity on Wellington Road. Aunt Edith, elder sister of my mother, was a member of that order, but was not there at the time as she was Reverend Mother in another house.

The next hurdle was Confirmation. Another matter altogether, and once more it was pressure and anxiety. This was a public affair, where the bishop might examine me. Accordingly, I had to learn the catechism from cover to cover, from 'Who made the world?' to 'Amen', which I proceeded to do, word-perfect. All this was to happen in May. I was fourteen, coming up to my fifteenth birthday on 23 June 1933. I was to be confirmed with a younger class of twelve-year-olds. We were all in St Patrick's Church, I was all dressed up in white poplin. (I don't know how my aunts could afford that, but the

BELOW:
My First Communion day with May Foley and Aunts Annie and Máire at the convent of the Irish Sisters of Charity on Wellington Road.

material of the frock had to be Irish, on principle!) We were all waiting in a panic for the bishop to question us, which of course he didn't. I think the least of our worries was whether the Holy Ghost descended or not.

The difference between going to school in Germany and my experiences in Scoil Íte was enormous. In Germany I had to leave the house at 6.30 in the morning to catch the train at 7.05am to the nearest town, Garmisch, to get to school, whereas in Scoil Íte we lived at the top of the house in which the school was located. If I rolled out of bed at 8.40am, I was still in time for classes. I adapted to this new school regime very readily.

In class I sat next to my friend, Máire de Róiste. She was the little girl who had been sent to play with me when I was six, when I returned for a month's holiday to Ireland (to be my last as a child) and could not speak a word of English after only nine months away. As Máire grew up in an Irish-speaking home, she was rushed up to play with me. I don't think I remembered her from before I left Ireland. I had

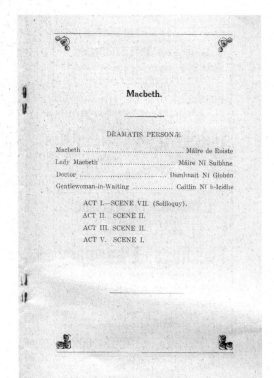

RIGHT:
Máire de Róiste as Macbeth (right) and me as Lady Macbeth in a performance of Shakespeare's play at the Fr Matthew Hall.
LEFT:
The programme.

lived a lifetime in between, but from the moment I sat next to her till the day she entered a convent we were inseparable!

Now finally, in September 1934, I entered my Matric year. This was to be the biggest hurdle I was to overcome. I had dropped Geography after fourth year, as I could use German as a fifth subject. While I was still studying Geography, in fourth year, I remember the evening before the mock exam walking round and round the table in the kitchen, learning all the rivers and mountains of Ireland off by heart without having a clue where they were. So giving up Geography was a good idea. I had six subjects – English, Maths, Latin, French, History and Irish – and in most of them I was quite competent, with the exception of Irish, of which I knew nothing.

I learned everything off by heart for the Matric Irish. Máire de Róiste's aunt, a native speaker, taught Irish in Scoil Íte. She sat me down one day and said, 'I'll tell you what we'll do. I'll write out four or five essays and you'll learn them by heart and you'll learn off passages of the texts.' These three texts were *Aesop's Fables*, *M'Asal Beag Dubh* by Padraic Ó Conaire and *Seilg i measc na nAlp* by Micheál Breathnach. This last book recalled some of my childhood in the Bavarian Alps. I learned enough off by heart to enable me to answer the questions on them.

The standard must have been much lower than it is today. However, there was one stumbling block on the exam paper. There were six small sentences to be translated from English into Irish. The one thing I had learned was that you could not say, *'Tá sé fear'* (literally, 'it is man'). So when I was confronted with the subjunctive in the sentence, 'If it were a dog, it would bite you', I had to get around it somehow or other. Finally I wrote, *'Dá mbeadh madra ann'* ('if there had been a dog there'). It must have worked out all right, as I actually passed Irish in my Matric. For weeks afterwards I had nightmares, thinking I would never get this exam – even after I had got the results and successfully matriculated. Still, from time to time I would start worrying that I would not pass.

When I had first returned to Ireland in 1932, Sr Laurentia, An tSiúr Lorcán, the sister in charge of Clothar Louis, the St Louis convent school in Monaghan, had asked Aunt Máire would she send me to the school on a scholarship; she said that she would consider it an honour if I would go to the school. My aunt replied that as she was running a school herself, it would look strange if she sent me to another school. But by all means when I matriculated, or if I were too young for college, she would be very happy to send me.

I was a very lucky girl to escape the fate of starting off secondary school in an enormous boarding school, where everything was taught through Irish when I was still trying to cope with learning English. This would probably have been beyond even my capabilities to deal with, in spite of my efforts and my MacSwiney determination!

BELOW:
The St Louis convent school in Monaghan went on an annual outing to Castle Leslie and I think this is where this photo of me, with my two friends, Máire de Róiste and Sheila O'Mahoney, was taken.

I suppose this determination was what carried the MacSwineys through hunger strikes and other vicissitudes. In my case, difficulties were more mundane, but in a way, for a young girl, almost as insurmountable. There was a cousin of my aunt's who was often in our house who used to say, 'Thank God I haven't inherited the indomitable will of the MacSwineys!'

Having succeeded in passing my Matric, I was prepared to go to Clothar Lughaidh. But I insisted my friend, Máire de Róiste, come with me. St Louis in Monaghan was a French order and therefore uncontaminated by influence from England! They had no bias against Irish. It is very interesting that those orders that came straight from France were different. Another such order was Les Soeurs de l'Enfant Jésu, also known as the Dames de St Maur because their provincial house was in the Rue de St Maur, in Paris. In Ireland they were always known as the Drishane nuns because their first convent in Ireland was in Drishane, County Cork. My Aunt Kit was a member of this order, and had been posted to Japan.

The St Louis sisters had founded the school in Monaghan in the nineteenth century. They came from Paris to teach the Irish poor, who had little or no education at the time. When I attended it had become an 'A' school, teaching everything through Irish. I joined *Rang a sé* (sixth year) and there I met a wonderful Irish teacher, An tSiúr Póilín (Sr Pauline), who taught me the basis of Irish grammar. She was mainly responsible for my being able to cope with Irish at university.

The Louis sisters were very Irish — not politically, but with regard to the language, dancing and culture. Going there was the makings of me in another area altogether. I was under no pressure with study, as I had already matriculated and had secured my entrance to university. Having the Matric meant we were very free, and as a result rather giggly. We had short gymslips up to our knees when everyone else's were nearly down to their ankles. One of the nuns didn't approve and

attached a piece of brown paper to the hem of my friend's slip to show how long it ought to be.

Since Máire and I had got Latin to Matric standard, we had reached Leaving Certificate standard, which was the same as the Matric. Sr Dorothea, the senior Latin teacher in St Louis, had always had an ambition to bring a class to Leaving Cert. Here she had the wonderful opportunity of two students who had reached said standard. She put us through our paces, to the point of conducting a lesson sitting on our beds when Máire twisted her ankle and was confined to her cubicle. We joined the class below us, *Rang a cúig* (fifth year), for Roman history. This class was preparing to do the exam the following year. Many years later I became very good friends with two of the girls from that class: one was Sheila Herlihy; the other was Bríd O'Doherty, who was the life and soul of the class.

By Christmas, with all this Leaving Cert. in the air I wrote to Aunt Máire asking if I could sit the exam as I was doing all the study for it anyway. She wrote back agreeing that I could. When it came to me and my welfare, I came first and the Republic came second. She had compromised her principles for me before when she had recognised the State by taking out a passport to visit me in Germany.

I sat my Leaving Cert. in June 1936, and on my results won a bursary to University College Cork. This was a great bonus as there was no money in the MacSwiney family. It would have been difficult to find my university fees, though I know my aunts would have made every sacrifice to do so.

I had one interesting experience after our Leaving Cert. exam was finished. All the other classes had gone on holidays and only the sixth-year girls remained behind. A special two-day retreat was laid on for us. The main theme of the retreat appeared to be that the world out there was a dangerous place. The priest suggested that we girls might consider returning to the convent as postulants in the autumn. This advice had no effect on me as I had already lived in this 'dangerous' world all my life. But it may explain why so many of the St Louis past pupils did enter the convent.

That was the only time I attended a convent school, or was taught by religious. I was happy to be able to add a new experience to my upbringing. Máire and I returned home to Cork to get ready to go to university in the autumn.

KERRY

The best part of my teenage years and afterwards was our summer holidays in Kerry, spent at our cottage in Gráig, Ballyferriter, on the Dingle Peninsula.

In 1924 or 1925, Monsignor Pádraig de Brún, Dr Paddy Browne (later President of University College Galway (UCG)), built his own bungalow on the hill overlooking Dunquin and the Blasket Islands. The summer of 1926 he invited my two aunts, Máire and Annie, to visit him there. They immediately fell in love with the place and wondered could he find them a little house to rent, which, in his efficient way, he immediately set about doing. He knew of a young farmer who had built a cottage in, I think, 1912, when he was getting married to a

local girl from the village of Gráig, just over the hill from Dunquin. This cottage also overlooked the beautiful, wide, sandy beach of Tráigh Clochair (Clogher strand), with a magnificent view of Sybil Head and three mountains towards Smerwick harbour and Mount Brandon in the distance.

The young farmer's name was Tomás Ó Cíobháin. He was a skilled carpenter. Sadly, his wife died at a very early age, leaving him with three small children. He couldn't manage on his own, so he had to put the children into the orphanage in Tralee. As a result, his cottage was free to rent. The cottage was of the traditional design: one large kitchen space and one smaller room for the parents' bedroom, with a loft for the children. It was

built of native stone with windows on either side, and the kitchen had a large, open fireplace with a crane for hanging the big iron pot and black kettle over a turf fire.

It needed internal reconstruction before my aunts could use it, which work Tomás was able to undertake. First, he knocked down the internal wall and then divided the whole inside with wooden partitions to create one small living-room, while retaining the fireplace and two windows at either end; this was to serve as a kitchen and living-room. We acquired an oil-burning stove for cooking. The rest of the house was

LEFT, TOP: Sitting by the open fire in Gráig. LEFT, BOTTOM: The cottage, built in 1912, was rented for £20 per annum with potatoes and turf included. RIGHT: Our neighbour saving the hay.

divided into three small bedrooms. One for the aunts, one small one, which was later to be occupied by my pal, Máire de Róiste, and myself, and a third, which was used by Sinéad Ní Bhriain, my aunts' friend.

That first summer Sinéad, who was then known as Jenny O'Brien, was spending a holiday in Cáit a' Rí's in Dunquin. She was called Cáit a' Rí (Cáit of the King) because her father was known as the *Rí*, or King, of the Blasket islands. A match had been made for Cáit with a young farmer from Dunquin and she moved across from the Island. She took in some paying guests. I don't know how Sinéad came to be there that summer, but she joined my aunts in the venture of renting the cottage in Gráig. She was probably the main financial contributor.

The rent for the house was to be £20 per annum, with potatoes and turf included. However, we did not take possession for a few years.

Later we rented out the cottage to Professor Busteed of UCC and his wife and family, and then to the Fleischmanns.

I got a quick tour of the house in the summer of 1932 when Aunt Máire and I spent a week with Sighle Humphreys in Baile na nGall. My aunt brought me over to see the cottage one morning and we walked in on the Busteeds when they didn't expect visitors. Mrs Busteed was probably disconcerted as the house was hardly tidied up at that early hour!

LEFT:
A simple, old-style cottage, still seen in the area at that time.
RIGHT:
Sinéad's photo of the high tide at Blennerville delaying the train's progress to Dingle – a regular occurrence.

Sighle Humphreys (niece of The O'Rahilly of the 1916 Rising) had built her own bungalow on the other side of Smerwick harbour a few years earlier. I was a complete stranger to the Humphreys family, but Emmet, Sighle's brother, took me under his wing. He brought me walking on the clifftops, where one day we found a mewling kitten, which had been thrown into the sea, and we rescued it.

Fíona Plunkett, daughter of Count Plunkett and sister of Joseph Mary Plunkett, one of the signatories of the Proclamation who was executed in 1916, was a friend of Sighle's and was also a guest in the house at the time. My memory of her is of seeing her walking around the house every morning sipping a cup of hot water. Sighle was a lovely person with beautiful blonde hair and was always smiling and laughing. We remained friends all her life.

The following summer the aunts and Sinéad took up residence in the cottage. Sinéad, in the meantime, had trained as a children's nurse at the Princess Charlotte Training College in London. Though a wealthy young woman, she did not intend to spend her time in idleness. As her first position after training she had taken charge of a little girl whose Irish father was in the British Diplomatic Service. He had been left a widower with a very young daughter, called Máirín Ní Ruairc. He had left Máirín in the charge of his sister-in-law, who was a Protestant. He had applied to Princess Charlotte College for a Catholic nanny to take care of his daughter, as he was anxious that she be brought up in that religion.

At the beginning of July 1933 my aunts, Sinéad, her little charge Máirín, who was now seven, and myself set out for Gráig. It was a memorable journey. First, the train from Cork to Tralee took three

hours. Then we continued onwards by the small Tralee to Dingle train; it was something like the West Clare train of Percy French fame. The trip to Dingle took another three hours, even though it was only thirty miles (58km) distant. This long delay was caused by the high tide at the village of Blennerville, where the seawater came over the tracks and held up the train for an hour. This was a common occurrence. All the passengers got out and sat waiting on the ditch. Sinéad, who was an amateur photographer, got out her camera and took a picture of the engine facing into the sea, which she sent to *The Irish Independent* as a curiosity. They promptly printed it and sent her ten shillings, which she hadn't expected.

Sitting on the ditch that day, we first met Fr Vincent Ryan, a young Dominican from Tallaght, who was on his way to spend a holiday in Dunquin. He was going to stay at the house of the local headmaster, Seán Ó Dálaigh, known as the 'Common Noun'. Seán's daughter, Han, kept house for him. Cáit a' Rí had by then built a large house next to the chapel in Dunquin. These two houses kept guests and had two special benches made for them in the chapel, at the front near the altar. All the rest of the congregation knelt on the bare floor — women

LEFT AND RIGHT: Travelling was arduous and fraught with mishaps.

on one side, and men on the other. When they first went to the chapel my aunts, naturally, marched up to the front and knelt on one of the benches, whereupon Cáit a' Rí graciously invited them to use her bench. Of course, my aunts had no knowledge of the custom.

When we arrived at Dingle train station, after frequent stops to pick up passengers, sometimes with small animals, Tomás Ó Cíobháin was waiting there with his horse and cart to transport our luggage to Gráig. We travelled by lorry another eleven miles (17km), Aunt Máire sitting in the front with the driver, the rest of us in the back. Going uphill we would all slide backwards amidst great laughter.

We finally arrived at our cottage and Tomás was there before us with his horse and cart and our entire luggage. Biddy, a little girl from the next farmhouse, immediately befriended Máirín. They remained pals throughout Máirín's summer holidays during her childhood, and by next summer Máirín was a fluent Irish speaker. In later years Biddy was to marry a local school teacher called Jackie Malone. She then became Bríd Bean Uí Maoileoin. Jackie and Bríd, our next-door

neighbours in Gráig, were to remain our good friends and allies in any domestic crisis. Jackie would come to our aid if there was a breakdown in the water supply, or any other difficulty.

The summer of 1933 I didn't venture out of the house, as I was still very timid. Although local children did try to entice me out by running around the house. In any case, I knew no Irish. The most outstanding memory of the summer was my first encounter with Dr Paddy Browne, my aunt's friend. He used to descend on us for 'afternoon tea', bringing with him the three MacEntee children – his nieces, Máire and Barbara, and his nephew, Séamus. He was a tall, imposing man with a big smiling face, a hearty laugh and a beautiful baritone voice. He also possessed a brilliant intellect. He had a PhD in Mathematics from the Sorbonne in Paris, where he had discovered, as a student, a new mathematical formula for which he received the distinction of the *Légion d'Honneur* from the French government. He had also

ABOVE:
**Green Street,
Dingle, in the 1930s.**
BELOW:
**Dr Paddy Browne
with his niece,
Barbara, and
her mother.**

attended Heidelberg University to study Celtic Studies and so was fluent in German. He used to sing all the German traditional songs to me.

As well as that, Dr Browne was a classical scholar and translated classic dramas from the original Greek straight into Irish verse. He wrote his own poetry, both in Irish and English. It was also Dr Paddy Browne who translated 'Stille Nacht, Heilige Nacht' into 'Oiche Chiúin, Oiche Mhic Dé', which is still sung at Irish Masses at Christmas. Who today realises that it was he who translated this German Christmas carol into Irish? He also wrote 'Sráideanna Naomhtha Átha Cliath' ('The Holy Streets of Dublin') in honour of the men and women of 1916.

The MacEntee children spent the six months between Easter and September every year with Dr Browne in his bungalow, attending Dunquin school for the summer term. A local girl, Bríd, was the housekeeper and looked after them all. Máire, his niece, was the apple of his eye and from him had imbibed all the classics and, when I met her, could recite from plays written in classical Greek.

One day, when Dr Browne and the children came to tea, he discovered I had learned no Irish. He said to my aunt, 'I'll bring her up to stay with us for a week and we'll teach her.' I was terrified at the prospect. I always felt intimidated in the presence of other children, and the MacEntees more than most as they were so self-confident. I went like a lamb to the slaughter! That was when I first got to know Máire MacEntee. She was twelve years old and I fifteen. She was a genius of a child, a true protégée of her uncle, whom they called Pábú. I had enough knowledge of the classics from my German school to appreciate the fact that she was able to recite from the original Greek. It was amazing to hear her do so.

When Máire MacEntee spoke at the launch of her autobiography, *The Same Age as the State*, she referred in her speech to our first meeting that week. She said her impression of me was that I was aloof and dignified. Little did she realise I was merely overawed! She remembers me in shorts, which was certainly not the case. My aunts would have been horrified at the thought of me wearing shorts. She also wrote in her book that my mother had a Nazi lover and that I had written to my aunts from a youth camp in Germany, where I was supposed to have been unhappy. These stories must have been circulating at the time and Máire obviously believed them, but they were untrue. In fact, my mother was an extreme communist and living in Paris with intellec-tuals and writers of her own way of thinking. I had never been in any youth camps. Actually, I had spent those years in the most modern, *avant garde* educational establishments in the country. My mother, to give her her due, saw to that! The cost of this school must have drained her, to a certain extent, of financial resources. I used to won-der, later, how she managed to go through so much of her money: my education must have been the cause of some of it!

Máire and I became friends, though I didn't see much of her throughout the years until recently. Not long ago I heard that Dr Browne also taught Máire in the ancient Bardic method of dialogue through verse. That is why she is one of the foremost poets in the Irish language today.

Looking back, I think Dr Paddy Browne must have been one of the greatest intellectual giants of twentieth-century Ireland, if not the greatest, and who appreciates that today? The last time Ruairí and I met him was in Sandymount, Dublin, where he had settled into his new home after retiring from the presidency of University College Galway. He was very happy there, overlooking Dublin Bay. We spent the evening there, with him reading Pierre Teilhard de Chardin to us and discussing his philosophy. On leaving, Ruairí made an appointment with him to play golf, but, alas, Dr Browne died a short time later of a heart attack, so the game never came off.

I consider it a privilege to have known Monsignor de Brún. *Beannacht Dé lena anam.*

BACKGROUND:
Our cottage overlooked the beautiful, sandy Clogher Strand (Tráigh Clochair) with a magnificent view of Sybil Head and Mount Brandon in the distance.

My Best Friend

The following year, 1934, my friend and companion, Máire de Róiste, came with us to Kerry. This made an enormous difference to my life there. We went out and about on our bicycles, spending time on Clogher and Coumeenole (Com Dhíneol) strands, or going on errands for my aunts. One task was to cycle to Eileen Ferriter's guesthouse at Béal Bán strand, to invite Mrs O'Callaghan and her sister, Eileen Ní Mhurchú, to tea. Mrs O'Callaghan was the widow of Michael O'Callaghan, Lord Mayor of Limerick, who had been murdered by the Black and Tans in front of his wife, as was Lord Mayor Tomás MacCurtain in Cork under similar circumstances. Eileen Ní Mhurchú was head of St Mary's Teacher Training College in Limerick, or Coláiste Muire gan Smál. She was a fluent Irish speaker. They stayed at Eileen Ferriter's every summer and were regular visitors to our cottage. To hear those two women and my two MacSwiney aunts talking and arguing was a treat.

Máire and I spent most of our time cycling around the countryside, she singing traditional songs in Irish, which she taught me, having learned them from her father. We met and got to know the local people on our visits to Ballyferriter to buy the basic groceries at the one small shop, owned by Pádraig Bodhlaeir, a great character. We also went to the post office (Aunt Annie always needed stamps). An old lady presided there who knew very little English. One day we heard her spelling out a telegram for Tralee and to explain the letter 'I' she said, to our great amusement, 'I far me', meaning 'I', for 'me'. There

was no English spoken in Ballyferriter at that time; very few people knew it. I began to understand and even to speak Irish with the help of Máire, though we always spoke English to one another when alone.

One of our most important entertainments was visiting Cáit a' Rí's, and sometimes one or two other houses. Cáit's regular summer visitors at that time were mainly Christian Brothers from the North Monastery school in Cork, known as the North Mon. There were four who came every summer. One of them was Bráthair Ó Briain, who later wrote a biography of my father. Cáit understood that they needed to improve their Irish, so she laid on a special night of entertainment, an *Oíche*, once a week, where we were both welcome because Máire had a beautiful soprano voice. Most importantly, the *Oíche* included a *seanachaí* (storyteller) from the local village of Dunquin. This man would speak Irish to the Brothers, including many old sayings, or *sean fhocail*. The Brothers would take down every word diligently into their little black notebooks, while Máire and I would giggle in the background, thinking a lot of it was rubbish. What we didn't appreciate was that that was what the Brothers wanted.

The *seanachaí* was known as Séamuisín a' Bhoiler. I always thought this had something to do with a violin, but later learned it was the

LEFT:
Máirín Ní Ruairc and Máire de Róiste by the fire, with the crane for hanging the big iron pot and black kettle.
RIGHT:
Enjoying the hay-making.

word 'boiler'. It came from the soup boilers during the nineteenth-century famine, when apparently Séamuisín's family and others turned Protestant. At that time people who needed food used to go to a centre where soup was served in big boilers, but to avail of this help they had to turn Protestant. By the time Séamuisín was twelve years old his family had returned to the Catholic Church, as had all the others. I still remember the little Protestant church in the heart of Dunquin that Máire and I used to pass, but it had been abandoned by then.

Life in our cottage was very simple when we were young as there was no electricity or running water. We had a little stream outside the gate for general purposes. Drinking water was carried by bucket from the nearest well: our job! Brown soda bread was baked in the bastable pot, called an *t-oigheann*, or oven, and potatoes were boiled in it. It was a big, black iron pot hanging over the open turf fire and the cooking was done by local girls from the village — and what wonderful potatoes!

Otherwise, Sinéad did the cooking on the paraffin stove. The black kettle also hung over the open fire and supplied hot water. We had an 'Aladdin's' oil lamp in the sitting-room, which had a thing called a 'mantle' that gave constant trouble as it was so delicate. For the toilet facilities we had an Elsinol container, since my aunts were very fastidious. This was housed in a little wooden annex attached to the house and known as '*an tigín*' (the little house); *an tigín* was the word for toilet in our house forever after. Every day a local farmer cleaned out this container.

BELOW:
Our bedroom.

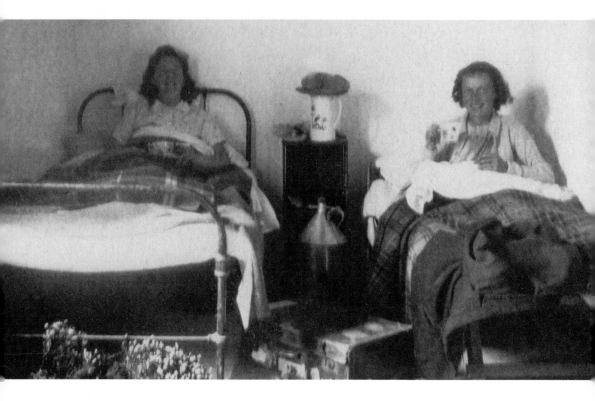

Sinéad, Máire and I would cycle into Dingle for our weekly shopping. Atkins was the main grocery store. It had a reputation that English-speaking customers were served first. All those living beyond Dingle, or west of the town, spoke only Irish. Whenever Sinéad would arrive in, she would speak only Irish on principle (although she knew very little!), but as she bought everything in bulk — oranges by the crate, boiled sweets in tins — she certainly was served first! A leg of lamb was bought once a week from the local butcher, Johnny Moore, and what lamb! This was delivered via the post office van to Ballyferriter, where Máire and I would collect it; there was no question of postal charges. Our main diet was heavenly lamb, potatoes and cabbage, followed by tinned fruit and fresh cream. The milk and cream were obtained fresh every day from the Cíobháin family.

Máire and I also visited the Caomhánach family in Baile na Rátha, Dunquin. This gave us an insight into the old lifestyle in the area. Liam was the eldest son of the family and had inherited the farm. He and his wife, plus four strapping sons and one daughter, lived there as well as his old mother, Máire Iosef, who used to throw her arms around me and Máire and kiss us warmly on our arrival. Their house was one of the few old two-storey houses in the parish, so they must have been one of the more substantial farmers. The family fished, mostly offshore, for lobster, crab and such from their small, black currach called a *naomhóg*. In the evening, the whole family gathered around the big scrubbed table, covered with a clean sackcloth, and turned the potatoes straight from the big pot on the fire onto the table, along with lobster, crab and other fish. There was milk or buttermilk to drink: a really healthy diet! Occasionally, Liam would offer the two of us, sitting at the fire, a lobster claw, taken straight out of the hot ashes, with the tongs, which I declined as I was allergic to lobster. He used to try to teach me Irish by repeating an old Irish saying about the fire, but I couldn't understand him. He would repeat it, raising his voice with each repetition.

One evening, there was great excitement. His younger brother, Séamus Caomhánach, was coming home for a holiday. Séamus was a student of Celtic Studies in Heidelberg University, where he had met and married a German-American. The main excitement was caused by the fact that his wife had a piano that had to be brought upstairs! Máire and I had to leave before this was accomplished, so we never saw the end of the venture.

Séamus Caomhánach, who was later Professor of Celtic Studies in UCC, was to have a great impact on my life when I enrolled in his class as a second-year student of honours Irish.

Máire de Róiste was like a very dear sister to me. From the time I met her when I first came to Scoil Íte we always sat next to one another, the same in Monaghan and again when we went to college. She came on holidays with me to Kerry, every summer, when we were in school together and later.

The cottage was very small. Usually we had my two aunts staying, as well as Sinéad Ní Bhriain and Máirín Ní Ruairc. So Máire and I did not have the luxury of single rooms! In fact, we always slept in the same room. The summer the two nuns spent with us, which shall be described presently, we had to rearrange the rooms, and Máire and I had to sleep in the kitchen.

I remember one night in particular, it was during our university career. She confided in me when we were in bed, in the dark, just before we were going to sleep. She said, 'Máire, I think I'm getting a vocation.' I said, 'Don't you dare!'

I was extremely upset to think that I might lose my dearest friend and companion. When I found that this vocation showed no sign of going away, I suggested that she might enter the order of the Drishane nuns. If she joined them, it would mean that I would not lose contact with her completely. The order had a boarding school in Drishane, County Cork, and a very good reputation as a teaching order. I also had a family connection with them, as my Aunt Kit was a member of the order; she spent her whole life on the missions in Tokyo. I knew the local Drishane nuns from when they first came to stay in Cáit a' Rí's in Dunquin. After that they had built a bungalow near

Ballyferriter, which they used for their summer holidays. They were frequent visitors to our cottage. The nuns had also opened a knitting factory in Ballyferriter, to give local girls employment, with Madame St Edmund in charge. Subsequently it was run by a local lady, Siobhán Fahy.

However, Máire felt that that would be too easy for her. I knew what she meant. In those days when somebody entered a religious order, they were supposed to distance themselves from their family and friends.

At this time, Máire and I were preparing for our BA degree examination in the autumn. There were always a number of nuns in our class, sitting in the front row, preparing for a teaching career. One of these was Sr Anthony, who belonged to the Mercy Convent in Doon, County Limerick, which was a very isolated place. Sr Anthony must have told her Reverend Mother that there was a possible candidate for the convent in her class. The Mercy nuns lost no time in their efforts to persuade Máire to enter their order. After another year, during which we were studying for our H. Dip. in Education as well as teaching full-time in Scoil Íte, Máire entered the convent in January 1941. I was invited to the ceremony. I wept secretly throughout. It felt as if we were burying her.

In the following years I only saw Sr Máire when on my way home from Kerry with the family. Ruairí would make a detour from Limerick to Doon so that I could visit her. However, I always felt she wasn't *my* Máire; she had become a Mercy nun. Sadly, she died of cancer before her time. I visited a few times when she was in hospital in Cork, where we said our goodbyes. I was at her funeral in the convent in Doon, again a very sad occasion. But I think I felt more broken-hearted when I attended her reception as a novice into the order, many years earlier.

I have never had a friend like her since. She was like a sister to me.

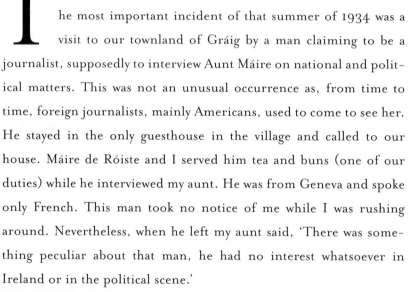

VISITORS

The most important incident of that summer of 1934 was a visit to our townland of Gráig by a man claiming to be a journalist, supposedly to interview Aunt Máire on national and political matters. This was not an unusual occurrence as, from time to time, foreign journalists, mainly Americans, used to come to see her. He stayed in the only guesthouse in the village and called to our house. Máire de Róiste and I served him tea and buns (one of our duties) while he interviewed my aunt. He was from Geneva and spoke only French. This man took no notice of me while I was rushing around. Nevertheless, when he left my aunt said, 'There was something peculiar about that man, he had no interest whatsoever in Ireland or in the political scene.'

BELOW:
My friend Síle O'Mahony and I enjoying a holiday break from college.

A few days later, Máire and I were on our bikes going to a strand some miles away. Not far from our house there was a completely isolated stretch of road, between our village and Dunquin, facing onto the Blasket Islands. This 'journalist' was walking along and when we caught up with him he gestured to me to stop. We both got down off our bikes, thinking he wanted some directions. He waved Máire further on – he insisted she move away. Here again there was a language barrier, he had no English and had interviewed my aunt in French. I had only schoolgirl French, though better than average. He told me he had a letter for me from my mother, which I was to read and give him the answer. This was the first communication from her since I had left Germany.

I read the letter, in which she explained that I was to accompany him back to Switzerland. To this she added what amounted to a threat: if I did not comply with her wishes and return with him to her, she would completely cut me out of her life and never speak to me again. Here I was again, supposed to make an irrevocable decision at a moment's notice. I did not hesitate, however. There was no way I was going to take off to Switzerland with a stranger, though I'm sure he was very respectable. I had spent two happy years of stability and safety and in my own country, had settled down properly at last and had a future. In Germany all those years I was a foreigner, even though I was indistinguishable from other German children. Neither did I quite believe her threat, although I was mistaken there as usual; she did carry out her decision. This was 1934. I was just sixteen and I never met my mother again, though she lived until 1982. Twice I caught a glimpse of her when she visited Dublin from London, where she was living during the war. On those occasions I did not reveal myself to her, as I didn't know what she would do.

Perhaps, if I had ever lived with my mother for an extended period, things might have been different. I probably did not take the threat seriously; I should have known better. She always did carry out these threats, but this one seemed too extreme. If I was prepared to comply with my mother's wishes, the man had a second letter that was to be given to me. If not, it was to remain unopened. I heard afterwards there were photographs in the second envelope and instructions on how to proceed. Since I would not go, this letter was not given to me. In the letter I did receive my mother asked me not to disclose any of this matter for at least three days, to give her friend the chance to get out of the country because, since I was a ward of court, abducting me would have been a criminal offence. I agreed to this very readily. Even though we could not communicate very well, I felt he was a nice person and was being used by my mother to undertake a mission at great personal risk to himself.

Then I got on my bike and rode on. Máire wanted to know what he wanted. I just passed it off. I always lived a double life! I kept this encounter to myself, not telling my aunt until several days later, giving this man, as promised, time to leave the country. And that was the end of it.

BELOW LEFT: I took this photo of Peig Sayers sitting at the gable wall of her two-storey house on the Great Blasket Island. BELOW RIGHT: Leaving the island in the *naomhóg*.

MacSWINEY AUNTS, MISSIONARY SISTERS

In 1937 my Aunt Kit and Aunt Peg, who were missionary nuns, were home at the same time in Ireland by coincidence. Aunt Kit, known as Katie outside our home, had entered the Drishane nuns' missionary order in Weybridge, where the English convent was situated. I think it was in the MacSwiney family tradition to join that order because her own aunt was already a sister there, a woman who was later known to me as Grandaunt Kate. I was told a story about her. During my father's hunger strike in Brixton, she was very old and bedridden and had lost most of her mental faculties. She kept murmuring, 'I can hear the banshee crying, there is somebody dying in our family'! When I returned to Ireland I was told this story, once more illustrating for me a weird aspect of Irish folklore.

The missionary work was mainly in the Far East, which included Japan. Aunt Kit was sent out to Tokyo as a young nun in the early part of the century and only returned to Europe once in her life, which was in the summer of 1937. The Reverend Mother in Tokyo had to attend an assembly in Paris and was to be accompanied by one sister, and Aunt Kit was chosen. She was very popular with her students and was laden down with gifts from them, among which was a porcelain tea set that she had decided not to bring. She brought many other wonderful things, however. There was a kimono that was reversible — oyster pink on one side and pale green on the other side and hand-painted. She brought hand-painted, perfumed fans. There were also two rolls of beautiful Japanese silk, one deep red and the other white voile with sprigs of rosebuds. And there were various lacquered boxes for trinkets and jewellery.

Aunt Peg, Mother Margaret MacSwiney, had entered the convent in Farnborough as a young woman. The order, known as Les Soeurs de l'Éducation Chrétienne, had originally come from Belgium where the education system was secularised. After some years the mother-house in England decided to set up a convent in America. My aunt and another choir nun, accompanied by one lay sister, were chosen to travel to America and found the order in Asheville, North Carolina. They set up a high school, St Genevieve-of-the-Pines. Later the order wished to establish a college, too. The US Department of Education informed them that the principal would have to hold a PhD. My aunt was given orders from her superiors to acquire this PhD. Being an obedient nun, she was immediately prepared to obey and take on the task. As she was endowed with the MacSwiney brains, she wrote a PhD thesis on the German philosopher Meister Eckhart, and so the order was able to open the college and prepare graduates for the university. Aunt Peg was allowed to visit Ireland on a few other occasions, the last being for her Golden Jubilee in 1958 when she was given a full month, which included a visit to Southwark Cathedral, where her brother Terence's body had been brought after his death in Brixton prison.

So now we had all four MacSwiney sisters in our cottage in Gráig.

LEFT:
Máire and I serve
tea and buns to
the older ladies.
ABOVE:
The four sisters,
Annie, Kit, Peg and
Máire, enjoying
the sun.

The two nuns slept in the little room off the porch. It was forever after known as 'The Nuns' Room'. One can imagine the discussions and arguments that went on in our sitting-room among the four of them. One time, Aunt Kit said to Aunt Máire, 'Well, you know, Min, the Union Jack is very useful on the missions for protection.' Aunt Máire replied in indignation, 'Wouldn't you consider doing your missionary work under the banner of Christ rather than under the protection of the Union Jack?' Aunt Kit also disapproved slightly of my smoking. I had spent a year in UCC, where I had acquired the habit; the main break in the day was coffee and cigarettes in the restaurant. I was never a heavy smoker, but Aunt Kit used to call me 'Vesuvius'.

All four sisters went to daily Mass in Dunquin, which was said by Dr Paddy Browne. His elderly sacristan, Mártan Ó hUalacháin, a local farmer, always served him. Mártan had acquired some unusual habits. For instance, any wine that was left in the cruet after Mass he would empty onto the floor beside the altar. We were well used to the smell, which was rather like the smell you would find in a pub, but we thought nothing of it. My two religious aunts were horrified: That dreadful man! Couldn't he be stopped? There was no question that any of us would talk to Dr Paddy Browne as in his eyes Mártan was special. And if he, the priest, was happy with the situation, it wasn't going to bother any of us. Sometime later, when four of the Drishane nuns were staying in Cáit a' Rí's, whose house was next to the church, they decided to go in and wash out the chapel floor one morning. Mártan happened to find them in action and was furious that anyone would encroach on his territory. He told them to get out and threw the buckets and scrubbing brushes after them.

Aunt Kit was in Tokyo during the earthquake of 1923. All communications with Tokyo had broken down. My Uncle Peter, who was living in New York, was frantically trying to find out what had happened to

LEFT:
Aunt Kit at the
dining table in her
convent in Tokyo.
She told us many
stories about her
life there.
ABOVE:
Aunt Kit brought
home some
wonderful gifts
from Japan. Here I
am modelling the
kimono and a sun-
shade, both of
which I still have.

his sister. Finally, in true MacSwiney fashion, he took what would appear to have been a drastic decision. He hitch-hiked from New York to San Francisco and there signed on as an able-bodied seaman with a cargo ship going to Yokohama, the main port for Tokyo. Uncle Peter, who hardly knew how to swim, was certainly no able-bodied seaman. Nonetheless, he was taken on as a general stevedore and was well able to cope with the manual labour involved. As the boat approached Yokohama harbour, my Uncle Peter must have been in the control room. The captain handed him the wheel and told him to bring the ship into the harbour. He was ordered not to turn the wheel until the captain gave the order. The ship was advancing directly towards a big, blank wall. My uncle was beginning to panic, thinking that the captain had forgotten and that the ship would surely collide with the wall. He decided that he would take action, whatever his instructions had been, but just at that moment the captain ordered him to turn sharp left and the ship was brought safely into Yokohama. This was a story Uncle Peter told me many years later.

Uncle Peter made his way to one of the convents in Yokohama, where he found that all of the nuns had died. In Japan the greatest danger was not, apparently, the collapse of buildings but the fire that would sweep through the city, because most of the houses were made of wood and paper. The nuns in the Yokohama convent had all taken refuge in the basement of their church to protect themselves from falling masonry. But when the fires had swept up the hill from the city, the flames and the carbon monoxide had engulfed the convent. Uncle Peter then made his way to Tokyo to discover, to his relief and delight, that all in Aunt Kit's convent were safe. In due course he returned to New York by the same method. But, hopefully, he knew a bit more about being an able-bodied seaman by then.

Aunt Kit had many other stories about her life in Tokyo. She explained to us that when the emperor was passing by, it was forbidden to wave, or to look out an upstairs window as no one was to be higher than the emperor. She also told us of her life as a teacher in the convent school. As the order was based in Paris they had excellent French teachers, and their connection with the English convent meant they had equally good English teachers. The wealthy and upper classes in

Tokyo attended the convent school. One of the conditions laid down for the order was that they were not allowed to teach any Christian doctrine during school hours. However, if any of the girls wished to return after school, the nuns could then give them religious instruction. Quite a number of the students became Christians. When it came to getting married, which in Japanese culture was by matchmaking, the bridegroom would always be of the Shinto religion. The brides were then expected to turn back to that religion. Aunt Kit, during her stay with us, would ask us to pray for Christian husbands because only if they married a Christian could the girls remain Christians. For quite a few years after my aunt's visit we included in our prayers, 'Please God, send Christian husbands to the girls in Tokyo.'

In 1939, at the outbreak of the war, the Japanese government interned all British subjects. As Aunt Kit had first travelled to Japan in the early part of the century, she held a British passport and therefore was included among the British internees. Those Irish sisters who had gone to Tokyo after 1921 and the foundation of the Free State held Irish passports and therefore were not involved. When Aunt Kit found herself interned, she was indignant that anyone would suggest that she was a British subject, so she promptly sat down and wrote a history of Ireland, which she handed to the authorities. She was released immediately.

REVISITING GERMANY

I was ready to start college in the autumn of 1936 and Máire de Róiste and I both enrolled in the Faculty of Arts at University College Cork. I was in a panic that I would not match up to expectations. I think my earlier years of schooling had left me with a lot of anxiety and a lack of confidence, so I studied like mad in order to pass, with the result that I got first-class honours all the way, right up to my degree; I also got an MA and won an All-Ireland Travelling Studentship!

In the second year I took honours German and Irish and pass French. The German wasn't going to be any problem except that I had to do the literature, which of course was an enormous task. As regards Irish, the most important factor was that Séamus Caomhánach came to my rescue. He was Professor of Celtic Studies and took our class for Old Irish. I remember the first day he stood in front of us and looked us over. Pushing his spectacles up on his forehead he announced: *'Ní hiad muintir na Nua Ghaoluinn a gheobhaidh an scrúdú seo'* (It is not the people who are fluent in modern Irish who will pass this exam). This was going to be 'old Irish'. None of the native Irish speakers, nor the brilliant Irish students from the North Monastery school in Cork, would have an advantage! I had a level playing field at last and could compete with the best. We studied the old Irish 'glosses', notes made in the margins of the Bible by medieval monks. These

RIGHT:
On arriving in Hamburg to spend the summer of 1938 in Germany, I was met by a member of the Krebs family.

152

were so concise that they were practically like mathematical formulae. As well as that there was medieval Irish-Scots Gaelic poetry.

One of the most interesting subjects Professor Caomhánach taught us was philology. I was fascinated. Not only did we learn the relationship between Indo-European languages but also the difference between the P-Celts and the Q-Celts. The Welsh, Cornish and Bretons were P-Celts, whereas the Irish and Western Scots were Q-Celts. No wonder I could never understand a word of Welsh! I always took for granted that Manx was a form of Welsh. Many years later, one evening while listening to BBC radio, I heard an announcement that they were giving a series of Manx lessons and this was the first one. It started off with counting: *aon, dó, trí, ceathair, cúig, sé, seacht, ocht, naoi, deich.* But that is Irish, I thought. Of course — it was obvious. Originally the Isle of Man had been populated by Irish tribes from eastern Ireland who had crossed the Irish Sea.

After passing Second Arts in 1938 we had our long summer vacation. It was decided I should spend the summer in Berlin to refresh my German. Aunt Annie had kept in touch with some girls she had taught at a finishing school for German girls on the Isle of Wight, before the outbreak of the 1914 war. She arranged that I should spend three weeks with three different families in Berlin, nine weeks altogether.

In the first family I stayed with, the father, Herr Krebs, was a wealthy businessman and was very interested in improving his English. He bought the English *Times* every day and would sometimes ask me to help him to read it. I discovered for the first time that I had a problem between German and English. When immersed in German, it completely wiped out my English. I found I was unable to help my host, Herr Krebs. He could not understand this and neither could I. Incidentally, he was very formal and always addressed me in 'Sie', the formal version of 'you', as in 'Miss MacSwiney'.

My second family was totally different. They were Herr and Frau

ABOVE:
During the
summer of 1938
I was able to
roam freely
around Berlin,
though scenes like
this were common
and the swastika was
visible everywhere.

Hess, who were of Bavarian origin. Dr Hess was a chemical scientist with his own business. He analysed the purity of foodstuffs in the supermarkets in Berlin. Their eldest child was their daughter, Hilde, two years younger than me and in her final school year. She was going to do her *Abitur* (Leaving Cert.) the following June. Hilde was friendly and completely informal. She immediately called me Máire and addressed me in *'Du'*, the informal version of 'you'. We became great friends and have remained so to this day.

During this period I was able to roam freely around Berlin. I visited the zoo and the art galleries, where I was greatly struck by the beauty of the bust of Nefertiti. I also noticed certain aspects of life under Hitler. Throughout the city there were German newspapers displayed in glass cases for the public to read. The newspaper was Goebbels's propaganda machine. These papers contained incitement against Jews.

Another incident occurred at this time. I was only twenty years old and therefore still a ward of court in Ireland, though I had forgotten all about this. The Dublin jurisdiction discovered that I had left the country and gone to Germany. This caused great excitement and I was summoned to the local police station in Berlin to clarify the position. Though I appeared to be a German, I was sitting there taking no part in this performance. As I waited my turn, I could see people coming and going, all raising their arms in the *Heil Hitler* salute. I was the only one present who didn't conform to this custom. My situation *vis-à-vis* the Irish government was quickly sorted out. This was my closest contact with officialdom in Germany. During my visit to Berlin at this time I never saw any mass rallies.

Later in my visit I accompanied the family I was staying with to a social occa-sion, and noticed some whispering and commotion at one end of the room. I asked my friends what it was all about. I was told it had been discovered that somebody there had a Jewish grandmother. This was bad news for the family in question. All these matters showed me the type of regime that was in place. Neville Chamberlain had come to Munich to negotiate with Hitler in the summer of 1938, and returned to England to announce 'Peace in our time' to the great relief of the English public. I remember the feeling of enormous relief also among the Germans I met at that party. They certainly did not want war, even though they could not have foreseen how great the horrors of it would become on all sides.

Catholics were not positively discriminated against, even though they were considered not favourably disposed to the regime. With regard to the first two Catholic families I stayed with, they were independent businessmen so this did not affect their situation. The children had to conform to the regulations of the time, one being to enrol in the boys' and girls' scouts. Hilde was not a member of the girl guides, the Bund Deutscher Mädel, but her younger brother, Benno, was a member of the Marine Corps, a branch of the boy scouts.

As regards the third Catholic family, the Pellengahrs, I understood the father was in some sort of State employment and, as such, he probably suffered some discrimination as far as career promotion was concerned. I don't think that any of the ordinary German people were aware of the extent of the concentration camps being set up for Jews. Of course, nobody could have foreseen the awful horrors of those camps during the war, ending in the appalling nightmare of the holocaust.

At the end of my sojourn in Berlin I returned from Hamburg on a German liner called the *Bremen*, which was headed for America via Cobh. I befriended a German Jewess who was escaping the country to join her family in New York. She carried all her worldly wealth on her person, in jewellery. As we stood on deck, one of her diamond rings slipped off her finger and into the water, losing no one knows how much money.

We spoke German all the time and I did not realise that I would have any difficulty with English until we were seated at our allocated places in the dining-room. There were some English and American people sitting at the same table. I discovered that I could not speak a word of English and promptly panicked. My German friend had to interpret for me. What was going to happen when I returned to Cork and had to go back to university? Thankfully, after landing in Cobh it all soon came back to me.

FINAL YEAR IN COLLEGE

Now we entered our final year of the BA and I, of course, was in a state of sheer panic. I studied from morning to evening, getting up every day at 6.00am and allowing myself only one hour for lunch and one hour for tea. This frenzy of work applied mainly to Irish and French. I set out the courses in detail, allocated a given time to each subject and the prescribed books. I kept a meticulous timetable. The result of all this was a first-class honours degree. Because of the high grades, I was called into President Merriman's office. I was told that, if I were willing, I would be granted a scholarship for two years, with £50 a year, to study for the All-Ireland Studentship. My first reaction was: who was I to turn down £50 a year? In the MacSwiney home such a sum was never dreamt of. It never occurred to me that there could be any possibility that I could actually achieve such a goal as getting a Studentship. I agreed with the proposal and then went off to sign on for my Higher Diploma course with the rest of my class. A few weeks into these studies, I was called back into the President's office. It was pointed out to me that I could not take up the scholarship and sign on for my Higher Diploma in Education as well. As far as I was concerned, I wanted to stay with my class doing this exam and, if necessary, would give up the scholarship. What to do?

As students, we were accustomed to going to Professor Alfred

158

O'Rahilly, the Registrar, with any difficulties we encountered. So I brought my problem to him. His solution was simple and the problem was immediately resolved. What he said to me was: 'Never mind the President, you do your Higher Diploma, girl, and the scholarship.' I went off happily to spend the year doing my H. Dip.

In June 1939, when Máire and I had just got our BA degrees, Aunt Máire fell ill with her last illness. We had to take over all her classes in Scoil Íte: I taught all the Latin and junior French; Máire taught the senior French. Some years later the parents asked me to teach German to the senior classes. When I first opened a German grammar, I couldn't believe how impossible this language was. In speaking it one doesn't realise the complications of its grammatical structure. However, my students were all successful at passing the Matric, and some took the subject at university level.

Being plunged into teaching suddenly like this was probably a great help to me as I might otherwise have lacked the confidence for teaching. As it turned out I was a very good teacher because I was able to communicate very well with the pupils. In the Higher Diploma course my favourite subjects had been Logic and Psychology, and I think I had a natural gift for both. My understanding of psychology helped me to foresee when a child would have a problem in a subject and explain it clearly before it became a problem. In all my years of teaching I hadn't a single failure in the Latin Matric examination.

Now I was faced with having to teach from 9.00am till 3.00pm, as well as studying for my H. Dip. I felt reasonably confident I would pass the H. Dip. The possibility of getting an MA arose also at this time. And in June 1941 two of us from UCC, Kathleen O'Flaherty and I, sat for the two All-Ireland Studentships: one was for English and a continental language; the other for Irish and a continental language. Kathleen took English and French; I took Irish and German. The exam, which lasted a whole week, was held in the rooms of the National University of Ireland (NUI) in Merrion Square. I had an

RIGHT:
Programme of events
to celebrate the silver
jubilee of the opening
of Scoil Íte,
1916–1941.

scoil íce

Silver Jubilee

1916 - 1941

cailíní scoil íce i sceicre vrámaí

CLÁR

(1) " an maiṡoean orleans "
(MAID OF ORLEANS)
(Translated from the English of Father Benson by
Mother Philomena, Ursuline Convent, Blackrock Cork)

(2) TRIAL SCENE (Merchant of Venice)
SCENES FROM-

(3)   MACBETH

(4) "LE VOYAGE de M. PERRICHON"

san halla maiciú

feabra 3av, 4av, 9av, 10av.

luaċ - - - - 3p.

Cló na Caṫraċ

oral exam in both Irish and German. I don't remember much about the Irish oral, but I know I was fluent. During the German oral I was asked questions about German literature. Sitting facing me at the table were the representatives of every university college. Since I had no expectations of getting the Studentship, I unburdened myself and spoke my mind, and said what I thought of German literature, especially Goethe and Schiller, both of whom I found boring. I was more interested in the poetry of Goethe as a younger man and the more modern part of German literature. I also liked Rainer Rilke's poetry. Anyway, I let them know what I thought. My examiners were left speechless, but thanked me and let me go.

There were students there from all over Ireland, from UCD and UCG. On the Saturday afternoon we all sat waiting for the results in the bright sunshine in the annex on the NUI half-landing. Kathleen then confided in me saying, 'Máire, would you ever wait for my result, as I have to go up to visit my brother in Mountjoy prison. I'm allowed only one visit a month and if I don't take it up, he will not have any visitors for two months.' I understood from her that only she and her brother had Republican leanings and therefore no other member of her family would dream of visiting him. There were others there who had high hopes of getting the English Studentship, but I was positive that Kathleen would be successful.

The results were announced eventually and, of course, Kathleen got the English/French Studentship. I was totally stunned at the announcement that I had won the Irish/German one. I went off to the Russell Hotel on the corner of St Stephen's Green. Kathleen and Mademoiselle Yvonne Servais, the French lecturer at UCC, were staying there for the week. Kathleen had returned from Mountjoy and they ordered sherry all round. I took one sip and promptly felt ill with indigestion and never touched the stuff again.

That evening I was invited to tea in the O'Rahilly home. I thought I had better ring up my German Professor, Mrs Boyle, to tell her that I had won the Studentship. I was unable to call the aunts, as they had no phone. Mrs Boyle was overjoyed and immediately went up to my aunts to give them the good news. It was quite a feat that that particular year UCC won both the English and Irish All-Ireland Studentships. The following year, 1942, I got my honours MA degree.

It was during this time that my companions and I used to go out on Saturday night for our weekly outing to the Savoy cinema on Patrick Street in Cork. We always had the same meal, salad and chips, which cost one shilling and sixpence each. This was all we could afford. At the time I was still on two shillings and sixpence pocket money, which was all I ever earned right through the six years of my teaching career.

AUNT MÁIRE DIES

The media sometimes portrayed my Aunt Máire as someone very cold, very harsh, ruthless and dogmatic – this is completely wrong. She was very hard on herself. The MacSwiney character made them all too hard on themselves insofar as, if they were in pain or sick, it counted for nothing. If you had a problem, the answer was not to ask, 'Can I solve it?' but 'How do I solve it?' and they went ahead regardless of any difficulty. Besides this toughness, Aunt Máire was the most kind, warmhearted woman I knew. She would not tolerate anything said about anyone that was in any way derogatory. When someone came chasing up to Scoil Íte at the time of the Treaty debates saying, 'Dick [General Richard Mulcahy] is going for the Treaty,' my aunt's answer was, 'Dick wouldn't do such a thing.' She refused to think what she would consider ill of anybody. She never criticised anybody, except in politics. If they deviated, they were wrong and she wasn't prepared to accept it.

Her political leanings were towards the nationalists with a Protestant background, men such as Wolfe Tone, Thomas Davis and the Young Irelanders, and Charles Stewart Parnell. She had a picture on the wall in our sitting-room of her hero, Erskine Childers, whose son later became President of Ireland.

I felt strongly irritated by the Republican cause and the way its members used Aunt Máire, who was obviously suffering from ill health towards the end of her life. Whenever they were holding a

LEFT:
**Mary MacSwiney
(Aunt Máire) in
1921. She was the
kindest, most
warm-hearted
woman I
ever knew.**

public meeting and wanted a speaker, they would call on her. They would expect her to climb on the back of a lorry to speak. The last time I remember was when Sinéad and I accompanied her to Milltown Malbay in County Clare, the greatest stronghold of de Valera supporters. We were all brought to the local garda station. Sinéad and I were absolutely furious, not necessarily with the gardaí but with those who brought about the situation. On our return, Sinéad immediately brought Aunt Máire to receive proper medical attention because of her failing health.

My Aunt Máire died on 8 March 1942. She was the only person at whose deathbed I attended. Aunt Annie, Sinéad and I were present as well as Fr Augustine, who gave her Extreme Unction. After the ceremony, in his fervour, Fr Augustine started to enrol her in the Third Order of St Francis. Aunt Máire, who, though dying, still retained all her mental faculties, started to shake her head. Sinéad and I looked at one another and Sinéad said, 'She doesn't like it.' I said, 'If she doesn't like it, she has a good reason. What could that be?' Since I knew she was a very devout Catholic, it had to be something based on her logical religious reasoning and knowledge. I thought this over carefully and came to the conclusion that it could be that when she was teaching as a young woman in a Benedictine convent in England, she was enrolled in the Third Order of St Benedict. I bent over and asked her, 'Aunt Máire, were you ever enrolled in the Third Order of St Benedict when you were a young woman?' She nodded and immediately I turned to Fr Augustine and explained the situation to him. Of course he understood — one cannot be enrolled in two different Third Orders.

That was the last sign of life from Aunt Máire. She died a few minutes later. Though all who looked after me always treated me with great affection, Aunt Máire was the first person to give me true love. I had spent ten years under her care. Looking back, I can truly say I never met another character to surpass her. She had a brilliant intellect, absolute integrity and never wavered in her political principles, no matter at what cost to herself. I understood how she arrived at these principles, but I felt her stance was leading nowhere. I remember saying to her once that she had gone up a cul-de-sac and there was no way forward. I understood she could not change her position, but I felt the situation should not be imposed on the next generation. We would have to find our own way forward.

Aunt Máire was buried from St Patrick's Church in the family grave in St Joseph's cemetery. Her mother was buried there. Her father had not because he had emigrated to Australia, after the business had failed in Cork, where he set up a business importing antiques. He was buried in Melbourne. After Terence's death the Irish in Melbourne erected a Celtic cross headstone over his father's grave. We had buried Seán that January, and now Aunt Máire. Hers was not a public funeral. Though the people of Cork held her in the highest esteem, they knew that she would not have wanted any demonstration. In fact, on the night of her removal the Lord Mayor of Cork, Patrick McGrath, approached me quietly and said that he had been asked to represent the Taoiseach, Éamon de Valera, at the funeral. I thanked him warmly and told him to convey my thanks and appreciation to the Taoiseach but added, 'Don't tell Aunt Annie.'

After my aunt's death in 1942 I missed her very much. She had been very close to me. I could never understand the public image by which she was portrayed as

LEFT:
Letter from my grandfather, John MacSwiney, to his daughter, Mary. He wrote from Australia, to congratulate her on getting a job.
RIGHT:
The Celtic cross on the grave of John MacSwiney, in Melbourne.

'merciless Minnie', a hard and unforgiving woman. The other person who was so maligned was Cathal Brugha, being portrayed as a ruthless killer, only considering violent solutions, where in fact he was a truthful and a thoughtful man who tried to find a solution to save the Republic. Pondering about the images created around these two people, I often wondered later had it to do with British propaganda. They obviously were the most prominent opponents of the Treaty, along with de Valera. So it was in the British interest to defame them and to laud people like Griffith and Collins.

It was not till much later that I understood how this came about. Peter Wright, who had been a member of the British Intelligence Service, revealed some relevant information in his famous book, *Spy Catcher*. I read all the extracts in *The Irish Times* where he explained that there was a section in the British Intelligence Service whose sole task it was to deal exclusively with black propaganda against those they considered to be the enemies of Britain.

It was then that I finally understood how people like my aunt and Cathal Brugha acquired this reputation. Of course de Valera, who had a long public life, was able to establish his own reputation. I could never understand why the Irish media, and later historians, followed the same British propaganda, nor why they have retained to this day the image of Cathal Brugha and Mary MacSwiney created at that time.

Hopefully a true account of their lives will be written at some time in the future.

During the Treaty debates I think my aunt was politically very close to de Valera. She used to tell me a story of how one day the two of them were having a

LEFT:
The sad day of Aunt Máire's funeral.

cup of coffee in a restaurant on Dawson Street. De Valera took a pencil and drew two separate circles on the paper tablecloth, one small one and one large one, and enclosed both within a larger circle. He then explained to my aunt that this was his idea of a solution to the British/Irish problem. The two circles represented Britain and Ireland, and the outer circle a new way of relating. He called this idea 'external association'. He explained that Ireland would be a completely independent country, but freely associated with Britain externally. He was prepared to accept the Crown as titular head of this association. In 1949, having attained her freedom, India based her political position with regard to Britain on the same idea that de Valera had put to my aunt that day in 1921. Out of this grew the British Commonwealth of Nations. I'm sure Mahatma Gandhi and India arrived at these conclusions by their own thinking.

My aunt listened carefully and did not fully argue against it. When events finally overtook them and civil war broke out, she remained a convinced Republican. De Valera had started to think politically and by 1926 he was fully convinced that the future lay in the democratic process. I think de Valera, like others in 1916, was not really of a military disposition. At that time there seemed to be no other way of solving the problem. They realised that Britain was not going to grant them home rule at the end of the war. In 1926 he formed a political party called Fianna Fáil, a name adopted from the title of a journal set up by my father and meaning 'Soldiers of Destiny'. De Valera hoped to enter Dáil Éireann and pursue the Republican ideals by democratic means.

Tommy Mullins, who was long-time General Secretary to Fianna Fáil and a senator, had been one of de Valera's earliest and most ardent followers. Many years later Tommy, who was a Cork man, told me a lovely story. He said to me, 'Máire, the hardest thing the chief ever asked me to do was to go down to Cork and explain to Mary MacSwiney that he was starting Fianna Fáil and contemplating going into Dáil Éireann.' Of course, my aunt couldn't go along with this as she claimed the Second Dáil had not been properly dissolved and she had totally rejected the Free State. During the 1930s she carried out debates with de Valera in the public press rejecting his policies. However, during the same period when it came to rescuing me from Germany, she was still very friendly with de Valera and accepted his kind assistance in the case of my homecoming.

At this time, de Valera held two general elections, in the summers of 1943 and 1944. He won the first election, but not with a sufficient majority to satisfy him. Owing to the war and to the precarious situation of the country at the time, I think he needed a larger majority to give him a stronger position in government. The final election rallies were held in Patrick Street, opposite the Savoy cinema. We girls used to hang out of the window of the Savoy watching the proceedings from a grandstand view. Billy Dwyer, one of the most prominent citizens of Cork and owner of the Sunbeam factory, was a candidate for Fine Gael. He made the tactical error of announcing from the platform, 'God bless the RAF for protecting us from the German bombers.' He promptly failed to win his seat, which was very unusual in Cork City where Fine Gael always topped the poll at the time. Cork, having been a garrison town, was a great Fine Gael stronghold. WT Cosgrave, a good Dublin Fine Gael man, always stood for election in Cork as it was considered the safest seat; I understand he rarely visited that city.

When de Valera called a second general election the following summer, Billy Dwyer, being the astute businessman that he was, handed over his campaign to a prominent Dublin advertising agency. He successfully headed the poll.

By now I had reached the age of twenty-one and my right to vote. I think it was during that time that I began to think politically. Even though I understood my aunt's position *vis-à-vis* the Free State, I came to the conclusion that the only way forward for the country was by political means and that I therefore had a duty to cast my vote. My aunt was still alive, so I had a problem: under no circumstances was I prepared to hurt her by letting her know that I was about to take part in a Free State election. I was always a problem-solver, so I figured out how to go about it. I went down to Fitzgerald's of the Grand Parade to ask the advice of George Buckley, who managed the shop for Seamus

MacGearailt TD, the senior TD in Cork at the time. I told George my problem was that I wanted to vote in the election, but didn't want to upset my aunt. Was there any way he could smuggle me in to the back of the polling booth so that I wouldn't be seen to vote? George said, 'Leave it to me.' Sure enough, he got me in and out without anyone seeing me and I did my duty by my country.

When I got to know Ruairí later, I found out he had arrived at the same conclusion during those elections. He was still on parole at the time and therefore technically a prisoner of the Fianna Fáil government. He too cast his vote for the de Valera government. We did not know one another at this time. Wasn't it strange that we should both have been on the same wavelength? Perhaps this was a good omen for our future together, that in such a fundamental matter we saw eye to eye. In his case the question of casting a vote wasn't so complicated because he was living in his married sister's house and could come and go as he wished without his family knowing what he was about.

AUNT ANNIE

Aunt Annie was quite a different personality from Aunt Máire. She always wore a locket, which held a lock of my father's hair that she had removed after his death. I think this was a Victorian custom. When I returned home to Ireland my aunts gave me a similar locket, also containing a lock of my father's hair, which I wore on a gold chain. The locket was gold and engraved on one side with '*Daidí*' and on the other, '*A "cailín deas"*' (His 'lovely girl'). I was told this is what he called me.

Though having inherited many of the same attributes as the MacSwineys, such as a considerable intellect, Annie was far less practical and organised than Máire. She could not have conducted the school affairs nor have run the household. During the war years, after Máire died in 1942, Annie never understood war conditions. One day she went down to the kitchen to tell our maid, Maggie, to go across the road and buy a pound of rice. Maggie said, 'Miss, rice hasn't been seen in this country for at least two years.' Another day she rang up Suttons Coal Merchants and ordered a ton of coal to be sent the following day. At this time coal was ordered by the half-ton, and three weeks in advance. Of course, the ton of coal arrived within a few days. I don't know whether this was because it was a school or because it was Miss MacSwiney; the man to whom she gave the order was the father of two of the children in the school.

Another incident was the day she went to the kitchen and asked Maggie to polish the brass nameplate on the front door. Maggie said,

ABOVE:
The locket my aunts gave me on my return to Ireland.
RIGHT:
Annie MacSwiney. My Aunt Annie taught me English when I returned from Germany by reading from Dickens in her educated English accent.

'I'll have to get more Brasso, Miss.' My aunt picked a container off the shelf saying, 'Will this not do?' Maggie replied, 'That's Bisto, Miss, for sauces.' Whereupon my aunt said, 'Am I not very ignorant?' Maggie replied, 'You're not ignorant at all, Miss, but ye knows nothin'!' I can understand what she meant; my aunt had a lot of academic learning but was not very practical.

Aunt Annie was very much her own person. She rarely left the house, leaving all such domestic matters as shopping for our weekly needs, small as they were, to Aunt Máire.

After Aunt Annie got her university degree, she went to England to teach in Ventnor, on the Isle of Wight, in the years before the 1914 war. This was a finishing school, conducted by the Benedictine nuns for continental students, mainly German and some Dutch, to improve their English. My aunt kept in touch with her past pupils throughout the following years. It was she who, in 1938, arranged for me to go to Berlin, after second year Arts in UCC, to stay with three different families – all relatives of her past pupils – to improve my German, which I had thought I had forgotten. Considering I had only left that country six years earlier, this was unlikely. These pupils were now grown-up and married, some with daughters of my age. They always remembered their former teacher, Miss MacSwiney, with affectionate admiration and were ready to accept me into their homes for the nine weeks of that summer.

Aunt Annie was a character in her own right. She read Charles Dickens's novels to me to improve my English. *Oliver Twist* was read in her Oxford accent, while at the same time I was beginning to learn 'Cork speak' from my school companions.

As she rarely left the house, apart from going to daily Mass, she was always sending people on messages. 'Run down to Brian Boru Street [the nearest Post Office] to post this.' She would also send messages to people to come up to see her in Scoil Íte. One way of doing this was to send them express letters. We had no telephone as it would have

RIGHT:
Three sisters, Annie, Mary and Peg. They spoke with Oxford accents because their mother was English and because they attended school in London.

meant paying a rent to the 'Free State Government'! We could not have afforded it anyway. Instead, a telegraph boy always delivered Aunt Annie's letters. One day, when the Irish Sweepstake results were due out, she sent such a letter to a teacher. The teacher's mother, seeing the telegraph boy coming up the path to the house, exclaimed, 'We have won the Sweep!' I don't think she forgave my aunt lightly.

Annie was an inveterate letter writer, which was a Victorian habit. One friend complained to me, 'As soon as I have worked myself up to answer her, she would write back by return of post, leaving me back where I was!' Though knowing little Irish, Aunt Annie always made a point of addressing her envelopes with 'Cork' written in Irish, 'Corcaig', which she did with a scrawl: C___g. She addressed one such express letter to a teacher in Douglas, a Cork suburb, who came rushing up to the school days later, apologising that it had only just arrived. It had been readdressed from Douglas, Isle of Man. Written across it was, 'Try Douglas, Cork'. She was indignant and immediately sent for the Post Master from the General Post Office in downtown Cork to come up and explain how the people on the Isle of Man could read Irish and not those in the post office in Cork! He duly came up to Scoil Íte to apologise to her; Aunt Máire would never have done that.

During the time of the Civil War, when all Republicans were excommunicated, she went to confession in St Patrick's Church. After giving her absolution, the young priest was chatting to her and discovered, to his consternation, that she was of Republican persuasion. He told her he wasn't allowed to give her absolution, as it was a reserved sin. She replied, 'Don't worry, Father, I came to confess my sins not my virtues. I consider my Republican principles to be one of my virtues,' and left the confessional! Some of these people excommunicated at the time, mainly men, never went back to the Church. The Church had a lot to answer for.

In 1942 Aunt Annie also lost her brother, Seán. He died some

ABOVE LEFT: Seán, the youngest and most brilliant in the family.

ABOVE RIGHT: Peter went back to New York after my father's funeral, where he died on 19 November 1949.

months before Máire of septic pneumonia. He was a very heavy smoker and he was suffering from emphysema. He had been moved to the private nursing home next door to Belgrave Place in Dublin. The matron there was Mrs Murphy, a great friend of the MacSwineys; all her daughters were past pupils of Scoil Íte. I still remember when he was laid out; his friends and former comrades came in to pay their respects.

Uncle Seán, the youngest of the MacSwineys, was the most brilliant in the family. He had won scholarships all the way through his school years. He went to Canada as a young man and established a very successful career. He was on the point of getting engaged when he returned home to Cork during my father's hunger strike. My Uncle Peter, who had earlier emigrated to New York and was in the insurance business, also returned at that time. A short while after my father's death, Peter went straight back to New York and continued his life and career there. Seán, however, felt he should stay on in Cork a little while longer to provide moral support for his sisters. In the meantime, the Treaty debates and the outbreak of Civil War occurred. Seán felt obliged to stay in Ireland so as not to abandon the Republican cause. That is why he never returned to Canada, thus ruining a very promising career and probably leaving a young girl broken-hearted. I consider my Uncle Seán another victim of the Republican cause. Because he couldn't recognise the Free State, he found that only casual employment was open to him. It makes me very sad to think that he died a broken man.

When Uncle Seán and Aunt Máire died, Aunt Annie was often on her own. I was a student at UCC. I decided to get a wireless for her as I thought she might find it company. We had no money, so I asked George Buckley, the General Manager of Fitzgerald's electrical shop on Grand Parade, if he had anything he could fix up that might otherwise be thrown out. It had to be cheap. It was a struggle even to come up with the ten shillings' annual licence fee for the 'Free State Government'. As my aunt would not recognise the Free State, I had to procure the licence fee.

Now, only Aunt Annie and myself were left to run the school. It was obvious we had a difficult financial situation on our hands because of the two funerals. I took no salary. I never saw a pay packet in my life, even though I taught all the Latin in the school. As well as that, some of the children attending were unable to pay the fees owing to their parents having fallen on hard times. Others had been taken in free because they were of a Republican background. The result was that the finances of the school were not in great shape.

Annie went to see her bank manager at Munster and Leinster Bank in Bridge Street, Cork, to see if she could get a little overdraft to cover the cost of the funerals. The manager received her graciously and said he would, of course, facilitate her. After chatting to her for a while on various subjects, he came to a form that had to be filled out with regard to the overdraft. He started to fill it in until the question of collateral came up. 'Now, Miss MacSwiney, what should we put down here for collateral?' 'What's that?' She had never heard of collateral because she had never had cause to borrow money from the bank before. The bank manager explained, 'Well, Miss MacSwiney, I have to put something down that will guarantee the loan; perhaps we could put the school building down as a guarantee?' 'But the building doesn't belong to us, it is only rented.' At that point the bank manager was a bit nonplussed and said the school furnishings 'might do', whereupon she replied, 'They are only cheap desks and benches.' He asked, 'What can we put down as guarantee?' 'My word of honour is my guarantee.' In the end, the manager gave up trying to sort it out and gave her the £350 loan anyway. I suppose he felt that she would be able to pay the loan off eventually and if not, the bank would hardly sue a MacSwiney for £350.

When she came home and explained all this to me I decided that drastic action was necessary! I told her that there could be no more free places for students, that we would have to amalgamate classes and reduce staff numbers by not replacing teachers who retired. This put the whole enterprise on a sound financial footing until we had paid off the overdraft. I reorganised the school, the timetables and the classes accordingly. In due course we were able to pay off the overdraft and the school was better organised financially.

For some years after I was married I used to spend my summer holidays in Kerry. Aunt Annie always asked me for help in reorganising timetables, or with any other problem that may have arisen. Of course, I never refused. But in spite of all this it must have been very difficult for her, though she had a very loyal and good staff. In 1953 she suffered a heart attack. At that time a Mrs Murphy owned Glenvera private hospital in Belgrave Place. Her daughter, Eleanor, a past pupil of Scoil Íte, had qualified as a doctor and was married to a young man who was a heart specialist. She and her mother, the matron of the hospital, kept an eye on my aunt and would call immediately if my aunt had any problems. The young heart specialist was called in and decided that she should be moved to the Bon Secours hospital. She said, 'What nonsense! I have my classes in the morning, I can't go to hospital.' He compromised and allowed her to take her class while lying on a couch.

In June 1954 Aunt Annie had to close Scoil Íte owing to her ill health. She was not prepared to hand over the school to anyone, as they would not have been able to continue with the same ethos. I went down to Cork to help finalise matters. My first concern was that the children attending the school, who were mainly at a primary level, would be accommodated elsewhere and that the staff, who were young, would find alternative employment. I worried particularly about what would happen to Iníon Ní Chaisligh (Nora Cassily), who was elderly and would have had no pension from the Department of Education.

BELOW:
Myself, Annie and Sinéad in Scoil Íte in 1954, the year the school closed.

Closing Of Scoil Ite

Scoil Ite will close at the end of the coming Summer Term with the retirement of its Principal, Eitne Nic Suibhne.

ITS PUPILS WILL BE INCORPORATED IN

scoil muire

Kindergarten (under the guidance of Miss Cassilly as heretofore) and lower classes, will form a Junior School in the present premises of Scoil Ite (4, Belgrave Place).

Intermediate classes will join parallel classes forming the Senior School in the premises of Scoil Mhuire, 2 Sidney Place henceforth to be distinguished from the Junior School as

coláiste muire

Enquiries for both Junior and Senior schools to:—

THE PRINCIPAL, K. M. CAHILL, M.A.,

2, Sidney Place, Wellington Road, Cork.

ABOVE:
Newspaper notice announcing the closure of Scoil Íte. Aunt Annie used the Irish form of her name here: Eithne Nic Suibhne.

A close friend of my two aunts, Miss Kathleen Cahill, had opened a secondary school, called Scoil Mhuire, nearby on Wellington Road. I asked if she could incorporate our primary children into her school. She readily agreed. Any of the young teachers who wished to remain on went with the younger pupils. I then asked her could she accommodate the kindergarten with Iníon Ní Chaisligh. She very kindly agreed to do so. I felt that Iníon Ní Chaisligh needed added financial support for when she would retire. I had learned from my sister-in-law, Nollaig, of a British organisation called RUKBA (the Royal United Kingdom Beneficent Association), which supported elderly ladies left in straitened circumstances. My sister-in-law was a member of the organisation and as such could vote to choose who would be a beneficiary.

At a past-pupils' reunion, when I had many of the girls present, I asked them to join RUKBA, which they all did, giving them the voting power when the question of choosing beneficiaries came up. This they all did, with the result that Iníon Ní Chaisligh was elected as a beneficiary in less than two years. Somebody remarked to my sister-in-law that they didn't know of anyone being elected so quickly. This organisation was of great assistance after she had to retire, both financially and in providing her with beautiful dresses. I encouraged the past pupils to continue their contributions to RUKBA for as long as possible.

RUAIRÍ

In September 1941 I returned to Cork and to my teaching duties. After Christmas I went to Dublin to study in the National Library for my MA. I stayed with the O'Donels in Eccles Street.

Although my Aunt Máire would have corresponded with Ruairí's mother, Mrs Kathleen Brugha, it was not a family that she visited, except on one occasion. Mrs Brugha and my aunt were both members of the Second Dáil (elected in May 1921), along with their very close friend Seán Ó Ceallaigh, otherwise known as Sceilg. Republicans maintained that at the time of the vote on the Treaty, on 7 January 1922, which they lost, the Second Dáil was not properly dissolved, as should have been done in accordance with correct procedures. They therefore insisted that the Second Dáil was still legally in existence. Whenever I came to Dublin, my aunt gave me written notes to be delivered to Sceilg, who worked in MH Gill's publishing company in Upper O'Connell Street. On this particular occasion she also gave me a note to be delivered to Mrs Kathleen Brugha in Kingston's menswear shop, which Mrs Brugha owned.

I had met Mrs Brugha previously, when I had accompanied Aunt

BELOW:
Ruairí, aged five, and his sisters at the funeral of their father, Cathal Brugha, in 1922.
RIGHT:
Cathal Brugha.

Máire one afternoon on a visit to her home on Upper Rathmines Road. When I took the letter to Mrs Brugha in her office upstairs, she was in the process of arranging with a friend, Tess Bruton (the sister of her son-in-law, John Bruton), to go to the Abbey Theatre the following Friday night. When Tess saw me she said, 'You must join us.' I did not want to do so, but I was swept along. Arrangements were made that they would meet after Kingston's closed, at the restaurant of the Savoy cinema in O'Connell Street.

When I duly arrived at Kingston's at 5.30pm, I was told there was a change of plan and we were all going out to Mrs Brugha's house for tea. That was the first time that I visited *Ros na Rí* in Temple Gardens. It was 2 January 1942 and my first official meeting with Ruairí, who at that time I knew as Rory.

According to him, we had met fleetingly twice before. Once was when Máire de Róiste and I were passing through Dublin on our way to Monaghan. We stayed with her Aunt Áine (the Irish teacher who had rescued me at the time of my Matric), who was by then married to Dónal Healy and lived on Cabra Road. Apparently, Ruairí Brugha was commandeered to take Rory O'Rahilly and us two girls for a drive. We girls sat in the back of the car, with the two Rorys in front. We took very little notice of the boys; possibly we were naïve for our age.

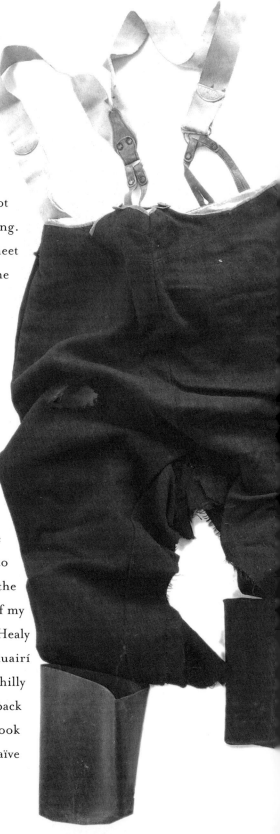

Caitlín bean Catail bruga, T.D
Elected Senior Member for Waterford City and County
August 27th, 1923.

When Ruairí was young the Brughas had spent a holiday in Árd Mór, County Waterford, where Fr Tadhg Ó Murchú, who was in his final year in Maynooth College, was also holidaying. They became friends. Fr Tadhg got the 'flu and Ruairí visited him a few times in his digs. Fr Tadhg invited Ruairí to attend his ordination the following June. The two of them remained friends from then on.

The second time Ruairí and I must have met was when Ruairí was on a bicycle tour around Ireland quite some years later and he visited Fr Tadhg in Gráig. Ruairí got permission to pitch his tent in the front garden of one of the local guesthouses. During the night a goat started to eat his tent, so Ruairí had to adjourn to the house and sleep the remainder of the night on the wooden settle in the kitchen.

One afternoon my aunts were holding their usual afternoon tea on the front lawn of our

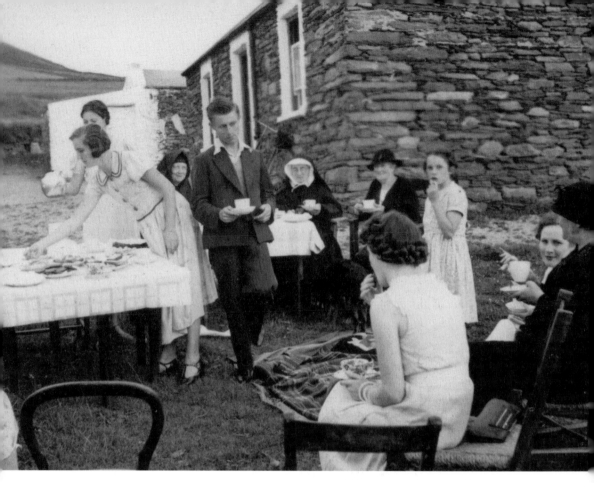

cottage. This was attended by quite a number of people, including two of the O'Rahilly boys, Maolmuire and Rory, and two of the MacCurtain girls, Síle and Eilís, sisters of Tomás Óg MacCurtain, who were staying in a guesthouse in the village. Máire de Róiste and I were fulfilling our duty of running around serving the guests with tea and buns. There were other friends of my aunts' present also, making quite a large gathering. All of them were sitting on the lawn, enjoying the refreshments. Apart from Máire and myself, the only other person on his feet was Ruairí, helping out and attending to the needs of the guests. As usual, neither Máire nor I, who were very busy at the time, took any special notice of any of the boys. I have a photograph (above), which shows I met him on that occasion.

As I have only a vague memory of these occasions, I speak of our meeting on 1 January 1942 as our first official encounter. After tea that evening, when Tess, Mrs Brugha and I were getting ready to go to the theatre, Ruairí suddenly decided that he would come along. After the theatre we returned to the Brugha home and I spent the night there, sleeping in the same room as Ruairí's older sister, Brenda, who never stopped chatting all night. I drifted in and out of sleep and said 'yes' from time to time. She was to become one of my best-loved sisters-in-law. The following morning, after breakfast, Ruairí stopped me on the landing outside her bedroom. He wanted to know if he could take me to the pictures the following night. I said I was busy. He asked what about Monday, I was still busy, and so he continued through the days of the week. By Thursday I ran out of excuses, so we fixed it for the Friday night and we met and went to the Savoy cinema.

The following Friday was the big annual Kingston's dance and the Brughas wanted me to stay over for that. I had to ring Cork and guarantee that I would be on the train at Kingsbridge at 8.30am the following day and would be in good time for the annual Scoil Íte past-pupils' reunion at 8.00pm. This was likely to be the last reunion for which Aunt Máire would be alive.

LEFT:
Ruairí helping Máire and myself to serve our guests with tea and buns at the cottage in Kerry.

As it turned out, the journey took from 8.30am till 11.30pm. The problem was wartime trains, which ran only twice a week and had to be fuelled by turf. This meant that at least twice the train had to stop, I think at Mallow and again at Limerick Junction. The stoker and the driver had to clean out the engine completely because turf produces a sticky, tarry substance. Alas, I was late for the reunion, which made me feel very guilty because Aunt Máire was in her last illness.

After my meeting with Ruairí in January 1942 I was invited to come back to Dublin at Easter. Of course I stayed again with the O'Donels. I visited Ruairí in a private nursing home, where he had undergone an operation. My reluctance with regard to any relationship with Ruairí was mainly founded on my determination not to get involved with any Republicans. As far as I could judge, from Ruairí's background and upbringing, one would take for granted that he would be

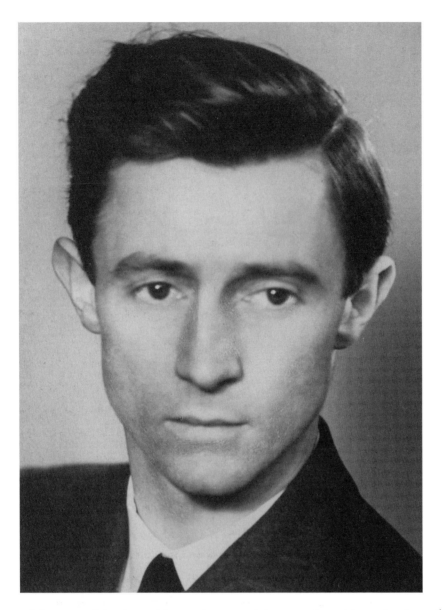

of that way of thinking. He was the son of the great Republican leader, Cathal Brugha. His mother, Caitlín (Kathleen Kingston), was left a widow with five daughters and an only son. The leaders of the IRA always frequented the house. Having been born into this milieu, there would appear to be no escape for the boy.

Ruairí's first encounter with the law was when he was about thirteen. He was told to go and put up posters to encourage people to

ABOVE:
Ruairí Brugha –
an election photo
when he was a
candidate for
Clann na
Poblachta.

wear the Easter lily. He was brought to a garda station. When they interrogated him and discovered who he was, they couldn't get rid of him fast enough. Another encounter Ruairí had was when he was told to join Na Fianna Éireann. He announced, 'No way, I'm not going to wear that silly skirt' – obviously he was not enamoured of the saffron kilt designed by Countess Markievicz!

By the time he reached sixteen it was inevitable that he would be enrolled in the IRA. He was put in charge of what was known as the college unit. It consisted mainly of young UCD and Trinity College students. He was supposed to take them out to the green fields of Tallaght on 'manoeuvres' and drilling. They had very few handguns and munitions between them, but at the end of every manoeuvre Ruairí would carefully collect all the weapons and every bullet from the young men before they went home.

When he was eighteen his mother had sent him to England to train for the family business, Kingston's. He spent over a year in Manchester and often spoke with affection of his time in digs. He also spent a few months in Austin Reed's store in London. His involvement with the IRA was, I think, at best very tenuous before he went to train in England. By the time he returned and went to work in the family business his involvement with the IRA had faded away altogether. He was now mainly concerned with helping his mother run Kingston's.

When his mother was left a widow she would not take any pension from the government. Lalor Bros., the candlemakers where Cathal Brugha had been the third partner, gave her a weekly allowance on which she brought up her children. But she was a strong and independent woman and wanted to earn her own living. She started a business, which she set up with the financial help of her brother, Charles Kingston. At the beginning they had a shop on Nassau Street that sold Irish leather goods, etc. Soon they moved to Upper O'Connell Street and founded the famous menswear shop,

Kingston's. She was very fortunate to have in her employment Dermot Anderson, a first-class manager and buyer. It was his skill at buying the right clothes that so quickly brought the business to such fame as a men's outfitters. It was Dermot who coined the famous slogan: 'A Kingston shirt makes all the difference.'

At the outbreak of the Second World War in 1939, de Valera declared strict neutrality to keep Ireland out of any involvement. One of the things that stood to his advantage was the fact that the last British ports, among them Spike Island, had been handed over by Chamberlain to the Irish State in 1938. The first problem de Valera had to confront was the possibility of difficulties arising out of activities of the IRA. He opened the Curragh camp to put any possible suspects under safekeeping.

Ruairí suspected that he might be considered for internment because of his family history. It would be presumed by the State that he had involvement with Republican activities. One morning, sure enough, he saw members of Special Branch coming down the street and, presuming they were coming to arrest him, Ruairí cleared out through the backdoor of the business premises and went on the run. He managed to elude them for over a year.

During that time Ruairí had met and shared a place of refuge for a short while with George Plunkett, eldest son of Count Plunkett, who also ended up in the Curragh. Ruairí was able to find refuge in the most unbelievable households, for instance, in the home of his uncle, Charles Kingston, who came from Anglo-Irish stock and still adhered to that tradition. Another house that looked after him was that of Mrs Beaumont, whose daughter, Máire, later married Dónall Ó Móráin. Mrs Beaumont was a friend of my aunt and was of strong Republican outlook. I remember her visiting us in Cork when she was acting as an extern to my H. Dip. class. She was Professor of Education in UCD. Later she used to tell me the story of when Ruairí was staying with her. When she was vacuuming her house, Ruairí would take the vacuum cleaner and finish the job for her, which was unusual at the time. That was typical of Ruairí, always helpful and considerate of others. During his period on the run he also stayed in houses where he saw, first-hand, how the poor had to struggle to make ends meet. But no matter how poor they were, there was always a welcome for him.

He was finally caught and put into the Curragh with the rest of them. By then Ruairí had had time to do a lot of thinking and had come to his own conclusion that the way forward for Ireland was not through physical force but by the political option. Of course, there were many people in the Curragh who were there only because their family was of a Republican tradition, but who would never have been involved in violence. One person in particular comes to mind. He was Seán Óg Ó Tuama, a beautiful singer and completely devoted to Irish music. He had his own choir in Cork and they frequently sang on Irish radio. Seán Óg would not hurt a fly. But his father, also Seán, was of a very strong Republican tradition and also involved in the Irish language. To his utter bewilderment, Seán Óg found himself in the Curragh.

Some inmates devoted themselves to crafts to while away the boredom. They made some beautiful Celtic crosses from matchsticks. They also produced leather goods with Celtic designs, such as handbags, missal covers and wallets. Others made jewellery from silver coins.

A great mixture of people ended up interned in the Curragh. There was George Plunkett, brother of Joseph Mary Plunkett, one of the signatories of the Proclamation and executed by the British after 1916. Their father was Count George Noble Plunkett, an anti-Treaty Sinn Féin TD until 1927. Some were prominent Republicans, such as Dom Adams, uncle of Gerry Adams. Others were native Irish speakers. Some of these set about teaching Irish to any internees who were interested. One such was Mairtín Ó Cadhain, the writer from the west of Ireland. Mairtín was a great Irish scholar. He taught the internees at university level. Later he was appointed a professor in Trinity College, even though he did not have university qualifications himself.

Another was Seán Ó Briain from Ballyferriter in the West Kerry Gaeltacht. He had been trained as a teacher in the training college run by the de la Salle order in Waterford and had been teaching in Dublin. Seán taught the Curragh internees at secondary level. He was an excellent teacher and should have returned to his teaching career, except that the Free State had a law preventing anyone who had been convicted from taking up State employment. One of his pupils in the Curragh was Brendan Behan; they became very close friends. Seán Ó Briain was of a strong Republican tradition, which he inherited from his father, Padraic Ó Briain, who was headmaster of Ballyferriter National School. With Seán's background and upbringing, he was bound to end up in the IRA and was very active.

Although not from the Gaeltacht, Ruairí had been brought up in Rathmines speaking Irish, a sort of 'Dublin Gaeltacht'! Ruairí taught Irish at primary level, 'beginners' Irish'.

When he arrived into the Curragh, George Plunkett, Seán Ó Briain, Dom Adams and others co-opted Ruairí onto the camp council, presumably because he was the son of Cathal Brugha, although he was only twenty-three years old. The inmates of the camp were a motley crowd, mostly people who themselves had no connection with the IRA or any organisation committed to violence.

Conditions in the camp were not too harsh, but confinement can have a bad effect on some people. Ruairí told me of one incident where one young man, in his frustration, lost his temper and decided he would take on the armed guard stationed on the perimeter wall. Ruairí said, 'What do you think you are doing? All you are going to achieve is to get yourself shot.' Ruairí always used his head. He carefully thought out any problems before making a decision. It was decided to start a general hunger strike to secure better conditions. Although he had been only a short time in the Curragh, Ruairí insisted that nobody would tell him to go on hunger strike. If he thought it correct, he would decide himself and would be able to stick it out to the end. However, he said, most of the boys there were very young and would not last a week. Such an action would end up demoralising everyone. They didn't go ahead with this proposal.

In time, boredom and frustration set in and the council decided it was necessary to organise some action. They decided to burn down one of the huts. Ruairí's suggestion that it did not make any sense went unheeded. They probably only meant to burn down one, but with the change of wind others caught fire. This had the unfortunate result of revealing a tunnel that was being dug! The upshot of all this was that they were all put into solitary confinement in what was known as the 'Glasshouse', a very cold and uncomfortable place.

Apparently, Ruairí did not mind this at all. He at last was alone, was able to read and make little paper chessmen and play chess alone. His only companion was a mouse that would peep at him over the head of the bed. One day a young man was put in with him who was obviously on the verge of a breakdown. Possibly the authorities thought Ruairí would be able to calm him, which turned out to be the correct assumption. The young man was threatening suicide and Ruairí was able to talk him out of it.

Finally, those who were involved in the burning of the huts were brought to trial in Dublin. As Ruairí was a member of the camp council, he was included. They were all sent to Mountjoy prison. While in 'the Joy' they were refused the Sacraments, as they had been officially excommunicated. Of course, there were always priests from some orders, such as the Capuchins, who would attend the prisoners and who gave them absolution.

One day Ruairí met one of his inmates storming out of the church because he had been refused absolution. The man was furious and announced he was going to have no more to do with the Catholic Church. Ruairí said to him, 'Don't be so stupid, you just went to the wrong confessional. Why don't you go over to that confessional and the priest will give you absolution?' That was sorted out! After some time Ruairí's health deteriorated and he was sent over to the Mater hospital for treatment on his stomach; he had had this problem before internment. On leaving hospital he was released on parole and went to live with his married sister, Nollaig.

After the war Brendan Behan remained in touch with Seán Ó Briain and they were very close friends. Many years later, Brendan's widow asked Seán to give the oration at the unveiling of a monument on his grave. Ruairí's sister, Noinín, married Seán and he came into the family business, Kingston's, as secretary of the company. Brendan Behan used to call in to see Seán in the main branch of Kingston's in O'Connell Street (very near where Cathal Brugha was shot in 1922).

Brendan was very generous, and would often give away his coat to some poor person he might meet. He would then come into Kingston's where Seán would provide him with a new coat. If Seán wasn't in the office, Ruairí would go down to meet him. The interactions between Ruairí and Brendan were always loud yet friendly. Ruairí would accuse Brendan of losing his coat, knowing full well that he had given it away to a deserving cause, and would probably do the same again with this one. Brendan would accuse Ruairí of being a capitalist.

On one of these occasions Brendan sent in a young man to be fully dressed: new suit, shirt, etc. The young man told Ruairí he did not want a new suit or anything else, but his father was outside in the taxi with Brendan, 'fluthered'. Ruairí went out and explained to Brendan that he would look after it. He went back to the son and said, 'Not to worry, they will probably forget all about it. But if you need anything, come back later.'

I saw Ruairí on a few more occasions and got to know him better. He commissioned an engagement ring for me while in the Curragh, made out of a silver shilling, although I hardly knew him at the time. I think he must have already had ideas in that direction. My problem in not making a commitment to him in the first few months was that, judging by his childhood and upbringing, I had no way of knowing whether he had been brought up to follow the same extreme Republican views that I had encountered in some other families, such as the MacCurtains of Cork, whom I had known slightly.

Even though Tomás MacCurtain and my father had together been the leaders of Sinn Féin and the Volunteers in Cork up to their deaths as Lord Mayor, one succeeding the other, the MacCurtain family had not remained close to the MacSwineys. In fact, none of the girls came to school in Scoil Íte, but passed by its door to attend St Angela's Ursuline school further up the road. They were a well-known family in Cork, especially Tomás Óg, who was a very popular student in UCC. The MacCurtain family grew up in a situation where they appeared to have no alternative but to follow a strict Republican path.

One daughter, Síle, remained at home with her mother and later I got to know her quite well when I used to visit Cork at least once a year to see Aunt Annie and my friends. Sometimes I took the opportunity to visit Síle, who was then working in the music department of Eason's on Patrick Street. She used to point out all the shelves crammed with records and say, 'I'm in charge of all this, Máire, and I don't know a thing about it' — because it was all contemporary music. Síle, like all the MacCurtains, had a great sense of humour and a visit to her was always a tonic. One day she complained to me, 'Máire, we're only supposed to marry Republicans, but where are these

Republicans?' This gave me a very clear insight into what their situation was.

For my own part, I did not want to be involved with Ruairí if it meant living life under the constraint of extreme Republicanism. As I got to know him during that summer of 1942, while he was still on parole from the previous year, I discovered that he had thought deeply on the political situation and would follow his own decisions. From then on I had no more worries about the kind of person he was. Ruairí was still on parole at that time and living in the house of his married sister, Nollaig, in order to avoid any possibility of breaking his parole by bumping into any Republicans who might be calling to his family home in Rathmines.

The German spy, Gunter Schütz, was harboured for a while in *Ros na Rí*, the Brugha house, because no one else would take him in. I think, as usual, the Republican movement was using Mrs Brugha. I actually met Gunter there one afternoon when I was visiting. He seemed to be very suave, well brought up and happily ensconced there. It struck me that he was very content to be living there rather than carrying out his mission as a spy, or indeed going back to Germany and his military duty. One evening, Maolmuire O'Rahilly invited me to dinner in Jammets of Grafton Street, the most elegant and expensive restaurant in Dublin at the time. There were posters of Gunter everywhere with the words, 'HAVE YOU SEEN THIS MAN?' As we were getting onto the tram Maolmuire said to me, 'I wonder where he is,' to which I answered, 'Yes, I wonder'! As I said before, I always lived a double life.

Sometime in the following winter, while Ruairí was still on parole, the Minister for Justice, Gerry Boland, sent for him and suggested that he should sign himself out of the Curragh. The regulation at that time was that if a prisoner signed a document saying he would not engage in any further Republican activities, he would be released. Of course, Ruairí would not sign any such thing – it would have been unheard of. He understood that the authorities were anxious to put an end to this embarrassing situation, but he wasn't going to help them out of their difficulties. Finally, they released him anyway.

In summer 1943 Ruairí visited Fr Tadhg Ó Murchú in Gráig while I was at my aunts' house. I have a nice snap taken of the two of us on

ABOVE:
Ruairí and me
sitting on Clogher
strand before
we were married.

Clogher strand. During the winter months, when I was teaching in Scoil Íte and Ruairí was working in Kingston's in Dublin, we had an arrangement whereby he telephoned me once a week at the office of a friend as we had no telephone at home. My friend was secretary to a rate collector in downtown Cork, and she would let me into her office at 8.00 at night and Ruairí and I would have a brief conversation.

On St Valentine's Day 1943 a card with a big, red, satin heart arrived. I looked at it in bemusement, not knowing much about St Valentine's Day. I also figured that Ruairí wouldn't have thought of it on his own accord: it must have been on the suggestion of one of his sisters. Neither Ruairí nor I were ever concerned with taking note of anniversaries. If only one partner is that way inclined it can give a lot of trouble, but where both are of the same way of thinking it doesn't make any difference.

Fr Tadhg's parents lived in Cork, in Montenotte, and he invited Ruairí to come and stay a few weeks in the summer of 1944. By then Ruairí and I were officially doing a line. We went on trips together on our bicycles. On one memorable occasion we took a trip out to Garryvoe, in East Cork. This was a strand I knew well because all the Scoil Íte picnics were held there. Halfway home, passing through Midleton, I decided this bicycle ride was too long. I got off the bike in the middle of the town and said I was not moving another inch until I got a cup of tea.

That summer, Ruairí proposed and I accepted. We were engaged at Christmas 1944 and set the date for our wedding for 10 July 1945. We were married in the Honan Chapel in UCC. It is in the Hiberno-

LEFT:
Our wedding day in Cork, 10 July 1945.
RIGHT, TOP:
The wedding party.
Seated: **Caitlín Brugha, Seán Ó Briain, Máirín Ní Ruairc, Aunt Annie.** *Standing*: **Nóinín Brugha, Fr Costello, Nessa Brugha, Uncle Norbert, Madame Stockley, Ruairí, Fr Augustine, Sinéad Ní Bhriain (hidden behind me), Dorothy Murphy, Fr Tadhg Ó Murchú, Mrs Norbert Murphy, Nollaig (Brugha) Bruton, May Foley, Gerry O'Donel and Rory O'Rahilly.**
RIGHT:
Me with Uncle Norbert who escorted me up the aisle.

Romanesque style, with striking Harry Clarke stained-glass windows and a beautiful mosaic floor. It is a copy of Cormac's Chapel in Cashel, County Tipperary. I asked my Uncle Norbert, my mother's brother, to give me away as there were no menfolk left in the MacSwiney family. He very kindly agreed to do so.

Fr Augustine, who had married my parents and prepared me for First Communion, married us. As he was elderly and not of good health he could not fast from midnight till 10.00am, so Fr Tadhg Ó Murchú said the Mass. It was a very quiet wedding because I was worried about too much publicity. I told no one the date. In fact, I had asked Ruairí could we get married in Dublin, but he thought that wouldn't do. I only told a few of my friends and they came to the church to see us.

The wedding breakfast was held in one of the ground-floor schoolrooms at Scoil Íte and caterers were employed. It was all very simple and rather austere. Ruairí made a lovely speech. He always knew what to say. It did not occur to me at the time that Aunt Annie never once complained about me leaving her alone to look after the school. It was really most unselfish of her not to hold me back.

In the first year of our marriage Ruairí suggested that we should get a copy of the Treaty debates and read them for ourselves. The first thing that surprised me was that most of the anti-Treaty speakers laid emphasis on the question of the oath of allegiance to the Crown rather than on partition. Apparently, only one lone voice, that of Seán MacEntee, had warned, 'Don't let them put a border through your country – don't cut off part of your national territory.' I felt that had been the devastating effect of the Treaty. Oaths or other political matters could be changed in later years; frontiers are very difficult to remove.

At this time (1945) I was still only thirteen years home from Germany and still saw many things, such as treaties, from a mainly continental point of view. I knew all about the Treaty of Versailles and its consequences. When I was living in Heidelberg, at the end of the 1920s, the Rhineland was still occupied by French troops and Germany had in many ways not recovered from the war. However, as the country had been completely defeated, it had to accept whatever conditions were laid down in the Treaty. Now it is generally accepted that Versailles laid the foundation of the 1939 war.

When I read the Irish Treaty of 1921 I was astounded to see the unfavourable conditions our negotiators had accepted – and this without bringing them back to Dublin to allow their colleagues in the Irish Government to examine them and give their judgement. After all, Ireland had not been defeated.

An Englishman, Mr Shine, a retired British civil servant and a close neighbour of ours on Roebuck Road, also brought this fact to my attention. He invited us to tea in his flat one day because he wished to tell me something. 'I want you to know, Máire,' he said, 'it was not the Irish Government but the British who asked for the truce.' Apparently, my father's hunger strike and death had repercussions in all corners of the world, and had brought discredit and ill-repute on Britain. In fact, immediately after his death the longshoremen in New York harbour refused to unload British cargo vessels. This came to light in recent years when the British archives of the time were opened to the public. Frank Costello, who wrote a biography of my father, refers to the correspondence between King George V and Prime Minister Lloyd George discussing the possibility of putting an end to the hunger strike by releasing my father – the adverse publicity was too damaging to Britain.

In the light of these circumstances, it seems inexplicable that Michael Collins and his delegation gave in on so many points which were disastrous for Ireland. The oath of allegiance to the Crown, which I understood to be of the greatest importance to unionists, was still in place. Not only did they accept a partitioning of the country but they allowed three-and-a-half counties, which were mainly Irish nationalist, to be cut off, *viz*. Derry, Fermanagh, Tyrone and South Armagh. It certainly brings to mind the old English proverb: 'Sow dragon's teeth and you reap a devil's crop.'

An interesting event occurred years later when Ruairí and I were invited to Cork for an Easter commemoration. As soon as we arrived at the City Hall, I found myself surrounded by a group of elderly men eager to speak to me. They assured me that their fathers had always maintained they would never have voted for the Treaty save that they had accepted Michael Collins's assurance that everything would be all right and the border would not remain.

The northeastern part of Ulster, which was mainly inhabited by Protestant settlers, could have been given some form of autonomy under the Dublin government. Personally, having got to know a large

number of Northern Protestants over thirty years and having discussed these issues with them, I feel that if representatives of
Northern Protestants had sat in an Irish parliament, they would have
played a significant role, perhaps even as government in partnership
with another party. This could not be said of their status in
Westminster today.

Years later, when we were holidaying with the children in the South
of France, I insisted that we should travel home via Lake Annecy in
the Alps, where the negotiations took place between France, under
General Charles de Gaulle, and the Algerians. It was reported in the
press that, as the conditions offered were unacceptable to the
Algerians, their delegation walked out saying, 'We are not going to
allow what happened to Ireland to happen to us.' Some months later
negotiations resumed and Algeria got full independence. How different was the fate of Ireland: the 1921 Treaty did not put an end to the
difficulties in Northern Ireland.

MARRIED LIFE

I settled into a life of looking after babies: Deirdre (born 1946), Cathal (1949), Terry (Traolach) (1953) and Ruairí (1955). My interest in them developed and became stronger as the children got a little older, when I could relate to them as rational beings who merely lacked experience. Our way of bringing up the children was based on the idea that they were capable of reasoning for themselves. If they were given an instruction and they asked, Why?, they were never given the answer: Because I told you so. The matter was always carefully explained to them: either it was for their

BELOW: My first-born, Deirdre, and me in 1946.

own safety or so as not to inconvenience others.

Once I became a mother, I began to look back on my own child-hood and the things I had enjoyed about it. I found that my early years still exerted an influence over me, an influence I passed on, in some ways, to my own sons and daughter. One of the effects of my early childhood was that we celebrated Christmas according to the German tradition. The children were never allowed to see the Christmas tree being decorated, which I always took care of. The door was kept locked until Christmas Eve when the tree was ready and all the candles were lighting on it, as I had known it in Germany. (After a few years I replaced the candles with electric Christmas lights, as they were safer.) When the door was finally unlocked, the children were allowed in, one by one: it was a magical moment. First, they knelt at the crib and said a little prayer. All their presents were lying at the foot of the tree. I explained to them that it was because we were celebrating the birth-day of the Christ Child (*Christkind*) that they were getting presents.

We had no Santa Claus coming down the chimney in our house. However, I was very conscious that I did not want the children to lose out compared to what their friends were getting. Every year I brought them to one of the big department stores in town to see 'Santa' and receive a little present. But they understood that it was only a man dressed up. I think I would have felt uncomfortable telling them the story about Santa Claus, only to have to tell them, some years later, that it was completely untrue. Peadar O'Donnell, who had a great sense of humour, once told us a story about a little boy, aged about seven, who had been informed by his friends at school that there was no such person as Santa Claus. When he arrived home, he demanded that his parents should tell him the truth: Was there *really* no Santa? After being told that that was so, he looked at them and said: 'Well, in that case I will have to look into the question of Jesus as well.' This brought home to me that one should never tell a child a lie.

My preference for German traditions was not unique. Through the Irish-German Society I was able to keep in touch with the language and culture of my childhood. I recall our family joining with the Society's members for their Christmas celebration in the Mansion House. There were candles on the Christmas tree, *Lebkuchen* ginger-bread, and we sang the hymns I knew in German. I felt at home with the children of German families living in Ireland and Irish families, such as ours, with German connections: the Clissmanns, the Mallins – whose grandmother, Madame Stockley, was half-German and half-French and who had come with my aunt to Germany when I escaped back to Ireland – and one of the founders of the Irish-German Society, Proinsias Ó Súilleabháin. The Society later founded St Kilian's, the German School, which is now on Roebuck Road in Dublin.

In time I lost contact with most of the people I had known in Germany. Erika Sommers, the youngest daughter of Frau Illig, the woman I had lived with in Heidelberg, wrote to me after the war asking could I help her by sending some clothes for her little daughter. Sighle (Humphreys) O'Donoghue, a life-long friend of the MacSwineys, gave me some beautiful dresses and a coat that her daughter, Cróine, had outgrown. I sent these to Erika, but lost touch with her after that.

Another person in Germany I made contact with was Gunter Schütz, whom I had met once in the Brugha household a long time previously. When my boys were young I wrote to him in Hamburg asking if he could send me two pairs of *lederhosen* for Cathal and Terry, then aged seven and three. These were the leather pants worn by Bavarian men and boys in summertime. They were indestructible and ideally suited to climbing trees in the backfields behind our house in Dublin, and for clambering on the rocks in Kerry when we were on our holidays.

Another effect of my childhood in Europe was that I felt a need to go back to the Continent regularly. One part of my life I particularly enjoyed, as a married woman with young children, were the bi-annual visits I organised to Paris and the south of France, where I thought the sun and seaside of the Riviera provided a good place for the children to spend a holiday. I felt at home in France, with the language and the people, because my mother had brought me on summer holidays to Paris and Normandy. I never felt like a tourist, and was not treated like one. We camped, like the French did, and I spoke their language.

On our return from the south of France I would always insist on spending a week in Paris because it was the only city in which I felt at home, apart from Dublin and Cork. Each time we stayed in the same small hotel near the Etoile, where the proprietor and his wife got to know us well. I introduced the children to the Eiffel Tower, the art galleries and museums, and Montmartre. After all this sightseeing I would treat them to a big ice cream from a café on the Champs-Elysées, near the Arc de Triomphe. Some of my happiest memories of Ruairí and the children are from these times.

In 1952 Ruairí and I, together with his mother, went on a holiday to Germany along with our friends, Paddy and Peggy O'Keeffe. (Páirc Uí Chaoimh in Cork is named after Paddy, who was Secretary of the GAA from 1929 to 1964.) I wanted very much to return to see what Germany was like after the war. We drove through the Rhineland, and all the big cities I had visited as a child, including Wiesbaden and Mainz, were still in ruins. When we arrived in Cologne the cathedral had been partly destroyed, but didn't look too bad. In Munich we found that only the walls and the two towers of its famous cathedral, the *Frauenkirche*, were left standing. We were told that all the stained glass and the mosaic floor had been removed at the beginning of the war for safekeeping. Apparently, towards the end of the war, the American bombers would fly up from Italy and drop all their bombs on Munich so as to return without what they called 'payload'.

I really wanted to visit Garmisch and Grainau, the last place I had lived in, but was anxious about what we would find there. In fact, we found the town intact; the Americans had made it one of their head-quarters and had built a large barracks there, thus it was spared the fate of so many other towns and villages in Germany. I took photo-graphs of the house where I had lived in Grainau and visited the Eibsee, the huge glacial lake nearby, at the foot of the Zugspitze. We tried to get lunch in the hotel on the lakeside, but found it occupied by American Forces who wouldn't let us have our meal there because it was still off-limits to civilians.

We went on our way to Heidelberg, another home of my childhood. Heidelberg had also been left intact, which I found astonishing — it was the only city in the area that wasn't in ruins. Somebody explained to me that when the Americans were in the Rhineland on their advance into Germany, they had set up their headquarters there. Not a single bomb was dropped on Heidelberg. Near the end of the war orders were sent from Berlin to the people of the town to blow up all the bridges over the Neckar River. The citizens discussed this com-mand and came to the conclusion that it would make no sense to blow up their own bridges with the end of the war in sight. They refused to comply with the orders from Berlin. Thus, Heidelberg stands today as it did in the Middle Ages — a sight that warmed my heart.

We spent every August in our cottage in Kerry, where people still lived in the old way, without running water or electricity. Drinking water still had to be collected in a bucket from a well some way up the mountain and carried back through the meadows. This task fell to the children. From time to time one might hear complaints regarding the weight of the buckets of water, but there was never open rebellion. A little stream ran past our house and Tomás Ó Cíobháin, from whom we had bought the cottage, had rigged up an ingenious device to sup-ply the cottage with water. He had constructed a little walkway on which he placed a pipe, through which water flowed into a little pool

within the stream. This water was very useful for domestic needs, such as cooking and washing. In fact, I used to stand a bucket under our little homemade waterfall and steep the babies' nappies in it. They came out very clean, though by the end of the summer they were slightly tinged as the water coming down the mountain came partly through turf.

In those days the farmers still supplied their own needs with milk, butter, eggs and potatoes. We were able to buy all these from the Cíobháins, our nearest neighbours, including buttermilk for baking soda bread, which I also learned to bake. The children used to collect these items for me and therefore were in regular contact with the Cíobháin children, from whom they learned to speak Irish, especially with the help of Bean Uí Chíobháin.

The old oil-burning stove we relied on at first eventually disintegrated and we had to fall back on two primus stoves. I was scared of

ABOVE: Sinéad Ní Bhriain was a great help running the house in Kerry. Here she and I are bringing Deirdre and Cathal to the strand. The cottage is in view behind us.

those stoves, and when Ruairí would bring the children to the strand or fishing, I would insist he light them before he left, even if it was ten o'clock in the morning. They rarely caught any fish on their excursions, but they did not know that I was up in the house praying that they would have no success because I had no idea how to fillet a fish or prepare it for cooking. Eventually we swapped the primus stoves for a second-hand Calor gas cooker, and cooking became a less stressful chore for me!

We used oil lamps for light, although we had an 'Aladdin' lamp for the living-room; to maintain the gas mantles required much skill and patience. After acquiring the Calor gas, Ruairí rigged up a complicated system to provide us with proper lighting from the gas. We had really advanced into the twentieth century!

Neil Ní Chinnéide, whose family had a farm nearby and with whom I became very close, taught me how to maintain a turf fire on a permanent basis. It was the custom to never let the fire go out. At night, before going to bed, the burning embers would be covered with ashes: this was known as '*ag coigilt an tine*', or saving the fire. The following morning the remaining burning embers were carefully raked out and set aside on the hearth while the ashes were removed. Then these embers were placed in the middle of the new turf sods, which lit up quickly. Neil taught me a prayer that the old people used to say when saving the fire:

Coiglím an tine seo mar a choigil Críost cách,
Muire ar mhullach an tí agus Bríd ina lár.

Save the fire like Christ saved all,
Mary at the summit of the house and Brigid in the middle.

When Aunt Annie died, in 1954, I was faced with having to close the MacSwiney home at 4 Belgrave Place, Wellington Road, Cork, and to

decide what to do with all the contents, the most important being the MacSwiney papers. Our great friend, Sinéad Ní Bhriain, with the help of a former member of Cumann na mBan, May Ahern, went through all the papers for me. May was able to recognise the many historical references, and between them they put everything in order.

I returned to Cork in February 1955 to make the final arrangements, staying in Sinéad's flat in Sidney Place on Wellington Road. The better items of furniture were either sent to my home in Dublin or housed temporarily by Sinéad. The less valuable furniture was sent to the cottage in Gráig. I remember, on my return to Dublin, the arrival of the Nat Ross furniture-removal van from Cork. I felt very nostalgic upon seeing it because this was the end of an era.

I kept all the MacSwiney papers in my own house, but I was always very worried about having them in case of mishap. Many years later Professor Robin Dudley Edwards was retiring from the Chair of History in UCD and taking over the Archives Department and he asked Seán Ó Briain, Ruairí's brother-in-law, if I would be willing to lodge the MacSwiney papers in the UCD Archives. I was delighted to

ABOVE:
My sons, Cathal (*standing*), Terry (both in *lederhosen*) and Ruairi, (*crawling away*), with the Cíobháin boys, Séamus, Tomáisín (*both standing*) and Pádraic.

hand them over into his safekeeping. Professor Dudley Edwards assured me at the time that he had excellent staff who would make a good job of cataloguing them, which they did.

Throughout these years I didn't work outside the home. It wasn't the done thing then, and four children were a lot of hard work anyway. The only occasion when I returned to teaching, the profession for which I had trained, was when the children were young and I used to make an annual visit to Cork each September to see my friends. I must have had a good reputation as a teacher because whenever the pupils heard I was back in Scoil Íte, they would persuade me to teach Latin to some of the classes.

I didn't proceed to PhD qualification, which I regret, although I did complete my thesis. After Aunt Máire died I couldn't leave Cork because Aunt Annie needed my help at Scoil Íte. I ought to have been studying at Trinity College in Dublin, under the Travelling Studentship, but instead I was in Cork, drafting my PhD thesis without academic guidance. I did complete it, but had no one to review it and approve it for submission to the faculty. By the summer of 1944 Ruairí was asking if this study was going to go on forever; he thought it was time to get married. I abandoned the project. We got engaged at Christmas 1944 and were married by the following summer.

I did, however, make an effort to get back to teaching in the mid-1960s. In 1964, University College Dublin had moved out to its new campus at Belfield, which was across the road from our house. I discussed with the Head of the German department the possibility of teaching tutorials, but received a negative response.

Mount Anville Secondary School, just a short distance from our home, also taught German. This was unusual at the time, and the Sacred Heart schools were among the few in Dublin that offered German as a subject; all the others taught French. When I learned this, I thought of going up and offering my services as a teacher. First, I would have had to get registered as a secondary school teacher, as I had taught only in Scoil Íte, which was an unregistered school. I made some attempts to get registered with the Department of Education, but gave up when they came to nothing. I never actually approached Mount Anville. Years later, St Kilian's, the German school, was set up on Roebuck Road, but I didn't approach them either. I was easily put off in those days, since I lacked confidence. Although I was accustomed to doing what was necessary to survive all my life, I still didn't have the self-confidence to look for something for myself.

This was, of course, an era when wives supported their husbands in their careers, and I was happy to support Ruairí. But if I were starting life over again, I think I would try to have a career of my own.

RUAIRÍ IN PUBLIC LIFE

For most of his working life Ruairí was Managing Director of Kingston's Department Store and ran it very happily with his brother-in-law, Seán Ó Briain. However, it was not enough for him: he had been brought up to serve his country. It became obvious that his life – our lives – were going to head in a new direction.

By the end of the 1940s, Ruairí felt that the only way forward for Ireland was through democratic means. Despite having grown up in a Republican family, he was increasingly convinced that the armed struggle was not the right way. Accordingly, he looked to the possibility of entering politics. In 1947 he went to see Éamon de Valera, a great friend and colleague of his father's, to ask his advice. De Valera's response was, 'I would have hoped you might have joined me.' Ruairí's reply was, 'Under the circumstances, it would be completely impossible since some of my friends are still in prison and it would be misunderstood.' De Valera appreciated his situation. Instead, Ruairí joined Seán MacBride, who was then forming a new party called Clann na Poblachta.

There was to be an election in 1948 and Seán invited Ruairí to

stand as a candidate in Waterford. The Brughas had a solid political background there: Ruairí's father had been elected to represent Waterford in the First Dáil in 1919 and after his death his widow, Kathleen, was elected by that constituency to the Second Dáil, in 1921. However, for Ruairí it didn't look as promising because Fianna Fáil had been able to retain only one seat there due to the small number of nationalist supporters; it was unlikely that a second nationalist would be elected. Clann na Poblachta campaigned on the platform of 'PUT THEM OUT', meaning Fianna Fáil. Ruairí objected strongly to this form of negative electioneering. During the campaign many people came up to speak to Ruairí, saying they very much regretted that they couldn't vote for him as they needed to hold the Fianna Fáil seat. In fact, one man actually spoiled his vote by writing Ruairí a poem on the ballot paper! As predicted, Fianna Fáil got the seat.

However, Clann na Poblachta did manage to get two TDs elected: Seán MacBride and Dr Noël Browne. Seán MacBride set out his manifesto for election with two main items: release of the remaining prisoners who had been interned during the war and the reforestation of Ireland. For centuries Ireland had had a luxuriant covering of oak and ash trees, but large areas had been denuded by the British for timber to build a fleet of ships to combat the Spanish Armada. In later centuries the remaining forest was cut down for use as pit props in the coalmining industry. (*Rape of Ireland*, by John Mackay, deals with this issue.) Seán MacBride was appointed Minister for Foreign Affairs and Noël Browne Minister for Health in John A Costello's coalition government. The remaining prisoners were released shortly afterwards.

Ruairí was a member of the Standing Committee of Clann na Poblachta. At one of the first of its weekly meetings, after the government was formed in 1948, Seán put forward the proposal that an organisation should be formed called Trees for Ireland, which would act as a pressure-group to persuade the government to put more effort and resources into tree-planting schemes. He asked Mac O'Rahilly and Ruairí to take charge of this project. Miss Sal Cahill, a member of the Forestry Department of Lands and Fisheries, was seconded to the organisation to act as secretary. She carried out this duty with great dedication and after her retirement from the Civil Service continued this work in a voluntary capacity.

Over the years many well-known people became members of Trees for Ireland, one of the most outstanding being tree expert Maurice Fitzpatrick. Other enthusiastic people, including David Luke, joined them later. After David's death his widow, Ann, gave unstintingly of her time and efforts to the organisation. Trees for Ireland published pamphlets and leaflets for schools, the most valuable being those written by Maurice Fitzpatrick. It organised tree-planting schemes throughout Dublin City during Arbour Week every year, in conjunction with Dublin Corporation. This was done with the assistance of primary schools and youth organisations.

Ruairí was the main force behind Trees for Ireland for over fifty years, right up to its final meeting in June 2002, at which they commemorated Maurice Fitzpatrick, who had contributed so much to the work of the organisation. The organisation's remaining funds were handed over to the Tree Council of Ireland, which now oversees the reforestation activities around the country very successfully.

Ruairí often sat next to Noël Browne at the Wednesday night meetings of the Standing Committee of Clann na Poblachta. Noël was a man of very strong personal convictions and at meetings it was sometimes difficult to persuade him to see other people's point of view. Ruairí could see all sides and would try to bring about some understanding between him and the others around the table. Despite his efforts, eventually the disagreements which arose between Noël and the other members of the Cabinet, and subsequently between Noël and Archbishop John Charles McQuaid, were a contributory factor to the collapse of the government in 1951 on foot of Noël's famous Mother-and-Child scheme.

Dr Browne's great crusade, and great achievement, was his contribution to the virtual elimination of TB, which had long been a scourge in Ireland. He built many TB sanatoria to treat and contain the disease. To achieve this aim, he diverted towards TB control the proceeds of the Irish Hospitals' Sweepstakes; they had been fundraising very successfully in America and the money raised was a major source of income for Irish hospitals. This diversion of funds had a detrimental impact on the financial position of the two major Dublin hospitals: the Mater Misericordiae and St Vincent's. The Sisters of Mercy, who were running the Mater, went to Archbishop McQuaid for advice as to how to resolve their financial difficulty. Dr McQuaid, in turn, called on the O'Connell Street Traders' Association, which included Clery's and Kingston's.

Ruairí became involved after we attended a lunch at Gerry

O'Donel's. Dr Seán Geraghty, a radiologist in the Mater and a friend of Peadar O'Donnell, was also invited to that luncheon. In 1922, as a young medical student, Seán had been one of the group that Cathal Brugha was evacuating from the Hammam Hotel in O'Connell Street when he was shot. When we were sitting around after lunch, Seán turned to Peadar and asked him, 'Do you know any businessmen? We are having a meeting next week in Guiney's to discuss how to raise money for the Mater.' Peadar pointed to my husband and said, 'What about Ruairí here?' Dr Geraghty invited Ruairí to attend the meeting.

Ruairí went to the meeting, and when he came home to me that night I asked him what had happened. He told me they had set up a Mater hospital fundraising committee and planned to start a pools scheme, based on the example of the Belfast Mater Hospital. I asked him who was on the committee. He told me there were five men, mainly leading doctors of the Mater: Dr Freeman [Chairman]; Dr Bryan Alton, an eminent physician; Mr Jack O'Sullivan, an eminent surgeon; the chemist Dermot Dolan, who was the chief supplier of pharmaceuticals to the hospital; and Ruairí as the fifth. Within a few years, the job of running the pools had fallen largely to Dr Bryan Alton and Ruairí. With only a small staff, it was a difficult undertaking. They had to monitor the sports results every Saturday night to be able to pay out the prize money on Monday. I remember one weekend, early on in this enterprise, waking up on Sunday morning to find that Ruairí had not come home. He had worked through the night.

The pools money was collected door-to-door, one shilling per week. After a few years, owing to the wonderful energy and ability of Dr Bryan Alton, he and Ruairí were able to expand their workforce and establish an efficient organisation, which successfully ran the Mater Hospital (MH) Pools for many years. Once they had helped put the hospital on a sound financial basis, the money raised was put towards the expansion of the Special Heart Unit and the purchasing of modern equipment. This contributed to the Mater Hospital being one of the top specialist units for the treatment of heart disease in Ireland. The MH Pools continued to function for many years. When Dr Bryan Alton came near retirement, an arrangement was made that the organisation be taken over by the Rehabilitation Centre Pools, on the basis of a small percentage of the profits being paid over to the Mater Hospital. Ruairí remained involved until recent years.

When the government set up the Tóstal Festival in the early 1950s to promote tourism for the whole of Ireland, Ruairí was invited onto the board that ran the festival in Dublin, presumably because he was a member of the O'Connell Street Traders' Association. The Tóstal functioned successfully for a few years, promoting theatre and other events countrywide to attract tourists, particularly Americans. Every year the festival's opening was marked by a Mass celebrated by the Archbishop of Dublin, Dr John Charles McQuaid, a particularly influential man.

In May 1957 a difficulty arose when the Pike Theatre in Dublin staged Tennessee Williams's *The Rose Tattoo* as part of the festival. The Archbishop found this play unsuitable and informed the Tóstal committee that he would not be prepared to celebrate Mass at the opening. Having joined the committee as an ordinary member, Ruairí suddenly found himself Chairman of the Dublin Tóstal Committee and, without taking sides in the row, having to save the festival from collapse. An impresario, Seymour Leslie — younger brother of the writer, Sir Shane Leslie — came to his rescue. He suggested that he would engage a famous ballet company and some theatre companies to tide him over that particular year. The ballet company performed in the Theatre Royal and the festival survived. Out of this evolved, finally, the Dublin Theatre Festival, which has been so successful ever since.

After the Tóstal, Ruairí became involved in Dublin Tourism where he served as Chairman for thirteen years. He worked mainly with its manager, Matt McNulty, to develop services for tourists in Dublin and to build up promotional events, such as the St Patrick's Day parade, which continue to flourish today. At a time when our national culture was not as accepted in 'The Pale' as it is now, he organised displays of Irish dancing in St Stephen's Green during the tourist season. These proved very popular with Irish-American tourists.

Ruairí's strength was to work in the background and bring a sensible approach to any organisation he was invited to join. He believed in being reasonable with everyone, always trying to come up with a policy or a solution that would reconcile the different groups. In this way, I think he was very like his father. Many of the policies that he helped to develop are now taken for granted.

In the mid-1960s there was bitter antagonism between the supporters of the Irish language and the Language Freedom Movement, which was opposed to the compulsory teaching of Irish in schools. Ruairí worked quietly on various committees to modernise the policy to restore the Irish language.

This dispute over the State's role in promoting Irish became focused on RTÉ, the national broadcasting authority, which was launched in 1962. On the one hand, there was the belief that to be a success it should follow the lead of Irish stars, such as Eamonn Andrews, who had been successful on British television. On the other hand, the War of Independence had grown out of a national movement to restore native culture. People whose families had been part of that movement, such as Dónall Ó Móráin, believed in Pearse's ideal of 'not free merely but Gaelic as well'.

As a member of the RTÉ Authority, Ruairí tried to develop a middle ground and encouraged programme-makers to develop a more positive attitude towards the Irish language. In 1969 he resigned from the Authority in order to run for election.

To mark the fiftieth anniversary of the Easter Rising, Ruairí was invited by the Irish community in London to give the formal oration in Trafalgar Square in 1966. In his address he stated that democratic means were the only way forward to solve the question of Irish unity. While this is widely accepted today, his analysis – almost forty years ago – was far ahead of his time.

After our brief sojourn in London, we returned to Dublin in time for the celebrations in Dublin Castle. One of my recollections of that occasion was watching old IRA men who had been comrades-in-arms, and who had parted company at the time of the Treaty to take opposite sides in the Civil War, meeting again for the first time in fifty years. It was a wonderful moment of reconciliation. They actually fell on one another's shoulders, weeping. Another thing that distinguished them from the rest of the company was that they only knew the national anthem, '*Amhrán na bhFiann*' (The Soldier's Song) in English.

During the 1950s, Clann na Poblachta was losing ground because there was room for only one nationalist party. Ruairí felt that he should continue to serve his country as he had been brought up to do. He went to see Seán Lemass who suggested that he join a local Fianna Fáil Cumann, which he did in 1962. In 1969 Kevin Boland invited him to stand for election with him in the Dublin South constituency, which Kevin represented as TD. Ruairí was very conscious of Kevin Boland's unselfish gesture. When he was canvassing and met a Fianna Fáil voter, he always told them that if they had intended voting for Kevin Boland, they must continue to do so as he didn't want to endanger Kevin's seat in any way. Ruairí wasn't elected and subsequently ran for the Seanad.

A message came from Gus Healy of the Fianna Fáil organisation in Cork, one of the main organisers of Ruairí's Seanad campaign, telling Ruairí that he didn't have to come to Cork to canvass: 'Just send down Máire Óg.' I went in Ruairí's stead and Gus took me around canvassing. We visited prominent citizens, including Gerald

Goldberg, whom we met in the Imperial Hotel where his son was holding an exhibition of paintings. Gus also introduced me to Anthony Barry. As we passed the office of his tea company, Barry's Tea, I went in and was given a great welcome. Anthony Barry was a leading member of Fine Gael, nevertheless he had been a great admirer of Mary MacSwiney; each respected the other's completely opposing political stand. My first introduction to canvassing was enjoyable as it was in Cork and was with Cork people. That year, Ruairí was elected to the Seanad. Generally, I didn't like campaigning in elections; although later I enjoyed canvassing in the referendum on our entry into the European Economic Community in 1972. Having grown up on the Continent, I felt confident that Ireland would compete successfully with these more advanced economies.

At the beginning of 1970 an acquaintance of Ruairí's discussed with him the need to end the ban on Catholics in the Dublin Diocese attending Trinity College. They visited Cardinal Conway in Armagh, who gave them a very positive reception and agreed to look into the issue. Soon after, on 25 June 1970, perhaps partly due to their representations, the ban on Catholics attending Trinity was lifted.

After the 1966 commemorations of the 1916 Rising, I was looking forward with some expectation to January 1969, which would mark the fiftieth anniversary of Dáil Éireann, the first sitting of an Irish Parliament in modern times. In the post-First World War election, in November 1918, Sinn Féin had stated in its manifesto that, given support, it would set up an independent government. After winning the election by a substantial majority, the party set about fulfilling its promise. The members gathered in the Mansion House in Dublin to set up the first free Irish government, which they called Dáil Éireann. They invited many foreign journalists, European and American, to attend the event. Éamon de Valera was to be elected as President, but as he was serving a prison sentence in Lincoln jail in England, Cathal

Brugha was selected to take the Chair in this First Dáil. Ministers were then appointed to the various Departments of State. Michael Collins became Minister for Finance and was in charge of collecting funds by issuing what were known as Republican Bonds.

To my mind this event had far greater significance than 1916 and so should earn at least some form of recognition in January 1969. However, I could discern no signs of preparation and I went to see the Taoiseach, Jack Lynch, to find out what, if anything, was being

ABOVE:
**Myself and Ruairí,
December 1976.**

proposed. Apparently nothing was being planned to mark the occasion. I pointed out to him that if this were the case, then obviously the date on which the Free State Parliament met in 1921 would be commemorated as the first meeting of an Irish Parliament. This would be a matter of consternation to many people. The Taoiseach assured me that he would look into the matter. True to his word, he organised a reception in the annex of the Mansion House, in January 1969, to which the surviving families of members of the First Dáil were invited.

RUAIRÍ IN POLITICS

In February 1973 Ruairí was elected Fianna Fáil TD for South County Dublin. Fianna Fáil went into opposition against the Fine Gael–Labour coalition government and Ruairí was appointed to the front bench as spokesman opposite Dr Conor Cruise O'Brien, Minister for Posts and Telegraphs. Debates in the Dáil between Ruairí and Dr Cruise O'Brien were amicable, because that is the way Ruairí always behaved.

In 1974 the leader of Fianna Fáil, Jack Lynch, appointed Ruairí as the Opposition Spokesman for Northern Ireland. He reshaped Fianna Fáil policy on Northern Ireland, basing it on reconciliation between the peoples of different traditions on the island. He also focused political attention on getting Britain to face up to its responsibilities in the area, and to working jointly with the Irish government.

In that same year Ruairí was invited to the annual conference of the British–Irish Association, which took place in Oxford and Cambridge on alternate years. When he first heard of this invitation we were on our way home to Ireland from France, driving to Le Havre to catch the ferry. Instead, we diverted from Calais to Dover and made our way to Oxford. The night before the conference, at a get-together in the bar, John Hume introduced Ruairí to David Trimble, who refused to shake hands with the 'son of a murderer'. John Hume took umbrage, but Ruairí intervened – he was ever a man to pour oil on troubled waters and to prevent conflict.

During the discussions at these conferences I got the feeling that the nationalist point of view was not fairly represented. It was understandable that English people might not comprehend the situation fully, as the consequences of Britain's involvement in Ireland over the centuries would not have been familiar to them. However, in many cases southerners, who should have had greater insight, also had a limited understanding of Irish nationalism. I disagreed with those who suggested that the IRA was the cause, rather than the result, of the Troubles in Northern Ireland.

During this period as Spokesman for Northern Ireland, Ruairí met most of the prominent figures in the Unionist party and British government officials in Northern Ireland, including Merlyn Rees.

Ruairí lost his seat in the 1977 election, mainly due to a constituency revision that left his voting base in three different constituencies and brought in votes from neighbouring Dún Laoghaire, where David Andrews was the TD. The seat went to David's brother, Niall, who was added on as an extra candidate by Fianna Fáil headquarters. If this had not happened, Ruairí might have been able to contribute more to holding people together in the following years of turmoil and splits in the Fianna Fáil party. His contribution to solving the problems in Northern Ireland would undoubtedly have been of great value, given the contacts and the trust he had built up with unionists.

After the 1977 results, John Hume was upset that Ruairí had lost his seat and he suggested to Taoiseach Jack Lynch that the least he could do was to appoint Ruairí as a Member of Parliament (MEP) in Europe. The first European Parliament was an appointed, not an elected, body. Jack Lynch followed John Hume's advice and Ruairí was appointed Vice-Chairman of the Foreign Affairs Committee of the European Parliament, and was involved in the negotiations for Greece's entry into the European Community in 1981.

Michael Yeats, a fluent French speaker and highly respected in the European Parliament, was leader of the Fianna Fáil group in the Parliament, which formed a political grouping with the Gaullists; this affiliation was due to the fact that recognition and access to facilities was dependent on having a minimum number of parliamentary representatives. Michael Yeats and Ruairí formed a warm friendship and always conversed with one another in Irish. Ruairí also made the effort to acquire a working knowledge of the French language. On the French Gaullist side, the delegates would not speak English, so most of the discussions took place in French. At this point, Michael and Ruairí decided something would have to be done. Since most of the Irish delegates were fluent Irish speakers, they decided that they would discuss matters in front of the Gaullists in Irish. This brought about the compromise that in future the group's discussions would be in the common language of English.

The first direct election to the European Parliament was held in June 1979. Michael Yeats, Ruairí, Joe Fox and Síle de Valera were selected as the candidates for Dublin. There were certain controversies at the time, not directly relevant to the European election but having an impact on it nonetheless. The main problem was the question of Wood Quay, where Dublin Corporation had opted to build its new offices, despite the fact that the site contained important archaeological remains dating back to the Viking era.

When this project was first mooted, Ruairí, in his capacity as Chairman of Dublin Tourism, had interviewed the officials in charge of the Corporation and had asked them if they would consider building the new offices in Smithfield. This alternative site had been vacated sometime previously and was owned by the Corporation. He was told that this would be impossible; one reason cited was that their staff would not cross the Liffey over to the northside! By June 1979 the furore was at its height. Despite his behind-the-scenes efforts, the Wood Quay development went ahead.

The Save Wood Quay campaign was led by the Augustinian priest Fr F X Martin, who suggested that one of the ways people could express their disapproval would be not to vote for Fianna Fáil in the forthcoming European election. An added problem for Fianna Fáil candidates was that, at the time, there was a postal strike and a bin strike. There were piles of refuse bags outside every door we knocked on during the canvass. When a door was opened, immediately there were complaints about the non-delivery of post, which sometimes meant people were not receiving their accustomed cheques from relatives abroad. It was not an easy campaign.

The outcome of all this bad publicity for Fianna Fáil was that only one MEP was elected for the party: obviously the name of de Valera impressed the Fianna Fáil voters. Indeed, we later met some Fianna Fáil supporters who said they had had great difficulty deciding between the names of Brugha and de Valera, but in the end felt they had to vote for the de Valera name.

Ruairí again ran for the Senate after the General Election in 1981. By this time Fianna Fáil had divided into two camps: one led by the Taoiseach, Jack Lynch, and the other by Charles Haughey. Ruairí was approached by some in the Taoiseach's camp who asked him if he would agree to go on their list, which would mean that Fianna Fáil TDs and county councillors who were part of that camp would be asked to vote for him. True to his principles, Ruairí refused to go on either list, saying, 'If I can't get elected as myself, then so be it.'

During the Senate canvass we got a great reception from a farmer in the hills above Killaloe in County Clare, who assured us of his vote. On the day of the count at the County Council head office in Ennis, this particular councillor said to Ruairí, 'I didn't care what orders I got. I had decided to vote for you and I did.' That gave us the first inkling as to how the election was being choreographed. County councillors were given instructions by their own party and were usually expected to vote en bloc. It became obvious that Ruairí's independent stance was going to tell against him. Refusing to join either faction meant that he wouldn't be elected, and that meant the end of his polit-ical career. In my opinion, his absence from national politics was a great loss to the country.

The fact that Ruairí's political career came to an abrupt and unexpected end did not mean that he left public life altogether. He continued to participate actively in various committees. We also joined several organisations together. One of these was the Irish branch of the European Movement, for which he served as Chairman. Another was the Irish Association for Economic, Social and Cultural Relations, which had been set up in 1938 by Northern

Protestants who wished to keep in touch with their friends and co-religionists in the new State. They may have been worried that the Protestant minority in the South would be discriminated against or in some way disadvantaged, but this did not happen.

Following independence in 1921, many big businesses were in the hands of Protestants, and remained so. Indeed, some Protestant companies in the South continued to practise employment discrimination against Catholics. I remember seeing a well-known shop in Patrick Street in Cork displaying a vacancy with the wording: No Catholics need apply. We were stunned because this was happening as late as the early 1940s.

It is true that the Catholic Church, which was the dominant Church, did discriminate against the Protestant minority in certain ways, such as the *Ne Temere* decree. On the other hand, Irish governments treated Protestants as equal citizens in every respect. Quite a few took part in public life and were excellent and prominent citizens in the new State.

Our membership of the Irish Association meant frequent trips to the North. We made many good friends in Belfast, but mostly among unionists. Meetings of the Irish Association were always held in Queen's University or in Queen's Elms, the university residence. There was little or no contact with nationalist West Belfast. This was brought home to me very forcibly in mid-September 1969 when, taking a break from the Annual Conference, we were brought on a visit to Bombay Street, off the Falls Road, a nationalist enclave in West Belfast that had been burnt down by a loyalist mob three weeks previously. The first sight that met us was a huge metal barrier, behind which the people were cowering, terrified. I was immediately reminded of the Polish ghettoes, about which I had read and seen photos, where the people had erected barricades to defend themselves against the rioting Nazi mobs.

When we were brought behind the barricades, the first thing that struck me was that the whole place had been completely cleared of debris, leaving just the bare earthen ground, and this just a few weeks after the place had been burnt down. This was in marked contrast to what I had seen in German cities in 1952 where, seven years after the end of the war, they were still clearing the rubble. It looked to me as if this clearing-up was deliberate, to suggest that nothing had happened there, wiping out the evidence. This was the first time I felt an understanding of the position of republicans in Northern Ireland.

We were told that on the night of the burning of Bombay Street and the Lower Falls, the RUC did not in any way defend the residents and in some cases, it was claimed, actually prevented people from putting out the fires. On the walls was written: 'IRA – I Ran Away'; this must have been written by people who felt themselves defenceless during that onslaught. Actually, there was no IRA in existence at that time – apparently young people were more inclined to leave the area and emigrate to Australia, England, or America to make a life for themselves rather than fight for a better life on the streets of Belfast. But after these terrible and terrifying events a new IRA sprang up and willing recruits volunteered in great numbers. There are two things that I could see in this: terrorist organisations are created as a reaction to injustices; people are not born terrorists, but once such an organisation comes into being it is difficult to control who joins up. Often the most enthusiastic members are people of a violent disposition, which creates its own problems. I think this occurs the world over.

As we surveyed the scene and met the residents, men who feared for the safety of their wives and children asked Ruairí for help. These men were from the Retired Catholic British Army Officers Club. As they were Catholics, they were not accepted by the main British Officers Club in Belfast, so they had formed their own.

This situation was a revelation to me, and in stark contrast to our previous experiences when visiting Belfast.

The person I found to have the most in-depth understanding of the difficulties in Northern Ireland was Dr John Robb, a well-known surgeon. He did not address himself merely to the professional and educated classes but went straight to the working classes, where the deepest gulf and greatest enmity stood in the way of reconciliation. In 1982 he founded an organisation called the New Ireland Movement. Mrs Louie O'Brien, formerly Seán MacBride's secretary, brought Ruairí and me to one of his meetings, which was held in the big hall opposite Queen's University. The place was packed. Various speakers addressed the audience and then we were divided into working groups.

I found myself at a table of twelve where the exchange of views went fairly smoothly. Then one of the contributors, who was obviously from a loyalist background, discovered that two people at our table, judging by their contributions, might be of a Sinn Féin persuasion. The loyalists were indignant, claiming that Dr Robb had promised that nobody from Sinn Féin would be invited, otherwise they would not have agreed to attend. It was explained that the members of Belfast Corporation had been invited, and these two men were members of that body. After a while the objections simmered down and our round-table discussion progressed.

At the end of the evening the conclusions of the various working groups were sought and written on the blackboard. The options were mainly: integration with the UK; direct rule from London; a Confederate Ireland along lines based on the Swiss model. A vote was taken and the majority opted for the Confederate model. It was the most successful meeting I ever attended in Belfast. I have found over the years of our contact with Belfast that Northern Ireland has many people with intelligence, understanding and goodwill who are very committed to finding solutions to enable society as a whole to move forward to a future of peace, stability and normal daily life. I cannot understand why their voices are neither heard nor heeded. We are still members of the New Ireland Movement and have kept in contact with Dr John Robb, although we are now unable to make the journey to Belfast to attend the meetings.

Few seem to understand how much the Protestant community in the Republic has contributed to Irish culture and public life over the years. Not only were Protestants, such as Erskine Childers, prominent in Irish politics, in Childers's case as government minister and later President, but often the leaders of the Protestant Churches had a greater commitment than had many in the Catholic hierarchy to the Irish language and traditions. I first learned this in memorable fashion at a social event in Cork in 1955. The Lord Mayor of Cork, Patrick McGrath — whom I had met when he represented Éamon de Valera at Aunt Máire's funeral — invited Ruairí and me to attend his official St Patrick's Day luncheon, an impressive occasion. After lunch the two bishops of Cork addressed the guests. The Catholic prelate, Bishop Cornelius Lucey, gave his solemn address in English, after which the Protestant bishop, George Otto Simms, delivered his oration in beautiful, fluent Irish. I was bowled over. Not very long afterwards, when Archbishop Simms was enthroned as the Archbishop of Dublin and Ruairí had entered public life as a senator and TD, we would often meet him at public receptions. We always had great admiration for him and were sorry when he was moved to the diocese of Armagh.

We were to become acquainted with other Protestant Church leaders during Ruairí's time as a public representative. As we were members of the Irish Association, Ruairí felt we should see off the Peace Train, which was leaving from Amiens Street station on its way to Belfast. There he met our friend Chris McGimpsey, whom we had met some years earlier at a dinner of the Irish Association. As Ruairí and Chris were chatting on the platform, Archbishop Caird hove into sight. He made a beeline for Ruairí, speaking in Irish, as usual. Ruairí turned to Chris and said, 'I would like to introduce you to the Protestant Archbishop of Dublin, Donal Caird.' Chris had been standing by as they chatted in Irish and, after the Archbishop departed, he asked Ruairí, 'Does he know any English?' Ruairí laughed and said, 'Of course he does.'

The Protestants we met in Dublin were wonderful citizens of the Irish State, for example, Douglas Gageby, editor of *The Irish Times*. Some of our closer Protestant friends were true nationalists, such as Bill and Muriel Porter. For instance, Muriel would become indignant if any Belfast unionist at the Irish Association suggested that Protestants in the South were ill-treated or even marginalised. Bill was the son of my former Professor of Classics at UCC. It was a strange coincidence that we should meet so many years later and become such warm friends.

Another activity in which Ruairí became involved, in later years, was as Chairman of the Management Committee of Coláiste an Phiarsaigh, the all-Irish school in Glanmire, County Cork. Unknown to any of us, Fr Tadhg Ó Murchú, a founder-member of the school, left his share in the organisation to his godson, our son Ruairí. At the request of our son and the other remaining active shareholders, Ruairí took on the committee chairmanship, on what was intended to be a temporary basis. However, it stretched out over many years, up to quite recently. With the help of a good committee he set about putting the school on a sound footing once again. Our monthly visits to Cork, in our late seventies and early eighties, were mutually rewarding. They were an opportunity for me to spend time again in what had been my first home in Ireland; and for Ruairí to continue to apply his experience and skills to advance what had long been a priority for him – promoting the cause of the Irish language. We made new friends, among them Jim Fitzgerald who, as treasurer, was a great help to Ruairí on the committee, and Siobhán Ní Dhúill, secretary of the school.

When the children had grown up and I had more time on my hands, I became involved with Ireland's first Third World aid organisation, Gorta. The United Nations' Freedom from Hunger campaign – under the section FAO (Food and Agriculture Organisation), which has its headquarters in Rome – asked each country throughout the western world to set up its own branch. The Irish Council was set up in 1965, under the aegis of the Department of Agriculture. The Council was to be chaired by the head of the Irish Red Cross, Leslie Bean de Barra, widow of Tom Barry, and she proposed the name Gorta in memory of the Great Famine. The Council comprised representatives of many of the main organisations in Ireland: the Federated Union of Employers (FUE), trade unions, sporting bodies – for example, the Gaelic Athletic Association (GAA) and the Football Association of Ireland (FAI) – Churches of all denominations and leaders from the world of business.

At the first meeting they discussed the question of how to raise funds for the project. With the exception of the chairperson and Mrs Swan, who was representing the Irish Countrywomen's Association (ICA), there were no other women on the Council. The men looked blankly around the table and asked, 'What do we do?' The reply came promptly, 'If you want to raise money, you can only do it with a ladies' committee.' Whereupon they decided that every member of the Council should ask his wife to come to the meeting the following week.

Our friend, Michael Birmingham, who was on the Council, suggested that I might join the committee, which somewhat reluctantly I did. We met the following week, as planned, and got to work. Mrs Noreen Feehan, wife of Matt Feehan who was the editor of the *Irish Press* and, as such, was a representative on the Council, was elected chairperson. Caitlín Ó Síocháin, the wife of Seán Ó Síocháin, General Secretary of the GAA, was elected as secretary. The treasurer, Marie O'Doherty, was the wife of the Secretary of the Department of Agriculture, Martin O'Doherty. Some years later I ended up as secretary of the Council.

Having tried different, but non-profitable ventures, such as fundraising social events, we came up with the idea of a charity shop. We opened our first charity shop in a vacant building that had been bought by the New Ireland Insurance Company for redevelopment. We never had to pay rent, rates or insurance, as the owners paid all these costs. The premises were a small, Georgian house on South Frederick Street. When we looked down into the basement from the stairs, we were convinced there were rats down there. Every committee member was asked to look after the shop for a half-day each week, and to provide her own assistant. I called on my sister-in-law, Nollaig, and her friends, with whom I had coffee once a week, for help. After seeing the premises, only Nollaig was prepared to come to my assistance. I then turned to my friend Teresa MacManus, who willingly came to help me with the shop. Supporting the Gorta shops became a life-long commitment for Teresa, which resulted in her later taking over as chairperson of the committee.

After some months we found more suitable premises on Merrion Row, which had previously been The Swiss Chalet Café. Of course it had defects, such as a leaking roof, but it was central and we really blossomed from then on. Directly across the road was O'Donoghue's pub, where The Dubliners began their career. Mrs O'Donoghue was a very kind lady and insisted that her contribution to our cause was to supply us every day with free bowls of soup and brown bread, which she often brought across the street herself. At this time we mainly sold costume jewellery, second-hand books and bric-a-brac — no clothes whatsoever at this point. In later years, an added benefit of the Gorta shop was that it was a source of affordable second-hand clothes for the people of Dublin. Our main source of income came from the contributions, in the form of second-hand items, made by people working in the area, in banks and offices.

In later years some of the other mainstays of our group included Kathleen Rochford, as treasurer of the committee, and Ruairí's cousin, Georgie Kingston. When my sight was failing in the early 1990s, I was no longer able to function as secretary and resigned from the committee, but continued to serve in the shop.

TRAVELS ABROAD

In the years after our children had grown up and left home, annual summer holidays for Ruairí and me always included a trip to Europe. I was determined to see the places of antiquity that I had learned about during my earliest education in the Odenwaldschule. My teachers there had given me a life-long fascination with the Classics and with the history of Europe and the Mediterranean region. Ruairí and I climbed the Acropolis in Athens to see the ruins of the ancient Greek temples, and visited the site of the Oracle at Delphi. We visited Tunisia to see the ruins of Carthage, which I had heard so much about at school in Germany. I had always had a soft spot for Hannibal because of the ingenuity and bravery he showed in his military expedition over the Alps and in the Battle of Cannae. Of course I understood that, with two powerful nations struggling for supremacy of the Mediterranean, in the long run it was better, from the point of view of Europe, that the Romans succeeded.

In 1990, after the fall of the Berlin Wall, we visited Berlin. Chunks of the wall were lying all over the ground, with graffiti still visible on them. I was able to walk through the Brandenburg Gate and down Unter den Linden. It was an emotional experience for me as I had been unable to go there since the summer of 1938, when I had last visited Berlin as a young student. I could understand what this meant for my good and longstanding friend, Hilde (Hildegard Hess), a native of Berlin whom I had first met in that last year before the Second World War. After 1945, East Berlin was forbidden territory and completely cut off. Hilde's father, who had died some months before the wall was erected in the early 1960s, was buried in a cemetery on the east side and their family was not able to visit his grave again until 1990.

In my later years, I had the opportunity to revisit and get to know the area around Grainau in southern Germany, where I had spent my youth. On alternate years Ruairí and I visited the south of France and my old home in the Bavarian Alps. In this way I kept in touch with both countries and their languages. The sleepy little village of Grainau had become a tourist destination, both in winter and summer, but I found that, although now a modern resort, it had not been spoilt. Many new houses had been built, but all were in the Swiss or Bavarian chalet style, with wooden verandas in front covered with scarlet geraniums. Inside were modern, self-contained holiday apartments, all made of pine.

We spent time swimming and picnicking at the Eibsee, the deep glacial lake at the foot of the Zugspitze, the highest mountain in the German Alps. On one such visit a local artist was painting at the lake and I bought a painting of the Alps from him. It has been a daily reminder of my youth in Germany. Ruairí and I also walked together in the deep woods where I had walked as a child so long ago. I remember, on a visit to Dublin (the first summer after my return to Ireland), being asked did I want to go anywhere special. I said I'd like to see a forest. I was brought to Glendalough in County Wicklow. I took one look at it and said: 'This is no forest, I can see through the trees!' In later years, after so many years away from Germany, it gave me great joy to revisit the places of my childhood. Everywhere I went – in shops and restaurants – the people thought I was German because I spoke the language like a native. I was delighted with myself! For a part of me, this will always be my home.

Now, with the advancing years, my travels (overseas at least!) have come to an end. At Easter 2004, my son Ruairí brought me for one last time to Germany. He flew direct from London to Munich, while his fiancée, Nicola Brennan, accompanied me from Dublin direct. I organised that my old friend, Hilde, would fly down from Berlin to join us. We had four great days together. Hilde and a friend of hers showed us all the sights. They brought me down to Garmisch for a whole day, the town where my school had been located; I remembered skiing to school in winter. I visited all my old haunts in Grainau and showed them the house I had lived in as a young girl. They took many photographs of me. To round off the day, we took the little Alpine train and the funicular to the top of the Zugspitze. As it was still the winter sports season, we were surrounded by skiers. It was a beautiful, clear, sunny day. I was able to look down on the whole vista, on all the places I had spent the last few years before leaving Germany, more than seventy years before, and then to return to Ireland, my first and last home, for good. And so, from the top of the Zugspitze, I said a final goodbye to all of it for the last time.

FINAL OBSERVATIONS

I must have been a very compliant child. Whenever I found myself in a new situation, my first anxiety was to find out what the rules were so that I could fit in and disappear into the background. There was never any question of disobedience or drawing notice to myself. On the other hand, I was always very determined, a characteristic I must have inherited from the MacSwineys, especially from my father and Aunt Máire. Whenever anything had to be done, I set out to do it, no matter what obstacles I had to overcome. If anybody tried to quarrel with me, which was very seldom, I just walked away. I always tried to avoid unpleasantness because I lacked confidence.

As to whether my growing-up years had any deleterious effect on my later life, I must admit I was wrong in asserting that it made no great difference. People, when they caught glimpses of my life abroad,

ABOVE:
In the City Hall
chamber, Cork, on
the occasion of the
rededication of
Terence MacSwiney
Quay in 2004.

would sometimes remark to me: How tragic, how sad, how you must have suffered growing up without knowing anything of normal family life. My answer was always: Not at all, I was perfectly happy; what you have not known, you do not miss. This was not altogether correct, however. It was when I left the Odenwaldschule and had to live in the real world that I began to lose confidence. This insecurity deepened when my mother decided to move me to Heidelberg. And after my return home to Ireland I strongly felt this lack of confidence.

The return to Ireland, when I was a teenager, was much more traumatic than earlier changes. I had become a foreigner, not knowing the language or anything else about this new country. I had also lost my anonymity. Suddenly, I was 'Máire Óg', the long-lost daughter of Terence MacSwiney, and I felt everybody was watching me. What heightened people's interest was that I was supposed to have been kidnapped by my Aunt Máire, who was also a well-known figure. I was unaware that the story of my supposed kidnapping was being told all over Cork, not to mention that it was recorded in the press not only in Ireland but in Britain and Germany, too. Of course, as I was unable to read English at the time and there were rarely newspapers in Scoil Íte, it was not difficult to keep these facts from me! I constantly felt overwhelmed by anxiety – how else to explain all that frantic studying in case I failed to pass any exams, or reach the standard necessary for entrance to university?

After my marriage in 1945, I had to adjust once more to a completely new life. This was reality now and I had to learn, fast! Throughout my life I soaked up knowledge and picked other people's brains, whenever necessary and whatever the circumstances, in order to find the skills I needed to fit in. But I still so often felt that I was out of step, dancing to a different tune that only I was aware of.

Of course, this led to some amusing episodes, such as the day I met my usual coffee companions and one of them had brought her five-year-old daughter with her. As the adults wished to discuss some matter regarding the child that they did not want her to understand, they began to spell out the words. The problem was that it was not only the child who could not understand: neither could I! I had never learned to spell in English. To this day I go through the alphabet in German. This gap in everyday knowledge followed me throughout life. So it is no wonder that some deep-seated anxiety has remained with me to this day. I was always confronted with problems. Whenever I had a difficulty, I would look for a solution and, if one wasn't forthcoming, would move on, unless it was absolutely necessary to solve it. This was probably the consequence of my early upbringing.

Whenever I have to undertake a project, such as planning for holidays, I meticulously see to every detail months ahead and anticipate any problems that might arise. In fact, I am a firm believer in: If things can go wrong, they will go wrong! Again, it is this underlying anxiety that urges me to anticipate problems and fret about tiny details. This has also helped me solve problems as I have gone through life. It was only after ten years or more of married life, when I had once more overcome all the obstacles in my path and acquired the knowledge and skills to fit me for this new situation, that my self-confidence was gradually restored.

I never lost my love of Germany and its language and I have never regretted my upbringing or my life in Germany. Undoubtedly, it would have been more difficult for me, as the only child of Terence MacSwiney, if I had spent my entire childhood in Cork. However, I received a broad and cultured education as a result of my twin identities. I think I benefited enormously from my years in Germany, particularly from the education I received in the early years at that wonderful school, the Odenwaldschule. Mine was a dual identity: I always felt partly German, yet wholly, deeply committed to Ireland. I quickly grew to love the people and language of my native country. I was at home.

When I returned to Ireland it was as a foreigner, and I was very detached in many ways from the political situation. But this too had definite advantages. For instance, I could regard the Irish political scene with objectivity because England never overshadowed my thinking. On the Continent, England was of very little significance, unless she was involved in a major war. Whereas in Ireland, she seemed to overshadow everything: some people loving her and wishing to emulate her; others hating and rejecting her. This seemed to give the Irish an enormous inferiority complex vis-à-vis their nearest neighbour. To me, England was irrelevant. Ireland was an independent nation, like all others, and would work out her own destiny. I had no trouble accepting completely the modern Irish identity and new concept of nationhood.

Do I have any regrets? Yes, I used to feel at times that I hadn't made any use of my academic achievements. I could have had a career in academia, something I think I would have enjoyed immensely. From the 1960s on, when Ruairí and I started to attend meetings and conferences at home and abroad, I found myself in contact again with people of intellectual and wide-ranging interests. I revelled in these new contacts. I was like a plant that had remained dormant during a long spell of drought and had suddenly come to life after the arrival of the rains. This realisation heightened my disappointment about my incomplete PhD. As my responsibilities for young children diminished, I could have had a career as a lecturer in German, or teaching in a secondary school. Sometimes, listening to the Gospel story on burying one's talents, I used to feel that I was the original example of somebody who had done that.

However, I was very happy with my family life, and I was especially interested in the intellectual training of my children and in developing their talents. I also got great satisfaction from accompanying Ruairí to many different events, and enjoyed the people I met through his public activities. Both Ruairí and I were very committed to our country and to making a contribution. Discussions at the dinner-table centred mainly on contemporary politics and Ruairí's activities in public bodies and organisations in which he played a leading role. We discussed public affairs and politics in front of the children, although not the split in the Republican movement which brought about the Civil War because we did not believe in placing this burden on our children, who were the next generation. We were of the same mind in this, having both spent our young adult lives getting away from that aspect of the Republican movement. By the 1970s, when Ruairí was in public life, family conversation turned more to current affairs, international and national economics and politics and often to Northern Ireland.

I was more concerned with rights, and the wrongs being done to our country, whereas Ruairí was always thoughtful and conciliatory, seeing the others' point of view. He wanted to serve his country. Maybe he was too idealistic for politics, as he never promoted himself. His only interest was in putting the country first. At the time I did not consider a political career for myself because this would have intruded into his territory. At home it was different. We were both very independent-minded and discussed everything. We had inherited a strong commitment to Ireland, and to working out what was best for the country. It was what we had most in common, and was the centre of our lives. I think these ongoing discussions at our dinner-table contributed to forming the intellectual atmosphere within which the children grew up.

I sometimes wonder if our two fathers played any role in our destiny, Ruairí's and mine. I feel I am still influenced by those two men, who dedicated themselves and their lives to the service of their country. And for their part, they would have been very concerned for our welfare. I certainly believe that my father kept an eye on me during the uncertain years of my childhood. It is a feeling that I have still.

I sometimes feel regret that half of the grandchildren of Cathal Brugha and Terence MacSwiney have spent most of their professional lives outside Ireland, and that their abilities and qualifications have been less available to this country as a result. I suppose I am still influenced by those people who dedicated their lives to the service of their country and whose attitude was that, where possible, Irish people ought to do that. My sons, Terry and Ruairí, take a view that is quite different, perhaps a global view, that wherever they can contribute something it does not matter whether the work is carried out in Ireland or abroad.

And so we come to the children, and to my most enduring and most fulfilling role, that of mother to Deirdre, Cathal, Terry and Ruairí. I may have regrets for myself, but I have no regrets regarding our children and how we raised them, and the people they have become. There was no question of encouraging any of the children to become interested in politics. Cathal was the only one to get involved, which he did when he was in college. At that time he was on the National Executive of Fianna Fáil, when Ruairí was in the Dáil and Seanad, and Cathal helped to run our election campaigns.

I suppose it was because of my influence on our children that all of them became, in part at least, academics, although I didn't try to influence their choice of careers. Each has specialised in research, in psychology, management science, mental health and international public health. They in turn have children who are part of a generation that has grown up independent-minded, confident and enterprising, who do not suffer from the inferiority complex that my Aunt Máire so decried. You could say that they have fulfilled the dreams and hopes of their great-grandfathers: that Ireland, once free, would successfully take charge of her own destiny.

When I arrived on the quayside in Cork, at the age of fourteen, I did not speak English and was a complete stranger in my own country and to my heritage. Now, after all these years, I feel totally at home. The people I came home to no longer feel like strangers, and our languages – Irish and English – are as familiar to me as my 'native' German.

So this, then, is the story of my life, growing up in a foreign country and then a foreigner in a country that was my home. Not what might have been expected for the daughter of Terence MacSwiney, the girl referred to in the ballad, 'Shall My Soul Pass through Old Ireland?'

Looking back on my life, I realise that I did not know my father or my mother as much or as well as a child normally would. History deprived me of my father. My mother deprived me of herself.

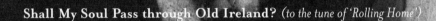

Shall My Soul Pass through Old Ireland? *(to the tune of 'Rolling Home')*

In a dreary British prison where an Irish rebel lay,
By his side a priest waits standing were his soul to pass away.
As he gently murmurs Father, the priest takes him by the hand,
Father, tell me, 'ere I die, shall my soul pass through Ireland?

Chorus:
Shall my soul pass through old Ireland, pass through Cork's old city grand?
Shall I see the old Cathedral where St Patrick made his stand?
Shall I see the little chapel where I placed my heart in hand?
Father, tell me when I die, shall my soul pass through Ireland?

Was for loving dear old Ireland in this prison cell I lie,
Was for loving dear old Ireland in this foreign land I die.
When you see my little daughter won't you make her understand.
Father, tell me if I die, shall my soul pass through Ireland?

With his soul pure as a lily and his body sanctified,
In the dreary British prison our brave Irish rebel died,
Prayed the priest his wish be granted as in blessing raised his hand,
Father grant this brave man's wish — may his soul pass through Ireland.

243

My Father
and My Mother

MY FATHER

After the Rising of 1916 — in which the Cork Brigade did not take an active part due to the countermanding order issued from Dublin — my father, Terence MacSwiney, and his comrade-in-arms, Tomás MacCurtain, were arrested. My Aunt Máire would never allow me to refer to 1916 as a 'rebellion'. A 'rebellion', according to her, was an uprising against lawful authority, whereas 1916 was an uprising against an unlawful authority — the unlawful occupation of Ireland by Britain.

In the years immediately preceding 1916 the national movement had been motivated and directed by cultural concerns, namely the renewal of traditional Gaelic theatre, language and sport. My father belonged to a generation where the cultural movement was the expression of their nationalism. Some devoted themselves to Irish

BELOW, LEFT:
Going to Mass in Ballingeary.
BELOW, RIGHT
AND ABOVE:
Card from 1909 on which my father wrote: 'This is a suggestion for a Xmas card from the Cuala Press, Dundrum, Dublin.'

ABOVE:
My parents in
July 1920 in
Ballingeary with
local girls and a
priest. I am sitting
on my father's
knee. I remember
my mother, some
years later, buying
ribbons for me and
for the little girl in
her arms here.

drama and literature, but mostly they joined the Gaelic League and made every effort to learn Irish. My father was writing poetry and drama at that time, but above all he was learning the Irish language. He did this by cycling to the West Cork Gaeltacht of Ballingeary (Béal Áth' an Ghaorthaigh) to learn the spoken language directly from the people, which is the best way since Irish grammar and written Irish are very difficult. In this way my father became fluent in spoken Irish and also, over time, became fluent in written Irish.

It must have been very difficult for him to master the language. His mother was English and only English would have been spoken in his family home, however he was determined to succeed. Indeed, when later he met my mother, he asked her to learn Irish too, which she did. It must have been even more difficult for her as she and all her family had been educated in England and the atmosphere in her home would have been decidedly Anglo-Irish. However, my father's diaries from this time show no sign of thoughts of armed struggle. Apart from describing normal life as it was lived in the early part of the twentieth century, his main activity was in the Celtic Literary Society.

It was to be many years, however, before I would get to read my father's personal diaries. His biographer, Moirin Chavasse (*Terence MacSwiney*, Dublin and London, 1961), would not let me see the diaries. She had some notion that I would thwart her in some way. Seemingly, my mother had told her I would confiscate them. Later, the editor of the Moirin Chavasse biography, Seán Feehan, went to Mayo with Florrie O'Donoghue, author of a book on Tomás MacCurtain, to ask her to return the diaries to me, and she refused. My main worry was that they were not safe in her house.

Years later, when I was losing my sight, I heard the diaries had been lodged in the National Library. My daughter-in-law, Catherine, arranged to have them sent on loan to the Archives Department in UCD, where she read them to me every week for a year. As we came closer to the period of the Rising, I was anticipating what would be revealed. But the diaries stopped suddenly. We couldn't believe it as we turned out the final box wondering, is that all? We had expected exciting events to start happening, but no, nothing to indicate preparations being made for 1916.

BELOW, LEFT:
My father (*front row, third from right*), with his school companions in the North Mon, Cork.

BELOW:
Some of my father's copybooks for his university studies.

RIGHT:
Official photograph of my father when receiving his degree in 1907.

One interesting thing I learned from the diaries was that it was a request to my father by Bulmer Hobson that resulted in his book, *Principles of Freedom*. Hobson was an influential figure in the cultural aspect of the movement and the editor of a monthly journal called *Irish Freedom*. He asked my father, who was mainly writing poetry at the

time, to contribute something in prose on freedom. My father had a degree in Mental and Moral Science and was well equipped to the task. These articles were written when he was a relatively young man, in 1912. However, it was only after my father's death in 1920 that an enterprising publisher in New York decided to publish them as a collection, in book form. Soon after that the Talbot Press published two editions in Ireland.

It is a strange way to get to 'know' one's father, but my father has been revealed to me, bit by bit, gradually over the years, and my way of knowing him is through others' memories and anecdotes. Nonetheless, I have always been surprised at the extent of his influence across the world. For example, a classmate of Aunt Annie's at university was Maggie Burke, later known as Margaret Burke Sheridan, the famous singer and diva at La Scala in Milan. I was to read in biographies of my father that on the day he died, she came out onto the stage of the famous opera house and explained that she could not sing that night as a compatriot had died. The Italian audience understood this perfectly. Also, the Italian parliament adjourned on hearing of his death.

In June 1948 Ruairí and I spent a night in the Grande Hotel, Place de L'Opéra in Paris. This was where Art O'Brien had set up offices in 1919 to represent the newly elected, independent Irish State. Here we discovered that when my father died, a queue had formed right around the whole block of the hotel of sympathisers wishing to sign the book of condolence.

In the Holy Year, 1950, Aunt Annie decided we should go to Rome for Easter on a tour organised by a travel agent in Cork, which was to be accompanied by Canon Bastible from the Cork diocese. Among those travelling were quite a few of my former companions from school and UCC. We had 'Irlanda' badges pinned to our coats. On seeing these the station personnel, such as baggage-handlers, signalmen and other staff, came crowding around our priestly guide, demanding to know immediately: *Irlanda*? Was that where Lord Mayor MacSwiney came from? Canon Bastible was delighted and told them it was and, like a magician pulling a rabbit out of a hat, he pointed to Aunt Annie and me, declaring he had Mr MacSwiney's sister and daughter here. I was astonished to realise that the word '*Irlanda*' would still recall my father's hunger strike after thirty years.

A similar incident occurred in the late 1950s. Friends of our family, Paddy O'Keeffe, and his wife, Peggy, were spending a few months in a quiet resort in Spain while he was recovering from a serious operation. They were accustomed to sending letters and cards to friends and relations, mainly in Cork. One day when they pushed their post across the counter, the postmistress peered at the address and asked was 'Irlanda in Cork' the place where MacSwiney came from? Peggy O'Keeffe told me this story on her return home and I took delight in telling this story to Cork people! I gradually got a sense of the stature of my father.

On 4 July 1958 we brought the children to the opening of the new St George's Catholic Cathedral in Southwark, London, which had been bombed during the war. Much of the money had been collected in Ireland and to a great extent in Cork, mainly because of the lying-in-state of Terence MacSwiney in the old cathedral in 1920. (There is a beautiful painting of this scene by Sir John Lavery in the Hugh Lane Municipal Gallery in Dublin.) The new cathedral had a side-chapel dedicated as the Terence MacSwiney Memorial Chapel. The Taoiseach, John A Costello, and former Taoiseach, Éamon de Valera, were there too, as was my aunt, Mother Margaret (Peg) MacSwiney, who was home from the USA to celebrate fifty years of religious life in the order of Les Soeurs de l'Éducation Chrétienne.

Another occasion we shared with Éamon de Valera was when he was scheduled to unveil a Celtic cross memorial to all those buried in the Republican plot in St Finbarr's cemetery in Cork, where my father was buried. Ruairí and I and our family were invited to attend the ceremony. On our way into the city, we stopped at a garage on the outskirts, in Tivoli, and the attendant asked us what we thought of the bomb the night before. Apparently, an IRA group had intended placing a bomb under the stand, timed to explode when de Valera was making his speech. This was the first we had heard of it. The mechanic told us that it had in fact exploded the previous night, while being assembled by the bombers, and that one of their party had been killed. We proceeded on our way to the Republican plot. I was thinking that if they had succeeded in their efforts to blow up de Valera and the Brugha families, which included four grandchildren of Terence MacSwiney, how would that have served the cause of Ireland?

The effects of my father's sacrifice had lasting and significant repercussions. In his life and death he had touched countless people with his steadfast, quiet heroism. The more people I met and talked with, the more connection I felt to him. In 1966, Ruairí and I attended the Easter commemoration in Trafalgar Square, London, at which Ruairí gave the formal oration. Introducing him, the MC, Abbey Theatre actor Eddie Golden, welcomed us as the son of Cathal Brugha and the daughter of Terence MacSwiney: it was a proud moment.

In 1969 my father's international reputation was again brought to

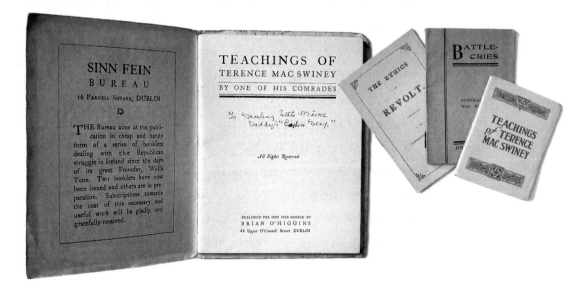

స్వాతంత్ర్యలక్షణము

ABOVE:
A copy of *Principles of Freedom* in the Indian language, Telugu, published in 1925.
BELOW LEFT:
Early books by and about my father.

my notice during the year of the Gandhi centenary, which the United Nations declared was to be observed worldwide. The Indian government sent a representative from their embassy in London to take part in the Dublin commemoration. One of the first things this envoy did upon his arrival was to enquire if any members of the MacSwiney family were still around. The Department of Foreign Affairs finally tracked me down through Bord Fáilte, and I was invited to the Indian embassy on Morehampton Road to meet Dr V Pachaiyappan. He told me that, as a young student, he had been a member of the Gandhi Movement. He explained to me that the example of MacSwiney and his hunger strike, as well as Ireland's struggle for freedom, was one of their main sources of inspiration for the Movement. In fact, MacSwiney's *Principles of Freedom* was considered essential reading for their members and had been translated into various Indian languages. I have a copy of it in Telugu, published in 1925. The preface reads: '*Principles of Freedom* has been translated into the Telugu language for the benefit of the Indian people as well as the remembrance of Terence MacSwiney who, during the period of Irish Chaos (around 1920), suggested peaceful means to achieve freedom.' This was kindly translated for me by Dr Pachaiyappan. The press took photographs of our meeting, which I kept, and I carefully wrote down everything that this envoy said. This was tangible evidence of the worldwide influence of my father's hunger strike and death.

India finally attained her independence in 1949. The form of constitutional settlement she had made with the Crown, when leaving the Empire, later became the Commonwealth of Nations. This was very similar to the idea de Valera had had during the Treaty debates and which he had explained to my aunt over coffee. India's attainment of her freedom was the beginning of the end of the Empire. If, as this gentleman told me, the hunger strike of MacSwiney and the example of Ireland's freedom struggle had an influence on that Movement at the beginning, one might consider that Ireland was the little pebble that, when it was loosened and fell out, caused the whole edifice to crumble.

From then on I received communications from other parts of the world, from people with the name MacSwiney who wondered if they were related to my father. In one case a very nice man from Florida was very insistent on his lineage, but as I had the written family tree I was able to tell him I didn't think that was the case. Up to as recently as September 2003, at a Sweeney clan gathering in Donegal, those attending from as far away as Nebraska, Minnesota and other States, as well as from Australia, came up to shake hands with me because I was the daughter of Terence MacSwiney. One gentleman had been invited into a home in Catalonia, in northeast Spain, and the first thing he noticed was a large portrait of my father on the wall — something similar to the picture of John F Kennedy one used to find in many Irish homes.

One memorable experience with one of my father's admirers occurred one summer's afternoon in the 1960s when Ruairí and I were having a cup of coffee in the Gresham Hotel, and it certainly served to remind me how strongly people felt about him. The waitress brought over a young man and asked if he could sit at our table as there was no room at any other table. We began asking him how he was enjoying his visit to Ireland. He told us that he was an Australian, with an English background, and that he had never had any intention of visiting Ireland. However, he was very friendly with Archbishop Mannix, who had insisted that he visit Cork, the birthplace of Terence MacSwiney. He began to tell us of his experience of that trip. He had checked into a hotel in Cork, and next morning asked for directions to the monument, presuming there would be one to

Terence MacSwiney. He was given directions to Patrick Street, to what the people of Cork call 'The Statue', which is a monument to Fr Theobald Mathew, the temperance priest. The Australian said, 'That is not the statue I am looking for, but the one to Terence MacSwiney.' He then discovered that nobody seemed to know anything about MacSwiney, and there was not so much as a plaque to commemorate the former Lord Mayor. At this point I spoke quietly to Ruairí in Irish, suggesting I tell our companion who I was, so that when he returned to Australia and Archbishop Mannix he would have something to tell and his journey would not have been in vain. I then said to him, 'As a matter of fact, I am Terence MacSwiney's only daughter.' I thought he would be delighted to hear this. Instead he answered very crossly, 'It is an utter disgrace, you should do something about it.' I replied, 'It is not up to me. I am living now in Dublin over twenty years. It is a matter for the Cork people.'

Since that time two busts, of Tomás MacCurtain and my father, have been placed on either side of the entrance to the City Hall; these were made by Donal Ó Murchú. Also, Albert Quay, which fronts the City Hall, has been renamed Terence MacSwiney Quay. In October 2004 the Lord Mayor and Cork Corporation rededicated it and unveiled a plaque. Now, anybody visiting Cork will see that my father, Terence MacSwiney, has been recognised by the city of his birth.

MY MOTHER

My mother was a beautiful woman of great intelligence and very strong opinions. She always felt very concerned for the underprivileged and the marginalised. One of the main reasons for her falling-out with the Catholic Church was its attitude to and treatment of unmarried mothers. Someone said to me years later, 'she was a woman before her time', and I had to agree with him. She always rebelled against her privileged upbringing, so it would seem she had formed her political ideas at a very early age.

My memories of my mother, Muriel, from the few holidays I spent with her when I was at school in the Odenwaldschule, are of a warm and loving mother and I dearly loved her. That was why I pleaded with her, when we were in Heidelberg, to allow me to live with her, but she couldn't cope with that. She was such a tragic figure; apart from loving her, one could only feel deeply sorry for her.

I remember very well that day at the railway station in Heidelberg. I was about eleven years old and I asked her to get a flat where we could live together. She said it was out of the question. After she had moved me to Garmisch, at the age of twelve, she came to visit me a year later. This was the last time I met her face to face, and she was proposing to move me yet again. I had just spent a very happy and stable year with Dr and Frau Kaltenbach, and I think it was then that I realised there was no future for me roaming around Germany with her. That was the moment I grew up.

My mother spent most of her life in Paris, with sojourns in Heidelberg and later in Geneva, where she may have been receiving medical help for her depressions, from which she suffered severely at times. As far as I ever knew, my mother lived happily in Paris amongst her friends, a coterie of French intelligentsia, journalists and writers who

IRISH COSTUME

REVIVAL. 1920.

LEFT:
My mother before she was married.
ABOVE:
A promotion of traditional Irish dress in 1920. My mother is seated fourth from the right, in the second row.

held the same views as herself: very left-wing and communist. Years later I read an article in *The Irish Times* written by a journalist who had visited Paris and met with the group there, ensconced in their favourite haunt, a café on the Left Bank. My mother was known among them as *'l'Irlandaise'*.

My mother spent the war years in England, visiting Dublin from time to time. On two of these visits I caught a glimpse of her. The first time was in the National Library on Kildare Street. She was chatting with someone on the landing. It would have been 1941, when I was studying for the Studentship. I sidled passed her, unseen, because I never knew how she might react. I was always nervous about that. It struck me at the time that she spoke beautifully. I had never heard her speak in English before and it was with an Oxford accent.

A few years later when Ruairí and I were getting married, in 1945, he suggested I write and tell her that I was marrying the son of Cathal Brugha, whom she admired greatly. We didn't hear back from her. The following year when our first child, Deirdre, was born, Ruairí again suggested I write and tell her. My mother, at this time, was staying in Buswell's Hotel on Molesworth Street. He delivered the letter personally, but we received no reply.

The second time I saw her was when I was married and was living in Dublin, probably in the 1960s. I was sitting upstairs in Bewley's café with my sister-in-law and her friends, having coffee. I heard my mother's voice on the other side of the room. She was with Kathy Barry, a sister of Kevin Barry. I pretended not to notice her and went on chatting with my friends.

Mrs Kathleen McDonnell of Bandon was a great friend and support to my mother during the years that she lived in London. Whenever my mother visited Dublin, Kathleen came up from Bandon to meet her. It so happened that Mrs McDonnell also knew me well and on her frequent visits to Dublin she often asked me to meet her in the Gresham Hotel. At one time she decided to make a valiant effort to bring my mother and me together. She did everything possible to persuade my mother to allow her to arrange a meeting between us, in her presence. She told my mother that she had seen me the day before and would my mother not allow her to arrange a meeting. My mother refused absolutely and told her that if she ever mentioned my name again, she would stop seeing her. Mrs McDonnell was then my mother's only friend in Dublin and, as she later explained to me, she 'decided your mother needed me more than you did, so I complied with her wishes.' I must say I was more relieved than anything; my mother was always unpredictable.

My mother went back to Paris after the war, returning again to London in later years to live the rest of her life there, where she found friends who were of her own way of thinking. She had a small income from shares which were left to me by my Grandmother Murphy, but which accrued to my mother during her lifetime. Later in life she received a pension from the Irish government, which supplemented her income. She had given strict instructions to her bank not to reveal her address to me, or to any other member of the Murphy family. This included my cousin Stephen Murphy, who was head of the Cork distillery that was owned by the Murphy family at that time.

In 1966 my mother was back living in Paris. We were passing through on the way home from holidaying in the south of France. Ruairí thought we should make an effort to see her as we had the four children with us, and it would be an opportunity for my mother to meet them. I called to the small hotel at 78 Rue Blomet where she was residing; Mrs McDonnell had given me that address. I was told at the desk that she had left the previous Easter and hadn't returned since. I thought it was probably just as well as she had expressed her wishes not to meet me again, but Ruairí always felt we should make the effort.

My mother died at the age of eighty-nine in 1982, having spent her final years in a nursing home. I was only informed of her death by her solicitor a week later. She certainly carried out her intention never to have anything more to do with me after I refused to return to her in 1934.

Later, I discovered a document amongst the MacSwiney papers recording my mother's account of my homecoming, from her point of view. It was totally inaccurate. I decided at that point that I would have to write the correct facts of the episode. If a document is written with the wrong information and not corrected, one must put on record the correct version otherwise the incorrect one becomes history. So I felt obliged to put the truth on record. I then lodged both my mother's document and mine in the Archives Department in UCD.

My mother's document made very sad reading. She very obviously suffered from her nerves and ill health, but it seems she was her own worst enemy. By removing herself abroad, far from friends and family, she found herself completely alone without any of the necessary supports she needed. I know her family, especially her mother, would have looked after her, but she, for whatever reason, would not consider it.

Some years ago I was at an exhibition of paintings by Sir John Lavery in the Hugh Lane Municipal Gallery in Dublin. I was admiring again the beautiful painting of my father's funeral in Southwark Cathedral, when I spotted my mother's portrait hanging nearby. I had not realised that Lavery had painted her, and on inspection saw that the painting was simply titled *Widow*.

Biographies

TERENCE MacSWINEY, M.I.P.
Lord Mayor Of Cork.

CATHAL BRUGHA

RIGHT:
**Painting of
Cathal Brugha
by John F Kelly
which hangs in
the entrance
hall of Leinster
House.**

Máire MacSwiney married Cathal Brugha's only son, Ruairí. Cathal Brugha and Máire's father, Terence MacSwiney, were friends and comrades in the struggle for Irish freedom. It was MacSwiney who most often seconded the motions that Brugha proposed in the First Dáil. Cathal Brugha was a passionate defender of his country's right to independence; he played a key role in the 1916 Rising and died while fighting for his beliefs.

The name Brugha is an Irish translation of Burgess. Cathal Brugha's forebears came from Picardy, in France, to Cornwall around 1600, and then to Borris (Buirghéis) in Carlow about 1650, where the name still survives.

The Burgesses were craftsmen and Protestants. Some of them moved to Dublin, possibly at the time of the Famine. Cathal's grandfather, Richard Burgess, owned a tobacconist shop in Dublin. He had four children, two girls and two boys, one of whom was Cathal's father, Thomas. When Thomas married a Catholic, Maryanne Flynn, his father disinherited him.

Thomas Burgess was a cabinetmaker who developed a successful business selling art and antiques, with shops in Dublin and London. Thomas and Maryanne had fourteen children, of which the tenth was Charles William St John Burgess, born in 1874. He attended secondary school in Belvedere College, Dublin, where he was known

for his sporting abilities. However, he was forced to leave school early in order to work after his father's business failed.

At the age of twenty-five, Charles Burgess joined the Keating branch of the Gaelic League. He began to devote much of his spare time to learning the Irish language and changed his name to Cathal Brugha. He became actively involved in the movement, travelling the country to promote the Irish language, Sinn Féin and the Irish Republican Brotherhood (IRB).

When he was thirty-five, Cathal Brugha, along with two brothers, Anthony and Vincent Lalor, set up a church candle manufacturing firm, taking on the role of travelling salesman. He met his future wife, Kathleen Kingston, at an Irish class in Birr, County Offaly. They married in 1912 and had six children over the next ten years: five girls — Nollaig, Noinín, Brenda, Delma and Nessa; and one son — Ruairí.

From 1913 onwards Cathal Brugha devoted much of his time to recruiting and training the Irish Volunteers. In 1914 he led a party of twenty Volunteers to receive the delivery of arms Erskine Childers had smuggled into Howth on board the yacht, *Asgard*. During a con-

frontation with the Dublin Metropolitan Police (DMP), one member of the force, Andrew O'Neill, prevented his colleagues from seizing the arms from the Volunteers. O'Neill was dismissed from the DMP the next day, but reinstated four months later after persistent appeals — which were even raised in the House of Commons. O'Neill's granddaughter, Catherine Jennings, was to marry Cathal Brugha's grandson, Cathal, sixty-three years later.

Brugha took a leading role in the 1916 Rising as second-in-command of the Fourth Dublin Battalion at the South Dublin Union, a 'Poor House' that is now St James's Hospital. Seriously wounded — he received twenty-five injuries from shrapnel and bullets, some of them life-threatening — he single-handedly held his position, even though his comrades had retreated. Later that night, when the British soldiers had given up attacking his position, his comrades heard his voice ringing out the song 'God Save Ireland' and went to his rescue. Fortunately, they found a nurse who was able to staunch the flow of blood. He recovered slowly over the next year, but was left with a permanent limp from his injuries.

As vice-commandant to Éamonn

Ceannt, Brugha was a senior leader in the Rising and might have been executed if he had not been so seriously wounded that the British believed he would not recover. His fame spread and is recorded in the song 'The Foggy Dew': 'O had they died by Pearse's side, or fought with Cathal Brugha ...' Even the British soldiers he fought against spoke of his bravery. After recovering from his injuries he organised an amalgamation of the Irish Volunteers and the Irish Citizen Army into one: the Irish Republican Army (IRA). At a Sinn Féin convention in 1917 he proposed a Republican constitution, which was unanimously accepted.

Sinn Féin won the general election in 1918. When the first meetings of the First Dáil Éireann took place in January 1919, Cathal Brugha was chosen as President of the Ministry on a *pro tem* basis, as Éamon de Valera was then serving a prison sentence.

The main aim of Sinn Féin was to establish the Republic of Ireland as a sovereign nation, with a government recognised by the people, and thereby to oust Britain after hundreds of years of English control over Ireland. The conflicting claims of the First Dáil and the Westminster parliament to the right to govern Ireland led to the War of Independence (1919–1921).

In April 1919, de Valera was elected as Head of State and Cathal Brugha was

BELOW:
Anti-Treaty deputies leaving the Dáil, 1921.

appointed Minister for Defence. As Minister, Brugha took a strategic view, believing that it was better for the IRA, who were poorly equipped, to avoid open military engagements with what was then one of the world's most powerful armies. He saw his role as being to recruit, equip, train, discipline and organise the many different groups of volunteers into one army, and to put that army under the authority of the Dáil. He felt that the IRB, which was under the control of Michael Collins, should not continue in existence and that the oath of allegiance to it should be replaced.

On 20 August 1919 Brugha proposed an oath of allegiance to the Irish Republic and to Dáil Éireann for the deputies, for the Irish Volunteers and for any others who, in the opinion of the Dáil, should take the oath. This requirement would make the Irish Volunteers a properly constituted army and would legitimise the war being waged by the IRA. Terence MacSwiney seconded this motion, and it was adopted.

The new oath of allegiance had military and political consequences. The military consequence was that allegiance to the Republic and to Dáil Éireann did not fully resolve the problem of control over the Volunteers because the IRB continued to exist, despite the obvious conflict of authority. This led to difficulties for Brugha. Michael Collins operated within the army structure, as Head of Intelligence, reporting to Dick Mulcahy, as Chief of Staff, who reported to Brugha, as Minister for Defence and Chairman of the Army Council. However, Collins was also operating independently, to some extent, as leader of the IRB.

This impasse had inevitable political implications. Collins was Minister for Finance, and as such was a senior government minister. Brugha, as Minister for Defence, focused on solidifying the country's military position, leaving de Valera to deal with political developments. Brugha became less interested in politics and his public image, concentrating instead on his role as commander of the army. As all the commandants throughout the country reported directly to him, Brugha felt that he should reduce his vulnerability to assassination by the British. He was very security conscious. He avoided being photographed. He always carried a gun. He rarely slept at home. He rarely used the offices of the Ministry for Defence, but generally met commandants in his upstairs office at

ABOVE:
Early morning, 6 December 1921, awaiting news of the Treaty outside Strand House, Limerick, home of Stephen O'Mara, where there was a telephone. *Front*: Mrs Rynne, President de Valera, Stephen O'Mara, Cathal Brugha, Minister for Defence. *Behind*: Michael Rynne, Richard Mulcahy.

Lalor Bros., where he still worked. He did not keep many written notes. Consequently, Brugha's increasingly non-political role reduced his influence within the Dáil and on popular opinion.

After a general election in May 1921,

the Second Dáil debated the Treaty in late 1921. There were at least three conflicting views amongst the leaders. Some, such as Arthur Griffith, wanted to negotiate and settle with the British. The de Valera/Brugha view was to keep the negotiations going as long as possible — reports from commandants were that the British were losing their grip on Munster and Connacht and therefore lengthy negotiations could lead to a stronger bargaining position. The Collins view — which gained hold during the Treaty negotiations and ultimately made the difference in getting support for the Treaty — was to make a settlement with the British, but then use it as a stepping-stone and restart military activities in the North of Ireland once the settlement had been ratified. Those members of the Dáil who were still under oath of allegiance to the IRB, and therefore obliged to obey instructions from Collins, may have made the difference in passing the vote on the Treaty. Brugha had heated exchanges with Michael Collins during the Dáil debates on the Treaty, his comments showing much irritation with Collins's stance on the issue.

After Dáil Éireann voted to ratify the Treaty, Cathal Brugha promised to maintain discipline in the army. Subsequently, however, he, Éamon de Valera and other anti-Treaty ministers resigned their portfolios. Most of the soldiers who had fought the War of Independence were anti-Treaty. These held an officers' convention and elected a sixteen-man executive. They met to discuss a motion to restart the war with England, hoping to unite the army to fight against the common enemy. Brugha, who now had no formal position, spoke from the floor against the motion and called on them not to carry out what amounted to a confrontation with the Dáil, to which they had sworn allegiance. A majority of 118 to 103 voted to accept his line. Three of the army leaders — Rory O'Connor, Liam Mellows and Joseph McKelvey — left the platform and walked out. As O'Connor was passing, Brugha called to him, 'Come back, Rory, you don't know where you are going.' Those who walked out, including twelve members of the sixteen-man executive, then established a military headquarters in the Four Courts on 15 April 1922, precipitating civil war. This led to Ireland's *cogadh na gcarad* (the war of friends).

One of these twelve was the socialist writer Peadar O'Donnell who, in later years, was one of a group of ex-Curragh internees, miscellaneous Republicans and Kerrymen who for many years met up on Saturday mornings over a cup of tea in various restaurants in the vicinity of Kingston's, O'Connell Street, where Ruairí was General Manager. Shortly before he died in 1987, Peadar said to Ruairí, who used to visit him regularly in his last years, 'The Four Courts was wrong, wasn't it?' A reason why some of them took this extreme action, which resulted in the Civil War, was the oath of allegiance they had taken to defend the Republic and Dáil Éireann. This was exacerbated by the inclusion in the Treaty of an oath of allegiance to the British Crown.

During May and June 1922 attempts were made to prevent a widening of the split between the pro-Treaty and anti-Treaty forces. There were numerous attempts to resolve the differences, which led to tensions on both sides. On the pro-Treaty side, Griffith felt honour-bound to implement his Treaty commitments and wanted a quick victory over the forces in the Four Courts. The British vigorously pushed Collins, Griffith and the Provisional government to follow this line, providing the Free State Army with arms and equipment to facilitate an attack on the Four Courts. However, Collins continued to negotiate with anti-Treaty forces, including exchanging with them equal amounts of (the same) arms and equipment, so that the British would not discover that he was pursuing his stepping-stone plan to continue the war in the Six Counties.

On the anti-Treaty side, Brugha and Liam Lynch set up headquarters in the Clarence Hotel, across the river from the Four Courts, and tried, unsuccessfully, to negotiate a reconciliation between the various groups. Lynch held several meetings with Collins, as both were senior members of the IRB.

On 25 June a Volunteer Convention was held at the Four Courts, but it changed nothing. A majority of the Volunteers sided with Brugha and Lynch, but a majority of the executive insisted on making a stand at the Four Courts, regardless of the consequences. This debate continued until Monday, 26 June, with Brugha taking the executive to task for insubordination. At this point Brugha wanted to walk out, but was dissuaded by Oscar Traynor, who was commanding officer of the Dublin Brigade of the anti-Treaty forces.

As it was apparent that the anti-Treaty side was divided, the British put further pressure on the new Irish Free State government to attack the Four Courts garrison. On 28 June the Free State, with the help of British artillery and a British warship on the River Liffey, commenced a bombardment of the Four Courts. Both Traynor and Brugha entered the Four Courts and entreated the anti-Treaty forces to leave, but they refused.

Traynor then ordered the occupation of many buildings centred on the

O'Connell Street area (then Sackville Street) in the hope that it might relieve the pressure on the Four Courts and force the Free State forces to negotiate. He called for support, whereupon Brugha, de Valera, Seán T Ó Ceallaigh and others reported for duty as privates, i.e., no longer acting as political leaders. Those who had been in the Clarence Hotel and many other Republicans joined, including some women, Muriel MacSwiney among them. Although these greatly outnumbered the Free State forces, they had no coherent chain of command, were poorly armed and without a plan of action. Within a short period the Free State Army would outnumber them as many of the unemployed joined up, including soldiers who had returned from fighting with the British Army in the First World War.

Traynor promoted Brugha to the position of commandant and put him in charge of the O'Connell Street area. Attacks by the Free State heavy-guns reduced many of the buildings to ruins, forcing the anti-Treaty forces to retreat. Brugha undertook to hold the position in the Hammam Hotel with a small group of men, allowing the others to escape. He indicated to de Valera

that he would join him later.

On the morning of Wednesday, 5 July 1922 two well-known members of the Dublin Brigade, Jack Rooney and Jack O'Beirne, made their way, fully armed, through the Free State lines into the back of the Hammam Hotel. They pointed out to Brugha that there would be no attempt made to relieve the Hammam garrison. At this point the hotel was in flames.

Cathal Brugha was left with three options: there was no question of fighting to the last; surrender was unpalatable; so he chose to attempt to escape back along the route that Rooney and O'Beirne had used to join their group. He asked them to check out the building to ensure that the rest of his men had got out safely. He then disarmed those who were left so that if they were arrested it would be clear that they were surrendering. He put the bullets from their guns in his pockets, threw the guns in the fire and ordered them to evacuate via the back of the hotel, to cross the lane and take cover in a large shed. But at that point it became apparent that the Free State troops had discovered the ruse and the back lane was no longer safe.

Brugha told Rooney and O'Beirne to wait while he assessed the situation

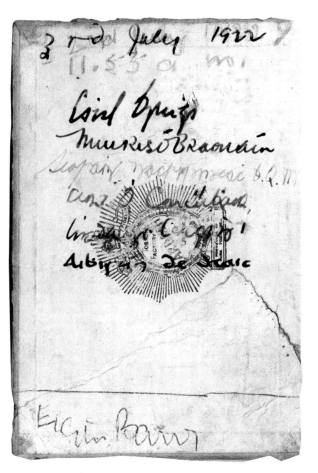

ABOVE:
Signatures of some of the Hammam Hotel garrison on the morning of 3 July 1922: Cathal Brugha, Maurice Brennan, Joseph MacM... (?) BQM (Battalion Quarter Master), Art O'Connor, Nurse Linda Kearns, Austin Stack and (*beneath*) Elgin Barry (sister of Kevin Barry; she later married Mac O'Rahilly).

femoral artery of his left leg, causing extensive bleeding. Medical personnel attended to him on the spot, including a young medical student, Seán Geraghty, who had been across the lane in the shed. He was moved to the nearby Mater Hospital, while Nurse Linda Kearns held his severed artery pinched closed between her fingers. He died two days later. He was almost forty-eight years old. Cathal Brugha was the first senior figure to die in the Civil War.

There are several other versions of what happened that day. One is unbelievable: that he died while charging at his enemies with guns blazing and shouting, 'No surrender'. Another is unprovable: that his gun was not loaded. The most credible alternative came from Art O'Connor, who was with Seán Geraghty. He thought that the group was surrendering, not trying to escape, but that Brugha was intent on making a heroic sacrifice. There are two views as to why he might have done this. One was to continue the fight; the other was that his death might wake people to the senselessness of the Civil War and somehow bring the pro- and anti-Treaty sides back together. In the end, Brugha came to be identified as a hero by one side, and an extremist by the other.

outside. As he crossed the lane he was seen to halt, kneel down on one knee and fire with his short rifle towards the block of houses in Parnell Street (then Great Britain Street). There was a responding burst of gunfire and Brugha was hit by one shot, severing the

ABOVE: Death-mask of Cathal Brugha by Albert Power.
BELOW: A page from the 15 July 1922 edition of *The Graphic* magazine.

1930s, during which time she was the leader of the diminishing group of members who were elected to the Second Dáil and retained allegiance to it.

When Ruairí Brugha became prominent in Irish politics in the 1960s and 1970s, his quiet, pragmatic approach contrasted with the public image of both his father and the MacSwineys. In years to come the focus for both Máire and Ruairí was on the reconciliation of all the people of many different traditions living on the island of Ireland, particularly through bodies such as the North–South Association. Ruairí's aim in politics was to help Ireland to play a constructive role within Europe.

Ruairí and Máire are moderates on

On the other side of the family, Máire MacSwiney Brugha's aunt, Mary MacSwiney, had taken the politically extreme position that the Dáil could not be disestablished because the members had taken an oath of allegiance to it. Consequently, she felt that the Third Dáil elections, held in June 1922, were illegal, and likewise all subsequent actions taken by the Free State and its successors. To her, only the Second Dáil was legal. She held this position into the

ABOVE: Seán T. Ó Ceallaigh (with spectacles, later President of Ireland) carrying the coffin of Cathal Brugha.

issues regarding Republicanism in Northern Ireland. This does not mean that they are any the less nationalists. Their moderation comes from their understanding of the historical events through which their families lived. Nor does it mean that they are inconsistent with the previous generation, even though it might appear so to some.

Both families are proud to have heroes in their genealogy. However, both families experienced personal and emotional difficulties as a result. This primarily affected the widows left behind. Kathleen (Kingston) Brugha was very loyal to her husband and would never have said anything against him, but she found it very difficult to run a business and raise six children without her husband. She indicated as much to her son, Ruairí, during her last days. Obviously, Máire MacSwiney Brugha was never in a position to have a similar conversation with her mother.

Cathal M. Brugha, 2005

Wilt thou yield up thy life unto my keeping
Nor fear to bend the world's ways with me
...
lives o'er its reign to Happiness and thee
Couldst thou find joy adown life's highway winding
If thou thy path with mine should interlace,
and let my loving care be ever finding

TERENCE MACSWINEY

Máire MacSwiney Brugha grew up knowing very little about her father. She was in her twenties before she began to realise the impact his death had worldwide, and how his personal stand against the authority of the British Empire did more than any other event to under-mine its authority and control over Ireland. The following extract, from an article by Rev. P MacCormac BA, which appeared in *The Catholic Herald* on 9 April 1921, best summarises Máire's father's achievement:

ETON

'In Eton, the well known English boys school, a prize was offered for the most satisfactory answering of the question: "Mention the name of the greatest man that ever lived, giving five reasons for saying so."

'The winner said;

"In my opinion Terence MacSwiney, Lord Mayor of Cork, was the greatest man that ever lived. My five reasons for saying so are: –

1. He overcame morally the most pow-erful Empire that has ever existed.

2. His last stand was the most heroic act in the 700 years' war, the longest war in history.

3. His agony was the longest, best known, and most universally discussed on record, lasting as it did for upwards of 73 days.

4. He made the supreme sacrifice for the most cherished cause of man.

5. His example was a lesson to all his race and the admiration of all peoples."'

Máire was gradually to learn about the international repercussions of her father's death; the following are some examples.

THE POPE

When Pope Benedict XV heard of MacSwiney's death he was deeply saddened and devoted himself to prayer. The British government had previously approached Rome to condemn the MacSwiney hunger strike as suicide. The reply that came was as follows: Bishop Shanahan, Nigeria's first bishop, brought a blessing from the Pope to MacSwiney on his deathbed.

PARIS AND ROME

In Paris and Rome the MacSwiney hunger strike was treated as the most important news item of the day. Indeed, some French newspapers ran a daily feature on MacSwiney's deteriorating condition. This story, along with British treatment of Ireland generally, revived a wave of anti-British feeling on the Continent not seen since the Boer War. The question of Irish repression raised by MacSwiney was seen as a potential threat to British–French relations.

THE TUC

A telegram on 6 September from the British Trade Union Congress to the British government stated: 'We, in the name of the whole organised labour movement, will hold the Government responsible for the death of the Lord Mayor of Cork and remind them that such blind stupidity will render a reconciliation between Ireland and Britain almost impossible.'

ITALY

After MacSwiney's death, a resolution was passed in Italy by the Popular party, 'In favour of the immediate settlement of the Irish Question in accordance with the principles of Justice and Liberty.'

LA SCALA, MILAN

La Scala opera house in Milan was closed in sympathy on the death of the Lord Mayor of Cork. The principal singer, Margaret Burke Sheridan, asked the audience to excuse her because she could not sing that night as her compatriot, Terence MacSwiney, had died.

BRITISH FOREIGN OFFICE

Within weeks of MacSwiney's death the first tentative discussions about peace were taking place in the Foreign Office in London.

VIETNAM

Ho Chi Minh, founder of the Democratic Republic of Vietnam, was greatly inspired by MacSwiney's actions and said of him: 'A nation which has such citizens will never surrender.'

GEORGIA

Zviad Gamsakhurdia, leader of the independence movement in Georgia, took inspiration from Roger Casement and Terence MacSwiney.

KING GEORGE V

Towards the end of the hunger strike King George V stated in a telegram to Prime Minister Lloyd George: 'Were he to be allowed to die in prison, results would be deplorable. His Majesty would be prepared to exercise clemency if you could so advise and believes that this would be a wise course.'

BRITAIN

Almost every English newspaper denounced the government's action in the MacSwiney case and a group of them, led by the Manchester Guardian, subsequently challenged the entire British war policy in Ireland.

NEW YORK

During his hunger strike the longshoremen in New York refused to unload British cargo ships.

INDIA

MacSwiney's book, Principles of Freedom, was translated into a number of Indian languages and had a profound influence on the Gandhi Movement.

BRAZIL

There were reports of calls for his release from large numbers of people in Brazil.

SPAIN

His actions were particularly important for the Catalan and Basque regions of Spain. The Catalan Trade Union (CADCI) and other associated groups organised public meetings of protest, with the highlight of one of the meetings being a recital of a poem commissioned in homage to MacSwiney.

TERENCE MacSWINEY was born on 28 March 1879, in Cork. He was an exemplary student in the North Monastery, where he was educated by the Christian Brothers. After the failure of the family's tobacco business, when Terence was six years old, his father emigrated to Australia in an unsuccessful pursuit of work, leaving seven children to be raised by his wife and his daughter, Mary (Máire). (An eighth child, Eugene, had died young.) To help support the family Terence left school at the age of fifteen and worked as an accountancy clerk, but did not neglect his academic studies and successfully matriculated for university. His study for his degree, which he combined with full-time employment, gave a good indication of the level of his determination when set upon a course: he would go to bed at 8.00pm and rise at 2.00am in order to study before leaving for work.

His mother, Mary Wilkinson, an Englishwoman, was a devout Catholic and passionate about Irish nationalism. Her death in 1904 affected Terence greatly. Although he had been lighthearted and sociable

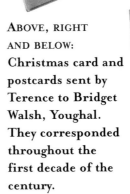

ABOVE, RIGHT AND BELOW:
Christmas card and postcards sent by Terence to Bridget Walsh, Youghal. They corresponded throughout the first decade of the century.

BELOW:
A poem written by Terence at this time.

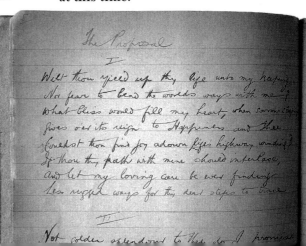

growing up, he now became more serious and withdrawn. Nevertheless he enjoyed the company of a group of friends who called themselves 'The Links', and around 1901 he fell in love with one of the group, Bridget Walsh of Youghal. In the years to come, however, he realised that the life choices he was making were not going to be easy for a wife to live with and that it would be unfair to burden her so. As a result, he ended the relationship.

In 1907 he was awarded a BA degree in Mental and Moral Science. He taught himself Irish and was active in the Gaelic League, frequently visiting Ballingeary in the Cork Gaeltacht in order to master the language. Throughout his political life he made every attempt to promote the use of the Irish language, particularly in official business. He was also interested in Fenianism and Irish history. He began to publish poems and articles, including a pamphlet in favour of Separatism in answer to one promoting another Grattan's Parliament. For his first book of poetry, *Music of Freedom* (1907), he used the pen-name Cuireadóir ('Sower') because he wished to sow the seed for the desire for freedom amongst the people.

Seeing a performance of the play *Macbeth* led to his wish to have a career as a dramatist and poet. He read widely and wrote poetry about love, nature, religion and, in particular, freedom. An early play he wrote and which reflected his lightness and enjoyment of social interaction was *Manners Masketh the Man*. As his political outlook became more focused, this was reflected both in his poetry and his plays, such as *Holocaust*, a short scene describing the suffering of the destitute and helpless in the slums of Cork.

He began to teach a few hours a week at the Municipal School of Commerce. He joined the Cork Dramatic Society (CDS), where he became friendly with Daniel Corkery, author of *The Hidden Ireland*, and in 1909 he started writing plays for the CDS. His fifth and most significant play, *The Revolutionist* (1914), focused on the nature of a political stand taken by one man.

In 1911, at the age of thirty-two, Terence left the job he had held for seventeen years to take up a post as 'commercial teacher', having been a part-time lecturer in Business Methods. He taught and organised classes for the towns of County Cork

Terence MacSwiney cycled the roads of County Cork as a travelling teacher.

for a salary of £200 a year. The travelling it involved gave him great insight into the lives and needs of the people of the county.

His greatest intellectual contribution came from his clear understanding that humankind has a hierarchy of freedoms. He realised that without political freedom the Irish people could not develop at the cultural, artistic and religious levels. Furthermore, while these higher levels of freedom provided the justification to seek freedom, they must also govern the behaviour of those involved in any independence movement. He refocused his energies to achieve political freedom for his country and became totally dedicated to this cause.

In 1913 he became a member of the organising committee of the Irish Volunteers and in that capacity collected money for arms and recruited and trained volunteers from all over County Cork. In less than a year there were 2,000 recruits. The first setback was

ABOVE: The newspaper *Fianna Fáil* was founded by Terence MacSwiney in 1914.
BELOW: Officer Volunteers in training at Coosan Camp, Athlone, September 1915; (L–R) William Mullins, Richard Mulcahy, Seán Lester (later governor of Danzig), unknown, Donal Barrett, Terence MacSwiney, John Griffin, Liam Langley, Pierce McCann, Austin Stack.

when war broke out in 1914, which saw 70 percent of the Volunteers throughout Ireland leaving to follow John Redmond's call to enlist in the British Army. In Cork, only fifty men remained with MacSwiney and Tomás MacCurtain. To try and stem this flow he founded a newspaper called *Fianna Fáil* (Soldiers of Destiny). This paper was suppressed, leaving him with debts that he paid off by selling his books. He was tried and acquitted on charges of sedition.

By 1916 the number of Volunteers in Cork was back up to 1,000 and they were ready to rise with Dublin. But Terence counselled obedience to Eoin MacNeill's countermanding of the orders to start the 1916 Rising, and subsequently regretted it intensely. By the time the Corkmen learned that Dublin had in fact risen, the element of surprise was lost and it was too late to follow suit without significant losses.

The confusion and upset associated with this led to MacSwiney being criticised and rebuked for not having led a rising in Cork. During these difficult times, and during extended periods in prison or internment, he increasingly turned to Thomas a' Kempis's *The*

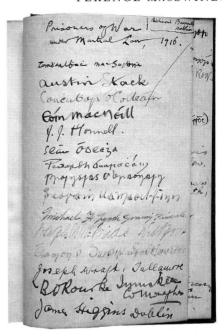

ABOVE: **Signatures of detainees at Richmond Barracks, Dublin, in 1916.** BELOW: **Terence MacSwiney and Muriel Murphy on their wedding day in 1917.**

Imitation of Christ for solace and inspiration. This book combines the ideas of the generosity of self-sacrifice with that of sowing seeds for the future, and seems to have further propelled him towards his destiny.

His intention not to marry was overturned by Muriel Murphy, the daughter of one of Cork's most prominent families, who won him with her dedication to the cause and her fearlessness. The Murphys, who were amongst Cork's wealthiest Catholics, were not best pleased with the marriage. Nonetheless,

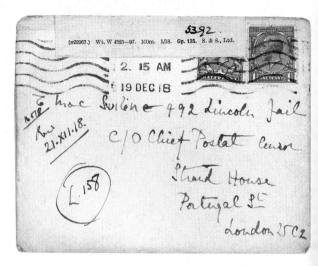

ABOVE, RIGHT:
The envelope of a letter Muriel sent to her husband, Terence, in Lincoln jail in 1918, six months after their daughter, Máire, was born.
BELOW:
A censored letter from Terence to his sister, Mary (Min), in 1919.

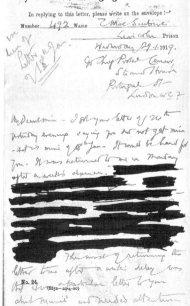

they married on 9 June 1917, during his internment at Frongoch, in Wales. MacSwiney was on the run or in prison for much of their married life; the first time he saw his baby daughter, Máire, was during his internment in Belfast Jail, in August 1918.

MacSwiney helped to build Sinn Féin into a strong political movement, which then won an overwhelming majority in the 1918 general elections. He was elected TD for Mid-Cork. The 1920 local elections saw a repeat of that success for Sinn Féin. He was elected to Cork Corporation as an Alderman. His comrade, Tomás MacCurtain, was selected as Lord Mayor of Cork, with Terence as deputy mayor. As a member of the Dáil and Cork Corporation he was particularly effective in organising the campaign for the Dáil Loan in his constituency of Mid-Cork, collecting

many more subscriptions than any other constituency in the Republic.

When MacCurtain was assassinated by the Royal Irish Constabulary (RIC), MacSwiney was chosen to succeed him as Lord Mayor. In one of Terence's articles in *Irish Freedom*, published after his death, he wrote:

> One day the consciousness of the country will be electrified with a great deed or sacrifice … A man who will be brave only if tramping with a legion will fail in courage if called to stand in the breach alone … There will be abundant need for men who will stand the single test.'

In the short period he served as Lord Mayor prior to his final arrest, MacSwiney was involved in numerous initiatives, many of which sowed the seeds for important developments since. These included: economic support for Catholics and Republicans suffering discrimination in Belfast; a report on the technical schools in Limerick; the institution of an income tax department; an industrial council to maintain peace in industry; a commission to establish a minimum wage; the appointment of commissioners to manage local hospitals; removal of all public appointments from patronage; grant support for child welfare; and the reorganisation of the Cork Municipal School of Music.

In August 1920 he was arrested by the British authorities and convicted of security offences while commandant of the Cork IRA, and received a two-year sentence for being in possession of 'seditious' documents. During his court martial (the country was under martial law) in Victoria Barracks he said: 'The position is that I am Lord Mayor of Cork and Chief Magistrate of this city and I declare this court illegal and those who take part in it liable to arrest under the laws of the Irish Republic.' He informed them that he would put a limit on his term of imprisonment by embarking on a hunger strike. Terence MacSwiney believed that the ultimate good of Ireland must be in perfect harmony with obedience to God, and those who truly sought God must also inevitably seek the good of their country. From a report sent to the Home Office on 29 August 1920 we know that while on hunger strike Terence told the prison doctor, Dr Higson, that the ethics of his strike had been 'fully considered by the Church, and it had been decided that his death would be a sacrificial one and not "suicidal", otherwise he could not have been given the blessing of the Church and the Sacraments by the Priest.'

Towards the end of the hunger strike Muriel suggested that baby Máire be brought to see him one last time. He replied, 'Oh no, it would only be cruelty to have her over', and Muriel added that Máire would not have recognised him as he was so changed.

Terence MacSwiney died in Brixton prison after surviving without food for seventy-four days. His body lay in state in Southwark Cathedral and thousands lined the streets of London and stood in respectful silence as the funeral

LEFT: Terence MacSwiney's crucifix. He had this with him in his last days.

cortège passed. Over 1,000 British Home Office files relating to the last days of his life were released in 2002. These show how it was a surprise to the medical world that someone could last so long without food. They suspected that his sister, Mary, was smuggling food in to him. However, the doctors

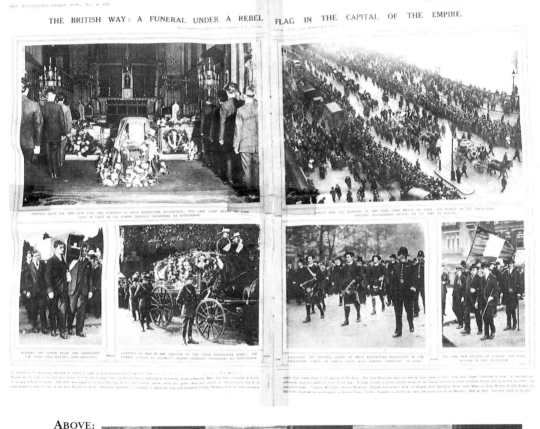

THE BRITISH WAY: A FUNERAL UNDER A REBEL FLAG IN THE CAPITAL OF THE EMPIRE.

ABOVE: *The Illustrated London News'* coverage of MacSwiney's funeral. **RIGHT:** Men from Cork who went to London to organise the removal of MacSwiney's body and accompany it back to Ireland.

carried out medical tests and reported that this was not so. The prison staff were also suspicious of what they called a 'tablet' dissolved in water that he received daily from Fr Dominic. This was clearly Holy Communion.

Terence MacSwiney's funeral took place in Cork on 31 October 1920.

*　　　*　　　*

Muriel MacSwiney spoke of Terence's final days in her testimony before the American Commission on Conditions in Ireland on 9 December 1920 in Washington DC:

> The next morning was the first time that I collapsed at all. I had kept up until then and really felt very well. But the next morning I felt ill and could not go and went to bed again. In the afternoon, since I was about the only person that was allowed in the room, Mr O'Brien took me down in a taxi. I opened the door and the nurse was there and she said, 'would you wait outside a few minutes?' I had not been there at all that day and my brother-in-law had not been there. I must tell you that the day before I had not been allowed in to see him until half-past twelve, although I had come about ten. This day the nurse said, 'would you wait just a little while?' They had a habit then of having a warder just inside the door. I opened the door again in about five minutes and I asked if I could go in, and he said he would ask the nurse and she said no, she was taking his temperature. In about five minutes more, about twenty minutes from the time I came, I sent in word again if I could see him and she said no, I could not. So I did not see my husband again until after his death.

His sister Annie wrote of him:

> He never spoke of what he wrote, and none could guess that such fires burned within. He was the quietest of us all in his comings and goings, easily pleased, easily amused, slipping off to his room and his books, except when Grand Opera or Shakespeare came to the theatre. The theatre was his home. He never missed a night. There was the Gaelic League, the Celtic Literary Society, the Dún, where

the plays of the Celtic Literary Society were produced. Those who were his friends at that time will remember him as enjoying these things in their company, and living through the days, as they did, with quiet purpose and little fuss. Now and again the hidden fire glowed outwardly, if only for a moment. One such flash I saw as, from the top of a city tram, I watched O'Donovan Rossa, the Fenian 'convict', drive through Patrick Street in an open carriage on his return from America.

Behind his carriage came a small group of those who had gone to welcome him home, and among them was Terry. His face was uplifted and shining. I had been thinking what a wretched crowd it was, how cold and indifferent the streets, until this glance at Terry startled me; the street, the people, the moving tram on which I sat, all faded. I carried that look with me, and wondered what he saw.

BELOW:
Letter to Cathal Brugha from Terence MacSwiney, and probably the last he wrote, on the 46th day of his hunger strike.

LETTER TO CATHAL BRUGHA WRITTEN WHILE ON HUNGER STRIKE

Brixton,
30.IX.20.

A Cathal,

Your letter went to my heart. It consoled and comforted me. God bless you for it. But I would not have you in my place here for anything. I'm praying that you will be among the survivors to lead the army of the Republic in the days of freedom. I feel final victory is coming in our time and pray earnestly that those who are most needed will survive to direct it. Those who are gone before will be with you in spirit to watch over the battle helping in unseen but powerful ways.

Will you give my loving remembrances to all at G.H.Q., and the officers and men of the Dublin Brigade of whom we are so proud and to the organisation as a whole. Its work goes on splendidly. Remember me especially to Mick C., Dick McKee, Diarmuid, Rory O'Connor, Gearóid, Austin — too many names come before me but don't forget Leo Henderson. I'm sending a line to Dick M. — too tired to go on.

Whatever I suffer here is more than repaid for by the fruit already reaped and if I die I know the fruit will exceed the cost a thousand-fold. The thought makes me happy and I thank God for it.

Ah, Cathal, the pain of Easter Week is properly dead at last.

I wish I could say all that's in my heart to thank you for your beautiful letters. God guard and preserve you for the future. God bless you again and again and God give you and yours long years of happiness under the victorious Republic.

With all a comrade's love. God bless you.

Toirdhealbhach.

EXTRACTS FROM *Principles of Freedom*

A spiritual necessity makes the true significance of our claim to freedom: the material aspect is only a secondary consideration. A man facing life is gifted with certain powers of soul and body. It is of vital importance to himself and the community that he be given a full opportunity to develop his powers, and to fill his place worthily. In a free state he is in the natural environment for full self-development. In an enslaved state it is the reverse. When one country holds another in subjection that other suffers materially and morally. It suffers materially, being a prey for plunder. It suffers morally, because of the corrupt influences the bigger nation sets at work to maintain its ascendancy.

We fight for freedom — not for the vanity of the world, not to have a fine conceit of ourselves, not to be as bad — or if we prefer to put it so, as big as our neighbours. The inspiration is drawn from a deeper element of our being. We stifle for self-development individually and as a nation. If we don't go forward we must go down. It is a matter of life and death; it is our soul's salvation ... A majority has no right to annul it, and no power to destroy it. Tyrannies may persecute, slay, or banish those who defend it; the thing itself is indestructible ...

If with our freedom to win, our country to open up, our future to develop, we learn no lesson from the mistakes of nations and live no better life than the great Powers, we shall have missed a golden opportunity, and shall be one of the failures of history.

I do not say we must settle now all disputes, such as capital, labour, and others, but that everyone should realise a duty to be high-minded and honourable in action; to regard his fellow not as a man to be circumvented, but as a brother to be sympathised with and uplifted. Neither kingdom, republic nor commune can regenerate us; it is in the beautiful mind and a great ideal we shall find the charter of our freedom; and this is the philosophy that it is most essential to preach. We must not ignore it now, for how we work today will decide how we shall live to-morrow.

QUOTATIONS FROM THE INAUGURAL SPEECH OF TERENCE MacSWINEY AS LORD MAYOR OF CORK, 20 MARCH 1920

This contest of ours is not on our side a rivalry of vengeance but one of endurance, it is not they who can inflict the most, but they who can suffer most who will conquer, though we do not abrogate our function to demand and see that evildoers and murderers be punished for their crimes. But it is conceivable that the army of occupation could stop our functioning for a time, then it becomes simply a question of endurance. Those whose faith is strong will endure to the end and triumph.

The shining hope of our time is that the great majority of our people are now strong in that faith. To you, gentlemen of the minority here, I would address a word. You seem to be hypnotized by the evil thing — usurpation that calls itself government. I ask you again to take courage and hope. To me it seems — and I do not say it to hurt you — that you have a lively faith in the power of the devil but little in the power of God.

But God is over us and in his Divine intervention we have perfect trust. Anyone surveying the events in Ireland for the past five years must see that it is approaching a miracle how our country has been preserved during a prosecution unexampled in history, culminating in the murder of the head of our great city [Tomás MacCurtain]. God has permitted this to be, to try our spirits, to prove us worthy of a noble line, to prepare us for a great and noble destiny.

You among us who have no vision of our future have been led astray by false prophets. I will give you a recent example. Only last week in our city a judge, acting for English usurpation in Ireland, speaking in the presumptuous manner of such people ventured to lecture us and he uttered this pagan sentiment: 'There is no beauty in liberty that comes to us dripping in innocent blood.'

At one stroke this English judge would shatter the foundations of Christianity, denying beauty to that spiritual liberty that comes to us dripping in the Blood of Christ Crucified, Who, by his voluntary sacrifices on Calvary, delivered us from the domination of the devil when the pall of evil was closing down and darkening the world.

The liberty for which we today strive is a sacred thing, inseparably entwined with that spiritual liberty for which the Saviour of man died and which is the foundation for all just government. Because it is sacred, and death for it is akin to the Sacrifice on Calvary, following far off but constant to that Divine Example, in every generation our best and bravest have died. Sometimes in our grief we cry out the foolish and unthinking words: 'The sacrifice is too great.'

But it is because they were our best and bravest that they had to die. No lesser sacrifice would save us. Because of it our struggle is holy, our battle is sanctified by their blood and our victory is assured by their martyrdom. We, taking up the work they left incomplete, confided in God, offer in turn sacrifice from ourselves.

It is not we who take innocent blood, but we offer it, sustained by the example of our immortal dead and that Divine Example which inspires us all for the redemption of our country.

Facing our enemy, we must declare our attitude simply. We see in their regime a thing of evil incarnate. With it there can be no parley any more than there can be a truce with the powers of hell. This is our simple resolution. We ask no mercy and we will accept no compromise. But to the Divine Author of mercy we appeal for strength to sustain us in our battle, whatever the persecution, that we may bring our people to victory in the end.

The civilized world dare not look on indifferent while new tortures are being prepared for our country, or they will see undermined the pillars of their own Governments and the world involved in unimaginable anarchy.

But, if the rulers of the earth fail us, we have yet sure succour in the Ruler of Heaven and though, to some impatient hearts the Judgments of God seem slow, they never fail and when they fall they are overwhelming and final.

Biographies

For more detailed biographies of the life and times of Terence MacSwiney, see: *Enduring the Most* by Francis J Costello (Brandon Books, 1995); *Traolach Mac Suibhne* le Diarmuid Ó Briain (FNT, 1979); *Terence MacSwiney* by Moirin Chavasse (Clonmore & Reynolds, 1961).

Catherine Jennings Brugha, 2005

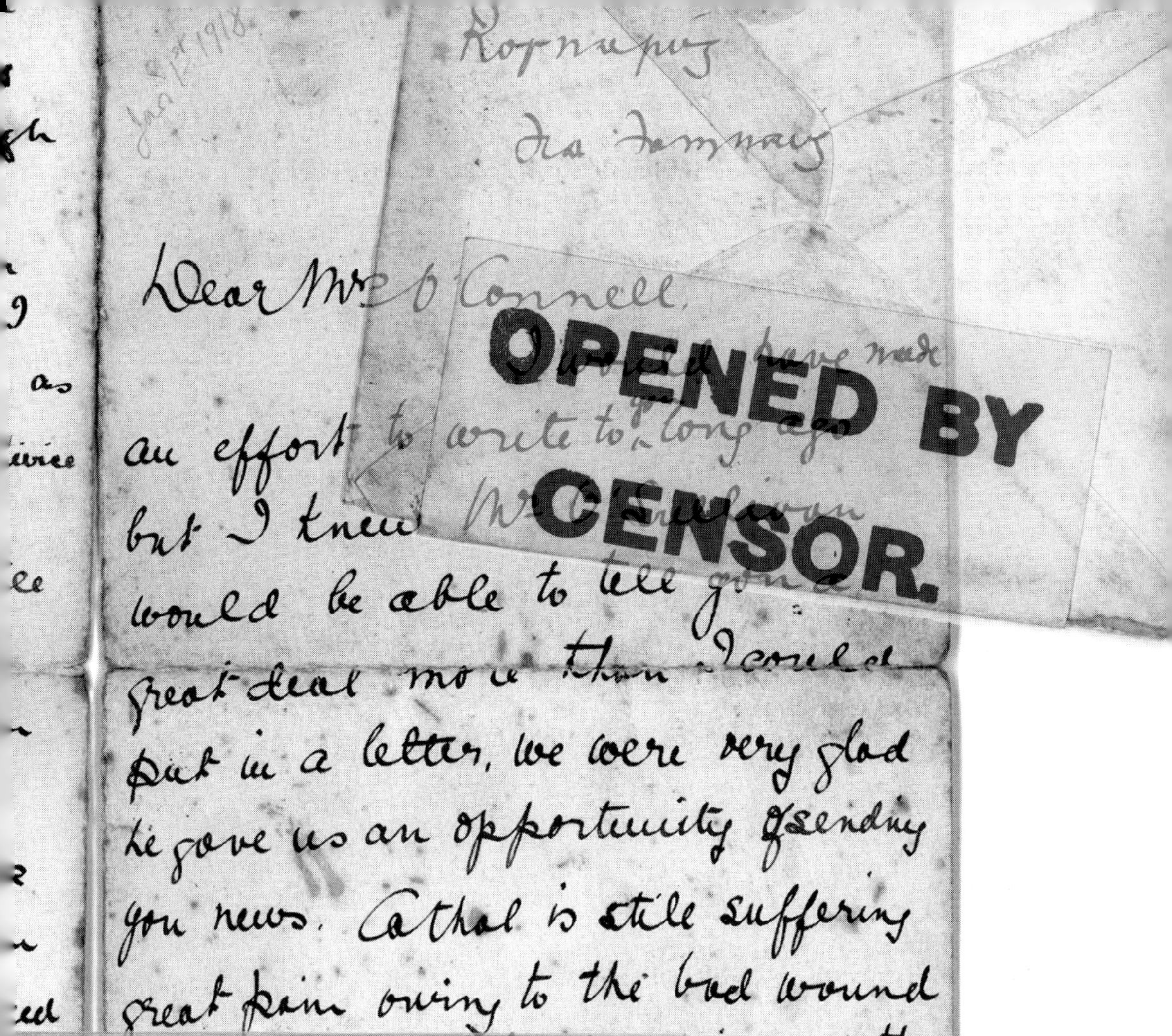

Jan 1st 1918

Dear Mrs O Connell,

an effort to write to long ago
but I knew Mr
would be able to tell you a
great deal more than I could
put in a letter, we were very glad
he gave us an opportunity of sending
you news. Cathal is still suffering
great pain owing to the bad wound
in the heel, the bullet pierced the
ankle bone right through & lodged
in the heel touching the nerves. As
weeks you
pain must

OPENED BY CENSOR.

Dublin.

LETTERS

Apart from this opening letter, which is from Caitlín Brugha, these letters are a selection from the personal letters kept by Terence MacSwiney and passed on to his daughter. Here we reproduce extracts to give an intimate flavour of the times and the personalities. These letters tell their own story. We have selected sections which are fairly legible, and provided introductions with occasional quotations from the letters (in *Italics*) for clarification. We have not corrected spellings but reproduced words as written.

1 January 1918

CAITLÍN BRUGHA TO MRS O'CONNELL

Having been badly wounded in 1916 Caitlín's husband, Cathal, is still in a lot of pain, which she describes here. He is in hospital under guard with many other Volunteers. She says elsewhere in this letter that '*St Mary's College was searched and an old, rusty rifle discovered that one of the priests told the Provost Marshal he would give him the British Empire if he could fire a shot from it.*' John MacNeill is in Dartmoor, she states, and so is Desmond FitzGerald. '*I should dread this for Cathal as they are only allowed letters twice a year and I do not think food could be sent to them.*' She adds that she likes the Dublin people for their kindness and that Cathal has not seen their newborn, Brenda. Caitlín says she is not strong enough to return to fundraising for the dependants.

1907 TERENCE TO HIS BROTHER, PETER

Postcards of Dublin sent by Terence MacSwiney to his brother, one thanking God his exams are over and saying he cannot judge if he passed, the other after his conferring: *'All went beautifully. "God Save the King" was wiped off the programme by the authorities. The students sang "God Save Ireland" instead and we all came home satisfied.'*

Kingstown Co Dublin.

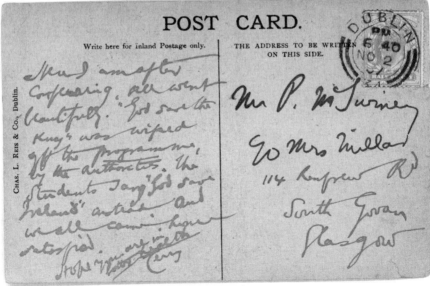

16 July 1915 **TERENCE TO HIS BROTHER, PETER**

Terence keeps Peter in Canada up-to-date on affairs in Ireland with newspapers and letters. Here he writes that things are getting critical. *'The country is right our way — don't believe anything to the contrary — but the repression is so vigorous a man can't open his mouth in public without the risk of being arrested — that is if he speaks his mind about the war.'* Elsewhere he says that a motion to put Home Rule into operation was defeated in Dublin Corporation by a vote of confidence in Redmond. He thinks that the coal strike in Wales may lead to trouble on a large scale and sees that England's problems may prove beneficial to Ireland.

came this week as mum told you. I trust we can keep in the exchange of news.

Things here grow more & more critical. The country is right our way — don't believe anything to the contrary — but the repression is so vigorous a man can't open his mouth in public without the risk of being arrested — that is if he speaks his mind about the war. It is all to the good for it is working the people up. The 'Loyalty' cry will fire its last shot soon. When men are being arrested or deported or expatriated north south, centre it will be too funny to 'keep on talking' of our

17 January 1916 **TERENCE TO PETER**

Terence tells Peter that he is no longer at liberty and has suspended his work organising Volunteers. He is on remand in the '*Male Prison*', Cork. He finds it very strange to be locked up having spent the previous six months cycling close to two thousand miles. Elsewhere in this letter he says: '*No charge has been made against me. I was simply arrested last Thursday on the orders of the Competent Military Authority and no one knows what is going to happen next. But whatever happens I stand where I always stood and my allegiance remains unchanged — Ireland first.*' He is ready to face any Tribunal that wishes to call him to account.

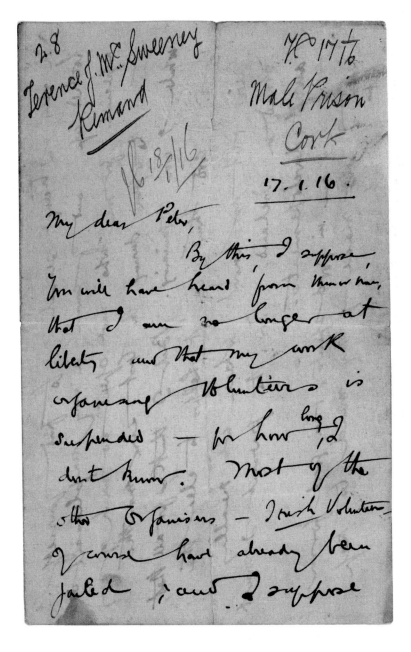

July 1916 MURIEL TO TERENCE

Muriel Murphy to Terence in prison in Frongoch, Wales (before they were married). She is trying to learn Irish and reports on her progress. She says she met a teacher from the North Mon who was very proud of having once taught Terence. She hopes that a branch of the Gaelic League will be started in Bandon where all the old people can speak Irish but don't use it. At the end she says: '*I must apologise for the only thing I sent you which was the unfortunate cake. I don't know whether you or Mr Curtin got it. I left it to the servants to cook, they are generally all right, but they had the oven too cool and to my horror I found it still cooking when I went down to the kitchen. I didn't know until after I had sent it that it was so terrible, it was not till one that was made with it was cut that I found out, I was raging. This means that I will have to get back my reputation for cake making by sending you more this week. I will sit in the kitchen and do my Irish, so they can't go wrong.*'

4 January 1917 **TILLY FLEISCHMANN TO MURIEL**

Frau Tilly Fleischmann starts her letter to Muriel with '*I cannot tell you what a relief your dear letter was to me. I have been terribly worried.*' All Muriel's friends have been worried, she says, as no one has heard anything for nearly a month. '*Dearest Muriel, no matter how depressed and miserable you feel in future do send me a little line, just a few words on a card to say you were at least alive.*' Here she says she hopes to be there for Muriel in times of trouble as Muriel has been for her.

9 March 1917 **TERENCE TO HIS SISTERS MARY AND ANNIE**

From Bromyard Prison, England, Terence sends this fourteen-page letter to his sisters, Mary and Annie, explaining why he has changed his mind about not marrying. Terence would not allow the comfort of marriage to draw him away from his allegiance and he knew his spouse would have a hard path. But Muriel had reached out to him. Through open and frank conversations he has discovered the mature, intelligent woman behind the open and almost child-like eagerness. *'I was set thinking. With it all was her indifference to consequences. I noticed with certain curiosity that fear was a thing that never seemed to touch her.'*

10 March 1917 THE BISHOP OF CORK TO MURIEL

Bishop Cohalan congratulates Muriel on her engagement but advises postponing the marriage to give her mother time to consider the matter; he advises her that it would be desirable to have her mother's consent.

10 March 1917

Dear Miss Murphy

To begin, I congratulate you very sincerely on your engagement. Immediately on receipt of your letter on yesterday I went to see your mother & gave her the letters & read the letter I had for (from) you. You will scarcely, I suppose, be perfectly satisfied with the result of my interview; but I hope you won't be altogether dissatisfied or displeased.

The announcement of your engagement to Terry came as a great surprise on your mother. She had heard rumours; but having heard nothing from yourself she thought there was nothing in the rumours. So the announcement of your engagement came with surprise. She would like some time to consider the matter; & this you will admit, is not unnatural for a mother.

She objects to such a hurried marriage as you contemplate, namely, on the 25th of this month. That, she thinks, would give her no time for consideration. What is engaging her attention most about your future is your spiritual & eternal welfare. And while the suddenness of the engagement has given her a shock she is much relieved by the thought that if you marry Terry you marry a good Catholic.

It would be most desirable to have your mother's consent to your marriage. In June you will be independent. But it would be nicer to have your mother's consent while you are still dependent on her. I would advise you to put off your marriage, say, for a month. You might have your mother's consent

2 April 1917 COPY BY MURIEL OF TERENCE'S LETTER TO THE BISHOP OF CORK
Earlier in this letter Terence points out Muriel's difficulties at home and why getting
married in Bromyard would simplify matters. He hopes the Bishop will forward his letter to Mrs Murphy. He assures the Bishop that Father Denys has facilitated their getting
married by helping to take care of all the regulations, and that they are conscious of
their duty to themselves as well as to others. He does not expect unpleasantness on their
return to Cork.

25 May 1917 **MURIEL TO ANNIE MacSWINEY**
Muriel writes of her wedding preparations to her soon-to-be sister-in-law, Annie.
There is a rumour (unspecified) in Cork about the Murphy family, and she is ashamed.
Elsewhere she says her mother has written and ignored the engagement and that she
hopes to buy a veil for £14 but cannot pay for it yet. Her exasperation is shown: '*Oh hang
and blow money, I'm not going to have a single thing to do with it once we're married.*'

what they think they are & try to be. Oh annie are n't you nearly
afraid to have anyone belonging to such an awful family in yours. I am
so terribly ashamed of them; but of course it may not be true.
I did not get an answer from the Bishop, I wrote to him on Wednesday.
Of course letters are delayed sometimes now & it was not a long
time ago. I am writing to him again tonight & asking him to write to
me on monday. I'm writing to Fr Augustine too today & saying
I'll wire to him on monday when I get the Bishops wire. Terry
sent Fr Augustine a letter card on Thursday from malvern when he came
to see me & said he would write to him when he got back to
Bromyard that night. The card should have caught him in
Dublin, he explained how we were situated. I'd love to have
him of course.
I saw Sp O Brien yesterday on my way. He is a dear. Paddy
is in manchester, there are five in Fairford two in Feltwisty.
Oh annie I wish we were married. Its only two weeks from today
Thursday. I had an awfully nice letter from mother Columba, she

HISTORY'S DAUGHTER

28 May 1917 THE BISHOP OF CORK TO TERENCE

The Bishop explains to Terence that distractions have led to a delay in replying to his letter. Elswhere in this letter he tells him that Mrs Murphy does not want to see the letter from Terence. The Bishop says he has to perform a Confirmation ceremony on 9 June and cannot attend their wedding. He hopes Terence may be freed with the Dublin Rising prisoners expected to be released to smooth the way for the Conference on the Constitution for Ireland.

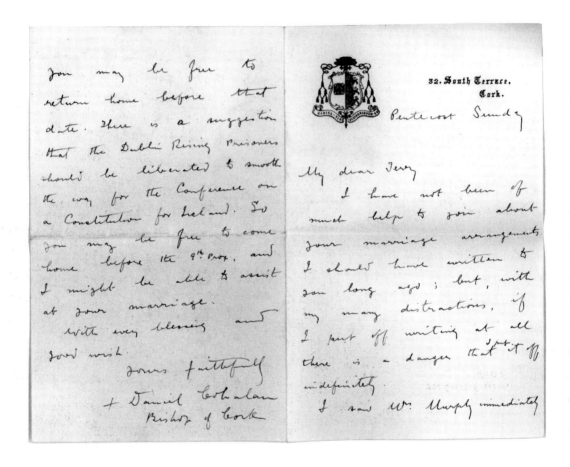

304

6 August 1917 **MRS MURPHY TO MURIEL**

Mrs Mary Murphy writes to her daughter on financial affairs and wants to guide her
even though management of her daughter's affairs has passed out of her hands now. '*You
should leave your money in the securities chosen for you by your dear father. Situated as you are I consider you owe
this respect to his memory.*' She tells Muriel she is '*impulsive and readily influenced*' and that she
should show this letter to her husband and ask him to write a reassurance that he will
not consent to her doing anything rash.

management of your affairs
has passed out of my hands
There is one point I feel very
strongly about on your account
namely That you should
leave your money in the
securities chosen for you by
your dear Father. Situated
as you are I consider you
owe this respect to his memory.
if once you begin to sell out
your capital I dread The
result — As at present safely
invested you have a good
income plenty for all your
needs & for those who may come
after you — You must know

I never cared for money
& how simple my wants &
Tastes have ever been,
but I always felt grateful
To God That my dear children
could have all that was
necessary for health &
comfort — You are very
impulsive & readily influenced.
I would like you to show this
letter to your husband Telling
him That I trust to his honour
not to consent to your doing
any thing rash — ask him
To write to me & if he gives me
his promise I am quite
Satisfied your loving
Mother —

22 May 1918 TERENCE TO MURIEL

Terence writes from Belfast prison to Muriel, now his wife, who is eight months pregnant. They write letters daily, but this tender letter is written after a visit. *'Darling I loved you today for being so sweet and brave.'* He prays for her and their unborn child, whom they presume is a boy.

6 September 1918 TERENCE TO MURIEL

Terence starts this censored letter to Muriel from Lincoln prison: '*Here I am having added another jail to my list.*' Here he tells her of the tiring train journey with many delays. He was glad to hear that all is well with his wife and baby daughter, Máire. Later he tells her that the advantage of this prison over the others is that the cell doors are not closed during the day and the prisoners can all gather to talk.

27 September 1918 MURIEL TO TERENCE

Muriel reports to Terence: *'the little love and I are both splendid'*. Muriel has returned to her
piano practice and plans to do Schumann's 'Kinderszenen'. She also tells him that she is
reading a book on the formation of character by Fr Hull which she doesn't like very
much, but approves of the notion that children should be let loose in a good library,
not just a children's library.

29 October 1918 **MURIEL TO TERENCE**
Muriel gives Terence all the domestic news about letters delayed and the comings and
goings of friends. She reports that Mrs Murphy adores her grandchild, Máire, and is
making new petticoats for her. Here she tells him that 'flu is raging in Cork so she will
avoid taking Máire to town and she puts '*Jey's fluid*' all over the place.

world + she will love you when
you come home to her. You are her own
darling distip.
The flue is raging here. all
the schools are closing, they had
less than half the children at
St)tas today + I'm sure they'll be
shut in a few days. I'm not going to
go anywhere. I'll just go for
a walk sometimes in the direction
of the country + never touch town
I'm minding her/pe altogether +
can't risk her getting it, but I really
don't see how she can if I am as
careful as that. I'm putting Jey's
fluid all over the place.
The sweet little lamp is fast
asleep now.
Seán Tóibín sent me a card saying
he had been three days in the house

HISTORY'S DAUGHTER

20 June 1919 TERENCE TO HIS DAUGHTER, MÁIRE

The opening page from a letter Terence writes to Máire on her first birthday. He admits
that they thought she would be a boy, but he reassures her she is loved deeply; he says
how happy he is with her and delighted that she is '*full of life and strength and joy*'. He loves to
watch her sleeping. '*You are our delight and our treasure and I pray that we may be worthy of such a blessing
and that we may raise you up to be a sweet and noble, true and loyal woman.*'

Summer 1919 **MRS MURPHY TO MURIEL**

Mrs Murphy writes to Muriel enclosing a Sweet Pea kissed by Máire and saying she is delighted with the child's health and happiness. On seeing a paper cutting of her parents Máire says her name and '*Da Da*'. Later in this letter she declares the child is full of intelligence but finishes: '*These are anxious days. We are praying for you. Baby prays for her father every night.*'

21 February 1920 **MRS MURPHY TO TERENCE**
A note from Mrs Murphy to Terence asking him to speak to a Dr FitzGerald about
Muriel's idea about *'electric treatment'*. She doesn't like her daughter being influenced by
advertisements.

1 May 1920 TERENCE TO HIS SISTER, KIT

Terence as Lord Mayor writes to Kit, in Japan, just to let her know he and his family are fine, but that it is an anxious time.

Seómpa an Apo Maoṁ,
ḥalla na Caṫpac,
Copcaiġ.

Lord Mayor's Room, City Hall, Cork.

1ˢᵗ May, 1920.

My dearest Kit,

I suppose you have got news in your papers of the murder of the Lord mayor of Cork and that I have been elected his successor. I am just a month at the post, and this is the first moment I can snatch to send you a line. I am only just sending a line as a sign of life. Later on I shall write at more length.

This is an anxious & trying time for us all & particularly for me in my present difficult post. So my dearest Kit you must pray for me

5 November 1920 **MURIEL TO MARY MacSWINEY**

Terence has died on hunger strike and Muriel tells Mary she would like all of her husband's work to be published and the story of his life written. She deals with Terence's effects and mortuary card. Art (O'Brien) has asked that Muriel go to the American Enquiry but she is reluctant to go and wonders who wants her to go. Here she appeals to Mary to go too. Later she says she is too upset to look after Máire and tells the story of the child whispering into the phone to her father.

half as good.

Art says you wrote something to him about the American enquiry or whatever it it

Personally I should not like to go at all, I did not think I would be any good either but Art seems to think I might.

What is your opinion about this?

I think you would be much better than I but perhaps you could go as well if I did go.

Art thinks you see that as I was all right on the day of the Inquest that I would be fall

7 November 1920 **MURIEL TO MARY MacSWINEY**

Muriel writes to Mary of concerns about Máire. Máire is with her grandmother in *Carrigmore* and Muriel would like her to go to the *Kindergarten*. She would like her to do things other than lessons, such as dancing, as she thinks Máire is too clever. She herself is hoping to go to Germany with the Fleischmanns.

her to go down every day instead.
I would wish her very much to go
to the Kindergarten when you reopen.
I like her to be with other children
a great deal, as much as possible
in fact. What I don't like &
don't think at all good for her
are a lot of grown ups

If she goes to the Kindergarten
every day for games you could
keep her on any time you wanted
to could'nt you.

If this heat continues I think the
less she is indoors the better but

11 November 1921 MURIEL TO MARY AND ANNIE MacSWINEY

Muriel writes from Germany: '*I was very glad to get your letters. Things seem sadder and sadder as time goes on. Last year is an absolute horror to me now.*' Máire is again in *Carrigmore* and elsewhere in the letter Muriel says she does not want her to be brought to the cemetery (Terence's grave) anymore. She ends the letter with: '*Everybody I meet is most sympathetic and sees that there will be no peace till Ireland is independent.*'

INDEX